SOCIAL CONTAGION
and Other Material on
Microbiological Class War in China

by Chuang

CHARLES H. KERR
PUBLISHING COMPANY

ISBN: 978-0-88286-007-7 (e-book: 978-0-88286-004-6)
Library of Congress cataloging in publication: 2021939155

Illustrations by Rafiki
Design and typesetting by J. Dakota Brown
Typefaces: Garamond Premier, Songti TC, Commune Nuit Debout

Printed in Canada on acid-free paper

Charles H. Kerr Publishing Company
8901 S. Exchange Ave.
Chicago, IL 60617
www.charleshkerr.com

Contents

Preface

Social Contagion provides a distinctly Chinese perspective on the COVID-19 pandemic that first appeared in Wuhan, China before spreading to the rest of the world. The authors, Chuang, are an international collective of communists. Many of their members currently live and work in China. They publish a theoretical journal of the same name that analyzes the Chinese economy and the struggles of the Chinese working class. In the present book, Chuang's analysis refutes the racist and xenophobic contention that the COVID-19 pandemic is some sort of "Chinese flu." In fact, they argue, there is nothing uniquely Chinese about the emergence and spread of this virus. During the past 20-plus years the world has experienced the onslaught of a range of new corona-viruses and other viruses originating in a number of different countries. These include Ebola (1996); SARS (2003); H5N1 or Avian Flu (2005); H1N1 or Swine Flu (2009); MERS (2012); Ebola 2 (2013); and the most devastating of all—SARS-COV-2, which causes the disease COVID-19 (2020). Many epidemiologists warn us that there are more to come. And the next one may be worse than the global catastrophe we are presently contending with.

All of these outbreaks have been the result of a number of factors associated with the insatiable need for global capitalism to accumulate surplus value through growth. These factors include: (1) the destruction of the habitat of species that had previously been kept isolated from humans; (2) the development of large-scale "factory farming" methods; (3) the use of institutional and political methods to achieve global capital mobility; (4) pollution and global warming that have enhanced the human spread of viruses by promoting diseases in humans, making them more vulnerable to virus outbreaks; (5) war and "natural" disasters that have forced people to migrate across the world; (6) rapid urbanization that has unleashed the mass migration of people within and among nations.

In China these factors take a specific form, which Chuang develops in the first chapter in this book. For Chuang, the COVID-19 outbreak represents a "social contagion" and "microbiological class warfare." They demonstrate how, in China, this social contagion was contained primarily through the actions of working people and local institutions. They argue that initially the Chinese state was overwhelmed by the appearance of the virus, which threatened to undermine capitalist development in China. Worker inquiries in chapter two of the book and interviews with people on the ground in chapter three show concretely how ordinary people made use of local institutions to control the virus. Chapter four focuses on how the Chinese central authority then used the crisis to strengthen their control over local institutions. Chuang calls the actions of China's central government "a melodramatic dress rehearsal for full mobilization of domestic counter insurgency." But the challenge of the pandemic to state control was not uniquely Chinese, and the dress rehearsal for domestic counterinsurgency is playing out around the world as capitalist states stumble and bumble in their efforts to stop the pandemic while preparing for future outbreaks of disease and challenges from working people who are finding that capitalism not only brings them disease, but is failing to adequately feed, clothe, house, educate, and care for increasing numbers of people.

Chuang argue that the outbreak of the COVID-19 pandemic in China was largely due to rapid urbanization and industrialization and subsequent changes in the diet of Chinese and other workers throughout Asia. These changes accompanied China's entry into global capitalist markets. Over the course of the late 1970s, the Chinese leadership began to pursue policies designed to liberalize rural production and gradually attract overseas investment. The end result was that, by the 2000s, China's economic growth became dependent on manufacturing goods for export in new "sunbelt" industries concentrated in the coastal provinces. Whole regions of the country participated in a building boom, and much of the rural population migrated to these regions to work in the new factories. Chuang notes that in the late 1970s only 20% of Chinese people lived in cities, while today the number is over 60%. The rapid construction of cities precipitated a massive destruction of habitat for many wild animals and brought a number of viruses into contact with human beings and domesticated animals.

These shifts, beginning in the late 1970s, were taking place in many parts of the world. But the thinking behind them started much earlier. Although I didn't realize it at the time, I sat in on some discussions in India that foreshadowed the major changes in economic development and agriculture that ultimately came to China and the rest of the world. In 1963 and 1964, I spent a year in Kolkata (then called Calcutta), India, working as a student intern for the West Bengal government and the Ford Foundation. We were working on a development plan for the region. The problem we faced in Kolkata was that too many people were coming into the city from rural villages in the region. Officials and planners considered Kolkata to be "over urbanized." The number of people migrating to the city was greater than the jobs and housing available to them. Sociologists and geographers called the problem "rural push." When I visited some rural villages near Kolkata, I learned that residents sustained themselves through subsistence farming. Rice, goats, and chickens were produced on small plots of land. But there wasn't enough food for the rapidly growing population. So some peasants left their villages to seek employment in Kolkata. The solution the planners came up with was to create a ring of industrial satellite cities where the villages stood. As global economic conditions changed in countries like India and China, the idea of converting urban hinterland into industrial cities became a model and key to economic growth.

At the end of the year I returned home, traveling through Asia. At that time, both the People's Republic and the US government banned US residents from traveling in China. Hong Kong, however, was still a

British colony, so we were able to stop there. I remember driving to the border between Hong Kong and China. We went through beautiful countryside. The border was heavily fortified, complete with gun towers manned by the Chinese military. Soldiers stood guard armed with automatic weapons. Our driver explained the closed border was a response to the fact that Chinese peasants had been streaming into Hong Kong because their fields were not adequate to sustain their growing population. Looking through the fence I saw a beautiful rural vista with small lakes and wetlands, rolling hills, and rice paddies.

In the mid 1990s, 30 years later, China was now open to the West. One of my students at the University of Illinois Chicago urban planning program went to China to teach English as a second language. She was working in the city of Shenzhen, which is located in Guangdong Province, bordering Hong Kong. She showed us slides when she got back. She explained that what had once been a rural border area was fully developed with factory farms and light industrial plants making goods for export. In the 1960s, Shenzhen, which is near where I stood on the Hong Kong side of the border, was a sleepy village. By 1970 it had grown to be a small city of 337,000. By 2006, the population of Shenzhen had grown to 8.5 million. She said that the entire year that she was there, heavy construction equipment was busy filling in wetlands, draining lakes, leveling hills, and building, building, building.

Urbanization and industrial development in China began to take off in the 1980s. Foreign investment played a significant role. China established four "special economic zones," of which Shenzhen was one. Wuhan, where the first outbreak of COVID-19 was discovered, is located far to the north of Shenzhen along the Yangtze River. Its position on the Yangtze enabled it to import the raw materials needed for it to become a major producer of the concrete and steel that was used to build urban infrastructure.

The urbanization and industrialization of China was a part of a much broader trend. In the 1960s, colonized nations and those depending on agriculture were often designated as "third world" or "underdeveloped." But beginning in the 1970s and 1980s, economists and political scientists began to use the term "Newly Industrialized Nations" (NICs) for countries undergoing a shift from agriculture to manufacturing. Initially the NICs included Hong Kong, Singapore, South Korea, and

Taiwan, which were also dubbed the "Four Asian Tigers." But very soon China, India and many other "third world" nations including Mexico, Brazil and Thailand were reclassified as NICs as well. Some of these nations also began to be centers of high tech industry. But in all cases the designation of a country as a "NIC" meant that these countries were undergoing rapid urbanization as well, which included both the destruction of the habitat of many animals and a movement of workers out of rural areas into the new cities.

As more and more "third world" nations joined the ranks of the NICs, there was a very different trend in high income nations with established industry and high levels of urbanization, including the US. Class struggles on factory floors throughout Europe and the US were on the rise. These struggles were often independent of the workers' unions and contrary to established labor law. Factory jobs at the time were plentiful. They paid reasonably well but working conditions were brutal as factory owners pushed for more production. Wildcat strikes and militant shop floor actions were happening almost daily. Many leftists, including myself, joined these struggles by taking factory jobs. Between 1976 and 1982, I worked in a number of factories located in Southeast Chicago and Northwest Indiana. And I participated in or observed many acts of resistance to the brutal conditions where I was working. For example, at Chicago Shortening, a factory that produced cooking oils, I participated in a wildcat strike that was fiercely contested by both the company and union. At issue was our contention that a contract ratification vote had been fixed and we demanded another vote. In the course of the two month strike I concluded that this was really a strike for human dignity. One action during the strike stands out. One day, 19 of us stood on the railroad tracks blocking an engine from pulling cars from the plant that were full of product. The president of the company in a coat and tie approached us flanked by cops in riot gear. They were led to our line by a huge cop in plainclothes with his badge and ID hung around his neck and a large pistol stuck in his belt. After he ordered us to disperse, one of the workers stepped forward. He stood inches away from the big cop and tilted his head up so he could look the cop directly in the eye. "All we want is a fair vote on the contract. For us this is about how we are goin' to feed our babies, man. Now that's something worth fighting for. So movin' us out of here... well it ain't goin' to be easy." The company backed down that day. The strike lasted over two months. Eventually we lost the strike but the workers took a stand.

Another example happened at the Foseco chemical plant. A production line had been automated using some very advanced technology for that time. One worker now ran a line that had once been run by 12. But the pace of work was inhumane. When the operator got behind, he stopped production and a loud alarm went off. When that happened a foreman came to the line and publicly berated him and warned him not to do it again. The next time he stopped the line the foreman began to scream at him. The worker grabbed the foreman by the shirt and pulled out a knife and said. "Leave me alone or I'll cut your fucking throat." Security guards appeared almost immediately and put the worker in handcuffs taking him to a lunchroom to await the police. Without a word, every worker in the plant who had been watching this shut down their machines and went into the lunchroom where the worker was being held. When the police and management appeared, one of the older workers demanded that the company negotiate with us. The aftermath was that the worker was released and returned to the shop floor with a helper and a promise that two workers would be assigned to the job in the future.

In the seven years I was working in the factories, I observed many instances of spontaneous worker militancy. At that time, this region had the largest concentration of heavy industry in the world. The region was anchored by ten steel mills, which, at their peak, employed two hundred thousand workers, half in the Chicago metropolitan area. It has been estimated that for every steel worker in the region, there were seven other manufacturing workers, bringing the total estimated manufacturing employment to over one-and-a-half-million workers. The presence of the Lake Michigan ports, rivers and canals bringing barges full of raw materials used by many industries, railroad spurs, highways and the mills themselves attracted firms that made steel products like automobiles, railroad cars, and steel structures. It also attracted industries that supplied products to the mills and other factories—chemicals, processed foods, tools, work boots, and welding equipment.

The development of this region began in the late 19th century. At the time, Northwest Indiana was a landscape of alternating sand dunes and forests, making it a major location for ornithologists' research and recreational bird watching. Southeast Chicago was a major wetland with lakes and marshes. The habitat destruction that went with industrial and urban development greatly reduced bird reproduction. Many of the sand dunes are gone forever. The marshes and lakes were soon heavily polluted. The destruction of the dunes and wetlands and their replacement by heavy industry and urban construction had major health impacts—tuberculosis, cholera, cancer, emphysema—to name a few. But living wage jobs that were won by the struggles of workers were plentiful, and there were large migrations from rural America and also from the American South, Europe, and Mexico.

The workers' insurgencies in the factories of the industrialized nations and those in which I directly participated in the 1970s appeared to be the beginnings of revolutionary change around the world. What the workers engaging in these struggles and the leftists like me who joined them didn't realize was that a process was well underway that would lead to a major shift in the way global capitalism would accumulate and distribute value. That process eventually took the form of a massive deindustrialization in the industrialized countries and the industrialization of the "third world" including China.

In Southeast Chicago and Northwest Indiana where I worked, much of the manufacturing activity that was going full blast when we made our stand on the railroad tracks at Chicago Shortening is gone. All the Chicago steel mills have been closed and demolished along with most of the factories whose locations were determined by the mills. While a few steel mills in Indiana are still producing as much steel as before, they are doing so with a fraction of the workers compared to this earlier era. Altogether, there are only about ten thousand steel workers left. The ground where the steel mills and other factories once stood is so polluted it is undevelopable. This same scene also played out in many of the large industrial cities in the US. They have been referred to as a "rust belt."

The specific reasons for this shift—the industrialization and urbanization of China and other nations designated as "NICS", and deindustrialization and urban decay in the industrialized nations—have been debated. I have written about my own views elsewhere, but I summarize them here.[1] In the 1960s and 1970s there were militant labor struggles throughout Europe and the US. In addition, in the US there were strong civil rights initiatives that impacted struggles in the nation's factories. In Southeast Chicago and Northwest Indiana, black and women's caucuses formed in the steel mills to demand an end to discriminatory work rules. Many of these struggles were independent of the labor unions. Black and Latino workers led the actions at both Chicago Shortening and the Foseco Chemical Corporation.[2]

As these struggles were going on in factories across the US and Europe, think tanks, foundations, international associations like the International Monetary Fund, World Bank, the Trilateral Commission, central banks, and others began to meet in the mid-seventies to discuss ways out of the crisis of both labor insurgency and falling profit rates. The global shift that resulted developed over time. It had many elements, but basically global capital needed greater mobility that would move production to areas of the world where wages were low and regulations protecting workers and the environment were nonexistent. Technological and institutional changes throughout the 1980s made such a strategy feasible. Process technologies made it possible to break up the production process and to produce pieces of products in different locations. These developments literally changed the metrics for scale economies. The big box containers and the new ships, trucks, and trains to move them made it feasible for these different places to be located long distances from one another. Computer technologies, robots, and now artificial intelligence not only automated production but offered innovations in inventory control to enable firms to get materials they used in production when they needed it ("just in time" or JIT). Meanwhile loans to "third world" nations included conditions that forced nations to open their economies to foreign investment. In the 1990s, institutional innovations arose to eliminate any barriers to the flow of capital around the world under the guise of "free trade." Finance became a highly profitable "product" during this period and was used to open nations to manufacturing. These developments were not

---

1. David Ranney, *New World Disorder: The Decline of US Power*, 2014.
2. David Ranney, *Living and Dying on the Factory Floor: From the Outside in and the Inside Out*, PM Press, 2019.

the product of some "master plan" or a conspiracy but the response of many actors asserting their class interests.

The rapid urbanization and industrialization of China discussed here by Chuang occurred in this broader context. So the global shift that I describe above is also the broader context of the pandemic. This restructuring also created new capitalist markets for a number of consumer goods. One shift that has contributed significantly to the zoonotic transfer of virus infections from animals to humans is the growing demand for meat in Asia and other parts of the world. That demand is in part due to former subsistence farmers migrating to cities and working in factories rather than growing their own food. It is also, in part, due to rising incomes that accompanied industrialization in the "NIC" nations. But meeting that demand required new agricultural methods and technologies, including the factory farm.

The method of factory farming for chickens and pigs did not originate in China. It was developed and still thrives in the US. Factory farming made the globalization of poultry, pork, and bovine production possible. The technique applied to poultry originated with US-based Tyson Foods. The giant corporations Smithfield and JBS USA initiated pork and bovine factory farming. In these cases a single firm usually controls all aspects of food production. This includes: the birth of animals; the feed that the animals eat (often using antibiotics and growth hormones); contracts with big farmers who use huge barns or cages in a confined space where they can raise the animals to precise specifications (size and weight); the meat packing operations where the animals are slaughtered, packed and shipped. The owner of the firm then contracts with marketers, sometimes owning some of the retail outlets. A Thailand-based firm called Charoen Pokphand or CP was the first corporation to implement factory farming methods in China. The owners of CP are a Chinese family who moved to Thailand many years ago from Guangdong Province in China. When China fully opened up its economy in 1978, the CP Group was among the first foreign investors in the country and became the first foreign company registered in the Shenzhen special economic zone. Then in 2013 a Chinese conglomerate, WH Group, bought Smithfield. The Smithfield CEO became general manager of WH Group. The other developer of factory farm methods, JBS, originated in the U.S but is now owned by a group of industrialists in Brazil.

The pork and chicken produced in China not only feeds Chinese industrial workers, but it is also exported all over Asia by CP. But like the other aspects of the social contagion, factory farming is part of global capital. And as Chuang demonstrates, drawing on the research of epidemiologists like Rob Wallace, the factory farm turns out to be a hotbed for the transmission of viruses. So the animal habitat destruction needed for the industrialization and urbanization of Guangdong Province releases viruses that are transmitted throughout China, Asia, and ultimately the world. The global nature of the factory farms is a good illustration of Chuang's point that the transmission of disease alongside urbanization and industrialization is not Chinese but is instead a product of global capitalist development.

Capitalist crisis, global shifts, and a global pandemic have had their impact on the capitalist state. The specifics of that impact vary from one nation to another. In China the government embraced foreign investment, global markets and the rapid industrialization-urbanization that ultimately fed virus outbreaks. In the US these forces resulted in deindustrialization. The US federal government played its role in the global shift by entering into a series of international agreements that would open up all nations to capitalist accumulation and enhance the mobility of capital. These agreements include IMF and World Bank conditions on loans to "third world" nations as well as trade policies such as those set by the North American Free Trade Agreement, the World Trade Organization, and a variety of bilateral agreements that opened nations to foreign investments. Politically they made use of various "blame the victim" theories of US economists and sociologists as justification for the destruction of the social safety net—especially public welfare and public housing. At the local level, cities adjusted to the decline of living wage jobs in different ways. During the manufacturing heyday in Chicago, Mayor Richard J. Daley, who was in power from 1955 to 1976, relied on the financial and political support of the CEOs of corporations and unions representing major manufacturing industries such as steel, food processing, apparel, meat packing, electricity generation, and farm equipment. By the time his son, Richard M. Daley, rose to power in 1989, that support had all but shifted to the elites in the so-called FIRE industries—Finance, Insurance, and Real Estate. Daley was re-elected five times and was in power until 2011. In addition, the 1980s saw the rise of community-based organizations to deal with poverty, housing deterioration, and crime. Many of these organizations were funded by governments at federal, state and local levels as well as by philanthropic foundations that were fully in tune with the emphasis of government programs supporting open markets and capital mobility.

When the present pandemic surfaced in China, Chuang argues that the Chinese central government was unable to contain it. In fact, they had disinvested in health care such that the system was not capable of caring for the huge numbers of people with COVID-19. The task of responding was largely taken up by a variety of institutions and citizens at the local level. But the central government began to take measures to bring these local institutions under the control of the Communist Party as part of a larger state-building effort already underway before the pandemic. Part four of this book has a very rich analysis of the changes in the Chinese state in relation to Chinese history and philosophy.

In the US the initial response of the federal government to the pandemic was to downplay its importance. And when that became impossible, President Trump tried to blame the Chinese. It remains to be seen at the time of this writing what to expect from the US moving forward. But mobilizations of military and pharmaceutical corporations to produce and distribute vaccines have gone hand in hand with repressive measures against both the far-right and far-left who oppose the power of the capitalist state in this nation. Perhaps, as Chuang argues with respect to China, we in the US are also witnessing a dress rehearsal for coming counter-insurgency measures. Such measures may be put into play in China soon after the pandemic is contained.

Chinese worker insurgency that has developed in recent years is reminiscent of what we experienced in the US in the 1960s and '70s. But the industrialization in China that contributed to the pandemic is starting to cool. Chuang notes that the steel mills and concrete factories that contributed to the earlier industrialization and urbanization in China have slowed down. The percentage of the Chinese workforce engaged in manufacturing has been on the decline since 2015.[3] The technological advances and global institutions that made it possible to de-industrialize regions like Southeast Chicago and Northwest Indiana will

3. Aaron Benanav, *Automation and the Future of Work*, Verso Press, 2020.

make it equally possible to move manufacturing out of China. And this has already begun to happen.

What Chuang clearly demonstrate is that the pandemic we are experiencing around the world today is a result of global capitalism's insatiable need to grow and find ways to accumulate the value created by the world working class. And while China's rapid industrialization over the last 30 years contributed to the current pandemic, a coming deindustrialization in Asia could make large areas like Wuhan and Shenzhen look more like Southeast Chicago and Northwest Indiana. And future pandemics may well originate elsewhere as capital finds new terrains to industrialize in other corners of the globe. Ultimately we face a global problem that needs a global solution.

— *David Ranney*

SOCIAL CONTAGION

社会传染

Introduction

Understanding China remains a central hurdle for anyone attempting an analysis of capitalism's trajectory or forecasting the potential for it to be overcome. On the one hand, this is because the gulf of language is here at its widest. Obtaining a working knowledge of Chinese beyond the most basic conversational level takes significantly longer than almost any other language and translation requires intricate contextual knowledge.[1] Even then, such topics often remain specialist affairs, opaque even to native speakers. On the other hand, China's unique history and its distinct position at the forefront of global accumulation have tended to generate an illusion of exceptionalism. The entire East Asian mainland has long been treated like a blank page, filled with the hopes, fears and political speculation of distant observers whose writings have less to do with China itself and more to do with their own position within local political conflicts.[2] The result is that minor epiphenomenal features of Chinese society are seized upon and built up into vast superstructures entirely ungrounded in reality. The effect is either to portray the nation as a totalitarian nemesis or a utopian ally—whichever bolsters one or another faction in domestic political battles. This is most egregiously visible in mass media, but it has been, if anything, even more pronounced among supposedly "anti-capitalist" theorists.

1. This difficulty is one reason that machine translation of Chinese is still so awful, even as it becomes increasingly functional for other languages. This fact also means that translators must make use of more skillful artifice in the translation process—not only restructuring the order of information but choosing proximate literary techniques in the destination language to emulate components of Chinese that are difficult or impossible to translate literally.

2. In fact, this situation is how the notion of "China" in its modern sense arose. The process is described in the preface to our first journal issue: "A Thousand Li," *Chuang Journal*, Issue 1: Dead Generations, 2016.

One of the founding missions of Chuang has been to burn through such illusions. We have sought to translate and interpret the actual character of China's recent history, its social and economic characteristics, its many multi-faceted class struggles, and the numerous new forms of cultural expression and intellectual inquiry emerging there—refusing to force-fit the prevailing conditions into inherited schemas designed with distant times and places in mind. This project began with an anglophone audience in mind, but rapid translation of our work has, in recent years, given it an influence beyond the English-speaking world. Chuang is, at its base, an international communist project unbound from any allegiance to the irrelevant factions of the extinct movements of the 20th century. We are committed to understanding actually-existing capitalism, identifying its core contradictions and emergent struggles, and thereby indicating points of leverage to be utilized and mapping out the limits to be overcome in the long battle to overturn this world and build the next. In this spirit, we have published two journal issues of long-form analysis—centered around an ongoing economic history of modern China—and regularly release shorter pieces and collaborative translations on our blog. Throughout, we have sought to connect with and publicize the work of Chinese radicals writing and organizing on the mainland today.

Any application of communist critique to make sense of the real flow of events in history and the present layout of global power must, in the end, have a practical orientation—as a means for building international connections between those engaged in struggles on the ground— while also contributing to the more general advance of communist theory as such. A purely "empirical" description of events is never possible. Theoretical positions are always taken, whether they are avowed or not. Even the most abstract and rarefied theory can often illuminate substantial connections between empirical data points that would otherwise remain in shadow. But, by the same measure, any purely "theoretical" description is quickly swallowed by the churning chaos of empirical reality. Theory thrives only as dynamic critique, sculpted in the churn of the very history that it seeks to shape. For Chuang, this means that our theoretical contributions should not be understood as the application to contemporary China of any preformulated body of theory, but instead as the dynamic production of new concepts hewn by our present moment of global crisis and strangled rebellion. The only true orthodoxy is that of a living theory that grapples with the world and, through this, maintains its political fidelity. In this way, China poses universal questions for communists today, not parochial ones. Similarly, the trajectory and character of Chinese capitalism can only be understood in relation to the larger dynamics of capitalism as a global social system, even as it also propels this system toward new and deadly heights.

The chapters below emphasize these more universal insights. Foremost among these is the way in which the emergence of the COVID-19 pandemic has again decisively demonstrated that capitalist production is founded on an ecological rift. Though most visible at the macroscopic level of climate change, in "Social Contagion," we show how this rift also manifests at the microbiological scale. This chapter demonstrates how the communist method of inquiry cannot be reduced to purely economic critique or even radical worker inquiry, but must instead offer a broad understanding of capitalism as an expansive social system that has transformed the anthropological coordinates of human life and devastated the ecological substrata of the biosphere and which now threatens the climatic system of the entire planet. At the same time, since we place such emphasis on the system's inherent tendency toward continual breakdown and recomposition—which creates the potential for its overcoming through escalating class conflict—subjective experience and emergent struggles are also of central relevance. After all, class conflict is not a hollow theoretical category, silent in its abstraction. It is instead a really-existing social war, cacophonous with contrasting voices. The second chapter, a translation of the article "Worker Organizing Under the Pandemic," offers a short summary of the recent experience of class conflict among Chinese workers, as retold by a mainland Chinese author involved in labor organizing. In chapter three, "As Soon as There's a Fire, We Run," we dig more deeply into the feeling of the lockdown in Wuhan, through an interview with friends who experienced it on the ground.

In every chapter, questions are raised about the capacity of the Chinese state and the nature of its response to the pandemic. These are not simple questions. Moreover, their answers are actively obscured by the widely accepted presumption that the state's authoritarian measures were what ultimately enabled it to contain the outbreak. Such a conclusion, we argue, is both factually wrong and politically naïve.[3] In the final chapter, "Plague Illuminates the Great Unity of All Under Heaven," we investigate this response in detail, exploring the intricate local anatomy of the state-building project in China and the ways in which the mass mobilization of volunteer labor was ultimately essential to the successful containment of the outbreak. The basic claim is that Chinese state capacity remains weak, but the pandemic also illustrated previously invisible dimensions of the ongoing effort to build new mechanisms for repression and administration down to the most local level. At the same time, the piece delves deeper into questions about the nature of the capitalist state as such and the influence of contemporary Chinese political philosophy on the actual practice of governance. As elsewhere, the results of this inquiry point beyond the Chinese case toward evolving techniques of class rule deployed across a world increasingly stricken by stagnation and crisis. By the end, then, we have come full circle: class war overspills its social bounds to reshape climate and microbiology. Microbial chaos then returns to its social form, spawning a new series of global rebellions, accompanied by more intimate subjective transformations among proletarians confined to their own meditation in lockdown. Finally, pandemic and insurrection together provide the justification for new forms of counterinsurgent governance. As the tongue-in-cheek title of our final piece suggests, however, the language of harmony and unity promoted in the state-building project is nothing but a classical veneer papering over the fissures that threaten class society. Rather than the unity of all under heaven, then, the twins of plague and insurrection hint at approaching havoc.

3. This conclusion is similar to the old adage that "Mussolini at least made the trains run on time." Beyond the reactionary politics evident in the phrase, it was also never actually true. Instead, the sentiment is revived almost exclusively as a justification for conservative political projects. It is deployed with such regularity (and so repeatedly debunked by historians) that there's even a name for the fallacy: "the myth of fascist efficiency."

1.
Social Contagion: Microbiological Class War in China

The Furnace

Wuhan is known colloquially as one of the "four furnaces" (四大火炉) of China for its oppressively hot humid summer, shared with Chongqing, Nanjing and alternately Nanchang or Changsha, all bustling cities with long histories along or near the Yangtze river valley. Among the four, Wuhan, however, is distinguished by its literal furnaces: the massive urban complex acts as a sort of nucleus for the steel, concrete and other construction-related industries of China, its landscape dotted with the slowly-cooling blast furnaces of the remnant state-owned iron and steel foundries, now plagued by overproduction[1] and forced into a contentious new round of downsizing,[2] privatization and general restructuring—resulting in several large strikes and protests in the last five years. The city is essentially the construction capital of China, which means it has played a particularly important role in the period after the global economic crisis, since these were the years in which Chinese growth was buoyed by the funneling of investment funds into infrastructure and real estate projects. Wuhan not only fed this bubble with its oversupply of building materials and civil engineers but also, in so doing, became a real estate boomtown of its own. According to our own calculations, in 2018–2019 the total area dedicated to construction sites in Wuhan was equivalent to the size of Hong Kong island as a whole.

1. Neil Hume, Anna Gross, and Christian Shepherd. "Chinese Group Sparks Oversupply Fears in Steel Market," *Financial Times*, April 25, 2019.
2. "Chinese Steel Trader Claims Wuhan Iron Slashed Workforce by 25%," *S&P Global Market Intelligence*, Nov. 1, 2016.

But now this furnace driving the post-crisis Chinese economy seems, much like those found in its iron and steel foundries, to be cooling. Though this process was already well underway, the metaphor is now no longer simply economic, either, as the once-bustling city was sealed off for over a month in the depths of winter, its flash-frozen streets emptied by government mandate: "The greatest contribution you can make is: don't gather together, don't cause chaos," read a headline in the *Guangming Daily*,[3] run by the Chinese Communist Party's propaganda department. Wuhan's broad new avenues and the glittering steel and glass buildings that crown them were cold and hollow, as winter dwindled through the Lunar New Year and the city stagnated under the constriction of the wide-ranging quarantine. Isolating oneself was sound advice for anyone in China, where the outbreak of the novel coronavirus (renamed "SARS-COV-2" and its disease "COVID-19") killed more than four thousand people—far more than its predecessor, the SARS epidemic of 2003, though far less than the 350,000 deaths in the US in 2020. The entire country locked down, as it did during SARS-COV-1. Schools closed, and people were cooped up in their homes nationwide. Nearly all economic activity stopped for the Lunar New Year holiday on January 25th, but the pause was extended for about two months to curb the spread of the epidemic. The furnaces of China seemed to have stopped burning, or at least to have been reduced to gently glowing coals. In a way, though, the city become another type of furnace, as the coronavirus burned through its massive population like a fever writ large.

The outbreak has been incorrectly blamed on everything from the conspiratorial release of a bioweapon virus from the Wuhan Institute of Virology,[4] to the propensity of Chinese people to consume "dirty" or "strange" types of food—since the virus outbreak was originally linked to either bats or snakes sold in a semi-illegal "wet market" specializing

---

3. "不聚集不添乱就是最大贡献-新华网," *Xinhua*, Feb. 5, 2020.
4. Bill Gertz, "Coronavirus May Have Originated in Lab Linked to China's Biowarfare Program," *The Washington Times*, Jan. 26, 2020. These theories, spread in initially by social media, particularly via paranoid Hong Kong and Taiwan Facebook posts, have sometimes been conflated with the more reasonable theory that the pandemic originated in an accidental lab leak linked to research on bat coronaviruses. Michael R. Gordon, Warren P. Strobel and Drew Hinshaw, "Intelligence on Sick Staff at Wuhan Lab Fuels Debate on COVID-19 Origin", *The Wall Street Journal*, May 23, 2021.

in wildlife and other rare animals[5] (though this was not the ultimate source).[6] Both major themes exhibit the obvious warmongering and orientalism common to reporting on China.[7] A slightly more complex variant of the critical response at least understands the economic consequences, even while it exaggerates the potential political repercussions for rhetorical effect. Here we find the usual suspects, ranging from hawkish dragon-slaying politicos to the spilled-latte pearl clutching of haute-liberalism: press agencies from the *National Review* to the *New York Times*[8] implied that the outbreak may bring a "crisis of legitimacy" to the CCP, despite the fact that there was barely a whiff of an uprising in the air.

But the kernel of truth in these predictions lay in their grasp of the economic dimensions of the quarantine—something that could hardly be lost on journalists with stock portfolios thicker than their skulls. Because the fact is that, despite the government's call to isolate oneself, people soon were forced to "gather together" to tend to the needs of production. In America, the consequences of this logic would take its fullest form, with hundreds of thousands literally sacrificed on the altar of the economy. But even in China, the epidemic caused the GDP growth rate to slow to an estimated 2 percent in 2020, below its already flagging growth rate of 6 percent in 2019, the lowest in three decades.[9] With its extension to Europe and the US, the pandemic triggered the global recession that had long been building. But in the midst of all this, a previously unthinkable question has been posed: what actually happens to the global economy when the Chinese furnace begins to grow cold?

Within China itself, the moment brought about a rare, collective

5. Christian Walzer and Aili Kang, "Abolish Asia's 'Wet Markets,' Where Pandemics Breed," *The Wall Street Journal*, Jan. 27, 2020.

6. Zhu Bochen and Wang Yiming, "Research Excludes Wuhan Seafood Market as Origin of SARS-CoV-2: CAS," China.Org.Cn, Feb. 23, 2020.

7. Timothy Brook, "Opinion: Blame China? Outbreak Orientalism, from the Plague to Coronavirus," *The Globe and Mail*, Feb. 13, 2020; James Palmer, "Don't Blame Bat Soup for the Coronavirus," *Foreign Policy*, Jan. 27, 2020.

8. Chris Buckley and Steven Lee Myers, "Where's Xi? China's Leader Commands Coronavirus Fight From Safe Heights," *The New York Times*, Feb. 8, 2020.

9. Amanda Lee and Cissy Zhou. "China's Economy May Expand by 9 percent in 2021, Helping to Overtake US Sooner," *South China Morning Post*, Jan. 1, 2021.

process of questioning and learning about society. The epidemic directly infected over 96,000 people (at relatively conservative estimates),[10]
but it delivered a shock to everyday life under capitalism for 1.4 billion,
trapped in a moment of precarious self-reflection. This moment, while
full of fear, caused everyone to simultaneously ask some deep questions: What will happen to me? My children, family and friends? Will
we have enough food? Will I get paid? Will I make rent? Who is responsible for all this? In a strange way, the subjective experience is somewhat
like that of a mass strike—but one which, in its non-spontaneous, top-
down character and, especially in its involuntary hyper-atomization,
illustrates the basic conundrums of our own strangled political present
as clearly as the true mass strikes of the previous century elucidated the
contradictions of their era. The quarantine, then, is like a strike hol-
lowed of its communal features but nonetheless capable of delivering a
deep shock to both psyche and economy. This fact alone makes it worthy
of reflection.

Of course, speculation on the imminent downfall of the CCP is
predictable nonsense, one of the favorite pastimes of *The New Yorker*
and *The Economist*. Meanwhile, the normal media suppression protocols ensued, in which overtly racist mass-media op-eds published in
legacy outlets were countered by a swarm of web-platform thinkpieces
polemicizing against orientalism and other facets of ideology. But
almost the entirety of this discussion remains at the level of *portrayal*—
or, at best, the politics of containment and the economic consequences
of the epidemic—without delving into the questions of how such diseases get *produced* in the first place, much less distributed. Even this,
however, is not quite enough. Now is not the time for a simple "Scooby-
Doo Marxist" exercise of pulling the mask off the villain to reveal that,
yes, indeed, it was capitalism that caused coronavirus all along! That
would be no better than foreign commentators sniffing about for regime
change. Of course capitalism is culpable—but how, exactly, does the
social-economic sphere interface with the biological, and what lessons
might we draw from the entire experience?

In this sense, the outbreak presents two opportunities for reflection:
First, it is an instructive opening in which we might review substantial

10. Johns Hopkins University Coronavirus Resource Center, Jan. 4, 2021.

questions about how capitalist production relates to the non-human world at a more fundamental level—how, in short, the "natural world," including its microbiological substrata, cannot be understood without reference to how society organizes production (because the two are not, in fact, separate). At the same time, this is a reminder that the only communism worth the name is one that includes the potential of a fully politicized naturalism. Second, we can also use this moment of isolation as an opportunity for a deeper reflection on the present state of Chinese society. Some things only become clear when everything grinds to an unexpected halt, and a slowdown of this sort cannot help but make previously obscured tensions visible. Below, then, we'll explore both these questions, showing not only how capitalist accumulation produces such plagues, but also how the moment of pandemic is itself a contradictory instance of political crisis, making visible to people the unseen potentials and dependencies of the world around them, while also offering yet another excuse for the extension of systems of control even further into everyday life.

The Production of Plagues

The virus behind the present epidemic (SARS-COV-2), was, like its 2003 predecessor SARS-COV-1, as well as the avian flu and swine flu before it, gestated at the nexus of economics and epidemiology. It's not coincidental that so many of these viruses have taken on the names of animals: The spread of new diseases to the human population is almost always the product zoonotic transfer, which is a technical way of saying that such infections jump from animals to humans. This leap from one species to another is conditioned by things like proximity and the regularity of contact, all of which construct the environment in which the disease is forced to evolve. When this interface between humans and animals changes, it also changes the conditions within which such diseases evolve. Beneath the four furnaces, then, lies a more fundamental furnace undergirding the industrial hubs of the world: the evolutionary pressure cooker of capitalist agriculture and urbanization. This provides the ideal medium through which ever-more-devastating plagues are born, transformed, induced to zoonotic leaps, and then aggressively vectored through the human population. To this is added similarly intensive processes occurring at the economy's fringes, where "wild" strains are encountered by people pushed to ever-more extensive agroeconomic incursions into local ecosystems. The most recent coronavirus, in its "wild" origins and its sudden spread through a heavily industrialized and urbanized core of the global economy, represents both dimensions of our new era of political-economic plagues.

The basic idea here is developed most thoroughly by left-wing biologists like Rob Wallace, whose 2016 book *Big Farms Make Big Flu*[11] provides an exhaustive case for the connection between capitalist agribusiness and the etiology of recent epidemics ranging from SARS to Ebola.[12] Even if the cause of such epidemics all trace back to similar sources, they can be loosely grouped into two, often intermixed categories: the first originating at the core of agroeconomic production, and the second in its hinterland. In tracing out the spread of H5N1, also known as the avian flu, he summarizes several key factors of geography for those epidemics that originate in the productive core:

Rural landscapes of many of the poorest countries are now characterized by unregulated agribusiness pressed against periuban slums. Unchecked transmission in vulnerable areas increases the genetic variation with which H5N1 can evolve human-specific characteristics. In spreading over three continents, fast-evolving H5N1 also contacts an increasing variety of socioecological environments, including locale-specific combinations of prevalent host types, modes of poultry farming, and animal health measures.[13]

This spread is, of course, driven by global commodity circuits and the regular labor migrations that define capitalist economic geography. The result is "a type of escalating demic selection" in which the virus is posed with a greater number of evolutionary pathways in a shorter time,

11. Rob Wallace, *Big Farms Make Big Flu. Dispatches on Infectious Disease, Agribusiness, and the Nature of Science*, Monthly Review Press, 2016.

12. Much of what we will explain in this section is simply a more concise summary of Wallace's own arguments, geared toward a more general audience and without the necessity of "making the case" to other biologists through the exposition of rigorous argumentation and extensive evidence. For those who would challenge the basic evidence, we refer throughout to the work of Wallace and his frequent coauthors, such as Rodrick Wallace, Luke Bergmann and Lenny Hogerwef. Below, we also draw from the work of historian and urban theorist Mike Davis and science writer David Quammen.

13. Ibid., p. 52.

enabling the most fit variants to outcompete the others.

This is a point already made in the mainstream press: the fact that "globalization" enables the spread of such diseases more quickly—albeit here with the important addition that this very process of circulation also stimulates the virus to mutate more rapidly. The real question, though, comes earlier: prior to circulation enhancing the resilience of such diseases, the basic logic of capital helps to take previously isolated or harmless viral strains and place them in hyper-competitive environments that favor the specific traits which cause epidemics, such as rapid viral lifecycles, the capacity for zoonotic jumping between carrier species, and the capacity to quickly evolve new transmission vectors. These strains tend to stand out precisely because of their virulence. In absolute terms, it seems like developing more virulent strains would have the opposite effect, since killing the host sooner provides less time for the virus to spread. The common cold is a good example of this principle, generally maintaining low levels of intensity that facilitate its widespread distribution through the population. But in certain environments, the opposite logic can make more sense: when a virus has numerous hosts of the same species in close proximity, and especially when these hosts may already have shortened lifecycles, increased virulence becomes an evolutionary advantage.

Again, the avian flu example is a salient one. Wallace points out that studies have shown "no endemic highly pathogenic strains [of influenza] in wild bird populations, the ultimate source reservoir of nearly all influenza subtypes."[14] Instead, domesticated populations packed together on industrial farms seem to have a clear causative relationship to such outbreaks, for obvious reasons:

Growing genetic monocultures of domestic animals removes whatever immune firebreaks may be available to slow down transmission. Larger population sizes and densities facilitate greater rates of transmission. Such crowded conditions depress immune response. High throughput, a part of any industrial production, provides a continually renewed supply of susceptibles, the fuel for the evolution of virulence.[15]

14. Ibid., p. 56.
15. Ibid., pp. 56–57.

And, of course, each of these characteristics is an outgrowth of the logic of industrial competition. In particular, the rapid rate of "through-put" in such contexts has a starkly biological dimension: "As soon as industrial animals reach the right bulk they are killed. Resident influenza infections must reach their transmission threshold quickly in any given animal... The quicker viruses are produced, the greater the damage to the animal."[16] Ironically, the attempt to suppress such outbreaks through mass culling—as in the recent cases of African swine fever, which resulted in the loss of almost a quarter of the world's pork supply[17]—can have the unintended effect of increasing this selection pressure even more, thereby inducing the evolution of hyper-virulent strains. Though such outbreaks have historically occurred in domesticated species, often following periods of warfare or environmental catastrophe that place enhanced pressure on livestock populations, increases in the intensity and virulence of such diseases have undeniably followed the spread of capitalist production.

The zoonotic transfer of disease is social in a broader sense as well. Urbanization has changed both eating habits and farming practices. China has to feed 1.4 billion people, almost 20% of the world's population but with under 10% of the world's arable land. These basic material facts have been made more complicated by the dramatic changes that China has undergone over the last several decades. In the late 1970s, the urban population of China was less than 20% of the total population; it is now around 60%. That is phenomenally fast urbanization. Nor is it just a distant phenomenon taking place in a far-off country. In many ways, we all come into contact with this urbanization in one way or another: For example, this process was driven by the migration of poor rural residents to new industrial complexes that were arising in places like the Pearl River Delta region of Guangdong Province in the South. There, these new workers flooded into factories producing exports for foreign markets. This means that what seems like a simple purchase of some piece of cheap consumer electronics at Target or Walmart is also essentially a social connection to these spaces. Nor is this a fanciful

16. Ibid., p. 57.
17. Dan Charles, "Swine Fever is Killing Vast Numbers of Pigs in China," *National Public Radio*, Aug. 15, 2019.

metaphor: it's a material link that manifests as a chain of social inter-actions between people and between people and their environment. Seemingly simple economic purchases have resounding consequences. In this case, fueling a wave of urbanization at a size and scope unprecedented in human history.[18]

Alongside this urbanization came changes in diet and in agriculture. We can call these changes the "livestock revolution."[19] As incomes in China rose, the urban population began to eat more and more meat. This was already happening in many parts of the world, with meat consumption growing outside China as well. Setting the stage for this livestock revolution, dramatic increases in production density was a key innovation in the industrialization of meat farming, in which farms were integrated with large industrial meat processors through contracting, rendering the farmer as a mere chicken or pig "custodian" on highly concentrated animal warehouses. As Mike Davis puts it, "the super-urbanization of the human population... has been paralleled by an equally dense urbanization of its meat supply."[20] And this concentration of animals has created new environments within which viruses can evolve. Urbanization within China only accelerated this trend. Guangdong Province isn't just home to factories producing commodities for the West, after all, it is also now one of the biggest producers of poultry for the domestic market. As human populations became much denser in Guangdong so too did animal populations: humans, chickens, ducks, and pigs.

Flu or influenza viruses find their ultimate reservoir in birds, and the farms of South China, where domesticated ducks, chickens, and pigs often cohabit, are the perfect environment for their spillover into human populations. Villagers who once engaged in subsistence farming gradually shifted more of their production to serve the market. At first this meant increasing yields of grain and planting more vegetables, but as urbanization accelerated these villages were encircled by industrial

18. This and the following four paragraphs are based on: Mike Davis, *The Monster at Our Door: The Global Threat of Avian Flu*, Verso, 2005; Wallace, *Big Farms Make Big Flu*; and, David Quammen, *Spillover: Animal Infections and the Next Human Pandemic*, WW Norton, 2018.

19. Davis, *The Monster at Our Door*, p. 81.

20. Ibid., p. 84.

development and increasingly incentivized to produce meat. The result was that many such farms have often replaced rice fields with ponds to produce ducks, leading to higher incomes. To place the scale of this shift into context: China now produces about 80% of the world's ducks. But this production is not just a shift from one land use to another on isolated plots, because these plots exist within a larger process of urbanization, with all its accompanying environmental consequences. Most relevant here is the fact that the destruction of native habitat and wetlands have forced wild birds to make use of these duck ponds on their migrations, and from there influenza viruses spread from the wild birds into the farmed birds.

While many of the avian influenzas cannot spread directly to humans, these viruses do often infect local pigs, putting them in contact with human viruses that infect pigs at the same time. This leads to what can be thought of (in somewhat imprecise terms) as a process of hybridization, with the body of the pig acting as a bridge between avian populations, with their specific viral mix, and human populations carrying human-adapted viruses. Because pigs are often susceptible to both avian and human viruses, those viruses remix across pig populations to create new varieties of influenza that can lead to epidemic diseases. This process is happening continuously: in fact, a new version of the H1N1 influenza has been spreading among pigs on Chinese farms over the last few years and infecting workers on those farms. Luckily, at this point it doesn't seem to be particularly virulent, nor is there any evidence that it is transmissible from human to human. Studies of Chinese pigs from 2011 to 2018, however, found 179 different influenza viruses. In 2009, another version of the H1N1 influenza virus killed between 150,000 and 575,000 people globally and afterwards spread back into world pig populations. China is home to half of the world's pigs, raised to feed its increasingly urban population, so it's no wonder that many of these viruses emerge there. But it's worth noting that this is not an exclusively Chinese problem in any sense: the 2009 H1N1 virus was first detected in the US, after all. Like the 2009 version, this newly found variant of H1N1 contains gene reassortments from humans, birds, and pigs.[21]

21. Sun Honglei et al., "Prevalent Eurasian Avian-like H1N1 Swine Influenza Virus with 2009 Pandemic Viral Genes Facilitating Human Infection," *Proceedings of the*

Another example signals the potential for a truly devastating pandemic to develop, capable of causing an almost unimaginable number of deaths: the H5N1 avian influenza first emerged in 1997 in Hong Kong, and then again in South China in 2003, at the same time that the first SARS coronavirus was spreading globally. The H5N1 influenza is highly virulent—it kills a high percentage of the people infected—but it doesn't spread easily to humans and almost never human to human. When it does spread to humans it comes from close contact with infected birds. The fear with H5N1, however, is that it might evolve in the bird or animal populations of South China to become much more transmissible from human to human. In fact, before the emergence of the first SARS coronavirus, most epidemiologists worried far more about the spillover of new influenza viruses than coronaviruses. This fear is more than justified, if we consider the actual death rate of H5N1, which has killed off roughly half of the small populations of humans it has infected. Even if that death rate were to diminish when spread across a wider, more varied population, it could still realistically result in more deaths than a nuclear war.

It was this fear that led to the upgrading of the Wuhan Institute for Virology (which was approved for construction a biosafety level 4 pathogen lab in 2003) and its pivot toward research on SARS-related coronaviruses. The lab would soon become the focus of conspiracy theories about "bioweapon" research, as well as more legitimate concerns that COVID-19 may have been accidentally released during the lab's research on coronaviruses. In early 2021, interest in the lab leak hypothesis began to spike as investigations of a natural origin came to a standstill and new information about the safety standards and the health histories of lab employees at the Institute came to light. In March of 2021, eighteen scientists penned a joint letter in *Science*, calling for a renewed investigation of this possibility.[22] In the end, the exact origins of the virus will likely never be determined. But the lab leak hypothesis is consistent with the fact that such diseases are becoming more virulent and

---

National Academy of Sciences, Vol. 117, no. 29, July 21, 2020, pp. 17204–10; and Mike Ives, "Scientists Say New Strain of Swine Flu Virus Is Spreading to Humans in China," *The New York Times*, Jun. 30, 2020.

22. Jesse D. Bloom et al., "Investigate the origins of COVID-19", *Science* 372(6543), May 14, 2021.

more prone to zoonotic spread. Indeed, this epidemiological trend—
already evident in China after SARS—was the very reason that such research on bat coronaviruses was initiated at the Institute in the first place.
Moreover, if a lab leak were found to be the cause, it would be due to a
spectacular failure of oversight linked to a general dearth of state capacity, as we will argue below.

History and Etiology

The connection between urbanization and the cultivation of epidemics is itself an old one. While the particularly rapid generation of new
plagues has attended capitalism specifically, the phenomenon as such is
better identified at the urban-agrarian roots of civilization as such. Here,
it becomes necessary to invoke the anti-civilizational underpinnings of
communist thought, emphasized repeatedly by Marx and Engels. Civilization has always been a machine for extermination: the movement of
settled agrarian states across mainland East Asia can be traced in the fos-
sil record, as in the retreat of the elephants to the mountainous south,[23]
and in the pollen record, which shows successive waves of deforestation like a tide ebbing and flowing with the rise and fall of dynasties.[24]
The most devastating pandemics to date (as measured by share of the
total world population that died), were gestated in the long-established
urban civilizations of Europe and Asia, with their spread amplified by
pre-capitalist mercantile networks. Neither the Black Death nor the
swarm of pandemics unleashed across the Western Hemisphere by
European colonization can be understood without reference to their
basic origins in civilization's agrarian structure, as intensified by global
trade.[25]

---

23. Mark Elvin, *The Retreat of the Elephants: An Environmental History of China*,
Yale University Press, 2004.

24. Kam-Biu Liu and Hong-Lie Qiu, "Late-Holocene Pollen Records of Vegeta-
tional Changes in China: Climate or Human Disturbance?" *Terrestrial, Atmospheric and
Oceanic Sciences*, Vol. 5, No. 3, 1994, pp. 393–410.

25. In the case of the bubonic plague, a certain Eurocentric focus has helped to obscure this relationship, since urbanization and agrarian expansion were relatively subdued
in the "middle ages" of the European subcontinent. But the development and distribution
of the plague was intricately linked to the urban, agrarian and mercantile expansions taking place across Asia in these years. In East and Central Asia, the groundwork was laid in

The emergence of capitalism itself was facilitated by these pandemics. The bubonic plague had helped to induce a demographic and, subsequently, economic and political transformation in Europe. As the sheer number of dead resulted in a scarcity of labor in both city and countryside, labor shortages conditioned shifts in production that saw pre-existing class relationships reaffirmed, expanded and consolidated in some places (creating what would later be seen as ideal cases of "feudalism") and overturned in others (as in the political ascent of merchant families in Northern Italy), all facilitated by shifts in agricultural practices to accommodate the scarcity of labor—in particular, the replacement of labor-intensive grains with livestock, most pronounced in England.[26] Similar phenomena occurred in East Asia, accompanying the rise of the Ming Dynasty. What was different in the European case was that the gradual turn to livestock-intensive agriculture among feudal landowners[27] and the turn to commerce among merchants[28] would ultimately fuse into what, retrospectively, can be identified as the first fully capitalist society in England.

---

the Tang dynasty's (618–907 CE) revival of the silk road and the Song dynasty's (960–1279 CE) more systematic colonization of the sub-tropical south, with both dynasties hosting some of the world's largest cities and sitting at the helm of expansive trade routes. These trends were completed by the Mongol conquest, resulting in the rise of the Yuan dynasty (1271–1368 CE) in mainland East Asia, now integrated into a single imperium stretching all the way to Europe. After the fall of the Yuan, the Ming (1368–1644 CE) retained many of these mercantile connections and even extended them, as in the famous voyages of Zheng He, which reached East Africa in the early 1400s.

26. Bruce Campbell, "The Demesne-Farming Systems of Post-Black Death England," *The Agricultural History Review*, Vol. 44, Issue 2, 1996; Christopher Dyer, "Changes in Diet in the Late Middle Ages: The Case of Harvest Workers," *The Agricultural History Review*, Vol. 36 Issue 1, 1988, pp. 21–37; Jessica Cordova, "Mortality and Meals: The Black Death's Impact on Diet in England," University of Washington Tacoma, Medieval History Commons, 2019.

27. It is in this process that Robert Brenner identifies the specific origin of capitalism in England.

28. The role of mercantile networks, such as those of Northern Italy or, later, Holland, are a key part of mainstream accounts of the origin of capitalism, most recently popularized by World Systems Theorists. These accounts, however, conflate commerce with capitalism as such and ignore the more definitive elements of capitalist production, which are found in wide-ranging transformations of production (and first agrarian production), not trade. Even more wide-ranging mercantile networks existed across the Middle East and East Asia, for instance, without leading to the emergence of capitalism.

One key difference that enabled this fusion in Europe, but not East Asia, was the bloody process of conquest and colonization in the Western Hemisphere and the accompanying rise of the Atlantic slave trade. Here we find a second major pandemic—really a wave of multiple pandemics—facilitating the emergence of capitalism, as diseases produced in the heart of civilization finally obtained channels for their transmission across the globe. On the one hand, the old conservative position that deaths in the Americas can be purely attributed to disease is a clear falsehood: disease was accompanied and enabled by warfare, induced famine, enslavement and numerous instances of the intentional pursuit of local genocides. But all of these things also amplified the spread of the pandemics. They're fundamentally inextricable, composing a single wave of mass extermination that traces the spread of Eurasian civilization throughout the world. This laid the immediate groundwork for the emergence of capitalism in England and its spread through later waves of colonization and an intensification of the transatlantic slave trade.

Plagues are very much the shadow of capitalist industrialization, then, while also acting as its harbinger. The cases of smallpox and other pandemics introduced to North America are, however, inadequate to illustrate the specificity of capitalist pandemics, since they were intensified by the long-term separation of populations through physical geography—and such diseases had, regardless, already gained their virulence via pre-capitalist mercantile networks and early urbanization in Asia and Europe, having been one of civilization's most enduring exports. If we instead look to England, where capitalism arose first in the countryside via the mass clearing of peasants from the land to be replaced by monocultures of livestock, we see the earliest examples of these distinctively capitalist plagues.[29] Three different livestock pandemics occurred in 18th century England, spanning 1709–1720, 1742–1760, and 1768–1786. The origin of each was imported cattle from Europe, gestated in prototypical, pre-capitalist epidemics that followed bouts of warfare. But in a rapidly urbanizing proto-capitalist England, cattle had begun to be concentrated in new ways, and the introduction of the infected

29. John Broad, "Cattle Plague in Eighteenth-Century England," *The Agricultural History Review* Vol. 31, no. 2, 1983, pp. 104–15.

stock would therefore rip through the population much more aggressively than it had in Europe. It's not coincidental, then, that the outbreaks were centered on the large London dairies, which provided ideal environments for the intensification of the virus.

Ultimately, the outbreaks were each contained through selective, smaller-scale early culling combined with the application of modern medical and scientific practices—in essence similar to how such epidemics are quelled today. This is the first instance of what would become a clear pattern, mimicking that of economic crisis itself: ever more intense collapses that seem to place the entire system on a precipice, but which are ultimately overcome via a combination of mass sacrifice that clears the market/population and an intensification of technological advances—in this case modern medical practices plus new vaccines, often arriving too little too late, but nonetheless helping to mop things up in the wake of devastation.

But this example from capitalism's homeland should be paired with the effects of capitalist agricultural practices on capitalism's periphery. While the cattle pandemics of early capitalist England were contained, the results elsewhere were far more devastating. The example with the largest historical impact is probably that of the rinderpest outbreak in Africa that took place in the 1890s.[30] The date itself is no coincidence: rinderpest had plagued Europe with an intensity that closely followed the growth of large-scale agriculture, only held in check by the advance of modern science. But the late 19th century saw the height of European imperialism, epitomized by the colonization of Africa. Rinderpest was brought from Europe into East Africa with the Italians, who were seeking to catch up with other imperial powers by colonizing the Horn of Africa through a series of military campaigns. These campaigns mostly ended in failure, but the disease then spread through the indigenous

30. Rinderpest is a viral disease that afflicts cattle, with a high mortality rate. It is thought to have originated in Asia and is closely related to measles and the canine distemper virus. It is now thought that the human measles virus may have emerged from rinderpest via zoonotic transfer in antiquity, since its genetic and geographic origins have been traced to the urban settlements that arose after the Neolithic revolution. For this history, see: Ariane Düx et. al., "Measles virus and rinderpest virus divergence dated to the rise of large cities," *Science*, Vol. 368, No. 6497, June 19, 2020. pp. 1367–1370; And for its relationship to imperialism in Africa, see: Fred Pearce, "Inventing Africa," *New Scientist*, Vol. 167, Issue 2251, Aug. 12, 2000.

cattle population and ultimately found its way into South Africa, where it devastated the early capitalist agricultural economy of the colony, even killing the herd on the estate of the infamous self-professed white supremacist Cecil Rhodes. The larger historical effect was undeniable: killing as many as 80–90% of all cattle, the plague resulted in an unprecedented famine across the predominantly pastoralist societies of Sub-Saharan Africa. This depopulation was then followed by the invasive colonization of the savannah by thornbush, which created a habitat for the tsetse fly which both carries sleeping sickness and prevents the grazing of livestock. This ensured that the repopulation of the region after the famine would be limited and enabled the further spread of European colonial powers across the continent.

Aside from periodically inducing agricultural crises and producing the apocalyptic conditions that helped capitalism surge beyond its early borders, such plagues have also haunted the proletariat in the industrial core itself. Before returning to the many more recent examples, it's worth noting again that there is nothing uniquely Chinese about the coronavirus outbreak. The explanations for why so many epidemics seem to arise in China is not cultural, it's a matter of economic geography. This is abundantly clear if we compare China to the US or Europe when the latter were hubs of global production and mass industrial employment.[31] The result was essentially identical, with all the same core features. Livestock die-offs in the countryside were met in the city by poor sanitary practices and widespread contamination. This became the focus of early liberal-progressive efforts at reform in working class areas, epitomized by the reception of Upton Sinclair's novel *The Jungle*, originally written to document the suffering of immigrant workers in the meat-packing industry, but taken up by wealthier liberals concerned about health violations and the generally unsanitary conditions in which their own food was prepared.

This liberal outrage at "uncleanliness," with all its implied racism, still defines what we might think of as the automatic ideology of most people when confronted with the political dimensions of something

---

31. This is not to say that comparisons of the US to China today are not also informative. Since the US has its own massive agro-industrial sector, it is itself a huge contributor to the production of dangerous new viruses, not to mention antibiotic-resistant bacterial infections.

like the coronavirus or SARS epidemics. But workers have little control over the conditions in which they work. More importantly, while unsanitary conditions do leak out of the factory through contamination of food supplies, this contamination is really just the tip of the iceberg. Such conditions are the ambient norm for those working in them or living in nearby proletarian settlements, and these conditions induce population-level declines in health that provide even better conditions for the spread of capitalism's many plagues.

Take, for example, the case of the Spanish Flu, one of the deadliest epidemics in history. This was one of the earliest outbreaks of H1N1 influenza (related to more recent outbreaks of swine and avian flu), and it was long assumed to have somehow been qualitatively different from other variants of influenza, given its high death toll. While this appears to be true in part (due to the flu's ability to induce an overreaction of the immune system), later reviews of the literature and historical epidemiological research found that it may not have been that much more virulent than other strains. Instead, its high death rate was probably caused primarily by widespread malnourishment, urban overcrowding, and generally unsanitary living conditions in the affected areas, which encouraged not only the spread of the flu itself but also the cultivation of bacterial superinfections on top of the underlying viral one.[32]

In other words, the death toll of Spanish Flu, though portrayed as an unpredictable aberration in the character of the virus, was inextricable from social conditions. Meanwhile, the rapid spread of the flu was enabled by global trade and global warfare, at that time centered around the rapidly shifting imperialisms that survived the first world war. And we find yet again a now-familiar story of how such a deadly strain of influenza was produced in the first place: though the exact origin is still somewhat murky, it's now widely assumed to have originated in domesticated swine or poultry, likely in Kansas. The time and location are notable, since the years following the war were a sort of inflection point for American agriculture, which saw the widespread application of

32. See: JF Brundage and GD Shanks, "What really happened during the 1918 influenza pandemic? The importance of bacterial secondary infections," *The Journal of Infectious Diseases*, Vol. 196, No. 11, Dec. 2007, pp. 1717–1718, author reply pp. 1718–1719; and: DM Morens and AS Fauci, "The 1918 influenza pandemic: Insights for the 21st century," *The Journal of Infectious Diseases*, Vol. 195, No. 7, April 2007, pp 1018–1028.

increasingly mechanized, factory-style methods of production. These trends only grew more intense through the 1920s, and the mass application of technologies like the combine harvester induced both gradual monopolization and ecological disaster, the combination of which resulted in the Dust Bowl crisis and the mass migration that followed. The intensive concentration of livestock that would mark later factory farms had not yet arisen, but the more basic forms of concentration and intensive throughput that had already created livestock epidemics across Europe were now the norm. If the English cattle epidemics of the 18th century were the first case of a distinctly capitalist livestock plague, and the rinderpest outbreak of 1890s Africa the largest of imperialism's epidemiological holocausts, the Spanish flu can then be understood as the first of capitalism's plagues on the proletariat.[33]

Gilded Age

COVID-19 can't be understood without taking into account the ways in which China's last few decades of development in and through the global capitalist system has molded the country's health care system and the state of public health more generally. The epidemic, however novel, is therefore similar to other public health crises that came before it, which tend to be produced with nearly the same regularity as economic

---

33. It's important to note here and throughout that these trends coexist with the very real advances in medical science that have also attended capitalist development, including the capacity to eliminate numerous diseases long endemic to the human species. The case we are making here in no way denies this. Instead, we argue that, even if the technical-scientific capacity to serve human needs and eliminate scarcity is more developed now than ever, those capacities are artificially hindered by the imperative to accumulate. In fact, they are even threatened in the long term by capitalism's tendency to repeatedly position humanity on the brink of extinction. In past decades, that extinction was threatened through global nuclear war. Today, it confronts us in the shape of an ecological catastrophe which is as much microbiological as macroecological. At a more mundane level, the limits capitalism poses to the further development of medical science are clear: endemic diseases that can be eliminated are not, so long as they mostly plague the world's poor. This has been made only more apparent by the rapid, massive mobilization of resources and expertise in the name of developing a vaccine. As always, the communist critique of capitalism is that every advance in the social, scientific and technical ability of the species to serve human needs and close the metabolic rift with the non-human world is simultaneously hindered by the imperatives of the mode of production itself. Every catastrophe averted lays the ground for a larger one to come.

crises, and to be regarded in similar ways within the popular press—as if they were random, "black swan" events, utterly unpredictable and unprecedented. The reality, however, is that these health crises follow their own chaotic, cyclical patterns of recurrence, made more probable by a series of structural contradictions built into the nature of production and proletarian life under capitalism. Much like the case of the Spanish Flu, the coronavirus was originally able to take hold and spread rapidly because of a general degradation of basic healthcare among the population at large. But precisely because this degradation has taken place in the midst of spectacular economic growth, it has been obscured behind the splendor of glittering cities and massive factories. The reality, however, is that expenditures on public goods like health care and education in China remain extremely low, while most public spending has been directed toward brick and mortar infrastructure—bridges, roads, and cheap electricity for production.

Meanwhile, the quality of domestic-market products is often dangerously poor. For decades, Chinese industry has produced high quality, high value exports, made to the highest global standards for the world market, like iPhones and computer chips. But those goods left for consumption on the domestic market have abysmal standards, causing regular scandals and deep public distrust. The many cases have an undeniable echo of Sinclair's *The Jungle* and other tales of Gilded Age America. The largest case in recent memory, the melamine milk scandal of 2008, left a dozen infants dead and tens of thousands hospitalized (though perhaps hundreds of thousands were affected). Since then, a number of scandals have rocked the public with regularity: in 2011 when "gutter oil" recycled from grease traps was found being used in restaurants across the country, or in 2018 when faulty vaccines killed several children, and then one year later when dozens were hospitalized when given fake HPV vaccines.[34] More mild stories are even more rampant, composing a familiar backdrop for anyone living in China: powdered instant soup mix cut with soap to keep costs down, entrepreneurs who sell pigs that died of mysterious causes to neighboring villages, detailed gossip about which street-side shops are most likely to get you sick.

34. Zhuang Pinghui, "Private Hospital Closed after Dozens of Patients given Fake HPV Vaccines," *South China Morning Post*, Apr. 28, 2019.

Before the country's piece-by-piece incorporation into the global capitalist system, services like healthcare in China were once provided (largely in the cities) under the *danwei* system of enterprise-based benefits or (mostly but not exclusively in the countryside) by local healthcare clinics staffed by plentiful "barefoot doctors," all provided as a free service.[35] The successes of socialist-era healthcare, like its successes in the field of basic education and literacy, were substantial enough that even the country's harshest critics had to acknowledge them.[36] Snail fever, plaguing the country for centuries, was essentially wiped out in much of its historical core, only to return in force once the socialist healthcare system began to be dismantled.[37] Infant mortality plummeted and, even despite the famine that accompanied the Great leap Forward, life expectancy jumped from 45 to 68 years between 1950 and the early 1980s. Immunization and general sanitary practices became widespread, and basic information on nutrition and public health, as well as access to rudimentary medicines, were free and available to all. Meanwhile, the barefoot doctor system helped to distribute fundamental, albeit limited, medical knowledge to a large portion of the population, helping to build a robust, bottom-up healthcare system in conditions of severe material poverty. It's worth remembering that all of this took place at a time when China was poorer, per capita, than your average Sub-Saharan African country today.

Since then, a combination of neglect and privatization has substantially degraded this system at the same time that rapid urbanization and unregulated industrial production of household goods and foodstuffs has made the need for widespread healthcare, not to mention food, drug and safety regulations, all the more necessary. Today, China's public spending on health is US $323 per capita, according to figures from the

---

35. Youngsub Lee and Hyoungsup Kim, "The Turning Point of China's Rural Public Health during the Cultural Revolution Period: Barefoot Doctors: A Narrative," *Iranian Journal of Public Health*, Vol. 47, no. Suppl. 1, July 2018, pp. 1–8.

36. Winnie Yip and William C. Hsiao, "What Drove the Cycles of Chinese Health System Reforms?" *Health Systems & Reform*, Vol. 1, no. 1, Jan. 2, 2015, pp. 52–61. Vikki Valentine, "Health for the Masses: China's 'Barefoot Doctors,'" National Public Radio, Nov. 4, 2005.

37. Donald P. McManus, et al, "Schistosomiasis in the People's Republic of China: The Era of the Three Gorges Dam," *Clinical Microbiology Reviews*, Vol. 23, no. 2, April 2010, pp. 442–66.

World Health Organization.[38] This figure is low even among other "upper-middle income" countries, and it's around half that spent by Brazil, Belarus and Bulgaria. Regulation is minimal to non-existent, resulting in numerous scandals of the type mentioned above. Meanwhile, the effects of all this are felt most strongly by the hundreds of millions of migrant workers, for whom any right to basic health care provisions completely evaporates when they leave their rural hometowns (where, under the *hukou* system, they are permanent residents regardless of their actual location, meaning that the remaining public resources can't be accessed elsewhere).

Ostensibly, public healthcare was supposed to have been replaced in the late 1990s by a more privatized system (albeit one managed through the state) in which a combination of employer and employee contributions would provide for medical care, pensions and housing insurance.[39] But this social insurance scheme has suffered from systematic underpayment, to the extent that supposedly "required" contributions on the part of employers are often simply ignored, leaving the overwhelming majority of workers to pay out of pocket. According to the latest available national estimate, only 22 percent of migrant workers had basic medical insurance. Lack of contributions to the social insurance system is not, however, simply a spiteful act by individually corrupt bosses, but is instead accounted for largely by the fact that slim profit margins leave no room for social benefits. In our own calculation, we found that coughing up unpaid social insurance in an industrial hub like Dongguan would cut industrial profits in half and push many firms to bankruptcy.[40] To make up for the massive gaps, China has instituted a bare-bones supplementary medical scheme to cover retirees and the self-employed, which only pays out a few hundred yuan per person per year on average.

This beleaguered medical system produces its own terrifying social tensions. Several medical staff are killed each year and dozens are injured in attacks by angry patients or, more often, the family members of

38. Matthew Jowett, et al, "Spending Targets for Health: No Magic Number," *Health Systems Governance and Finance*, World Health Organization, 2016, p. 34.
39. China Labour Bulletin, "China's Social Security System," Oct. 15, 2019.
40. Chuang, "Picking Quarrels: Lu Yuyu, Li Tingyu and the Changing Cadence of Class Struggle in China," *Chuang Journal*, Issue 2, 2019.

patients who die in their care. Such an attack occurred on Christmas Eve, 2019, when a doctor in Beijing was stabbed to death by the son of a patient who believed his mother died from poor care at the hospital.[41] One survey of doctors found that a staggering 85 percent had experienced workplace violence,[42] and another, from 2015, said that 13 percent of doctors in China had been physically assaulted the previous year.[43] Chinese doctors see four times the number of patients per year than US doctors, while being paid less than US $15,000 per year—for perspective, that's less than per capita income (US $16,760), while in the US an average doctor's salary (about US $300,000) is almost five times as much as per capita income (US $60,200).[44] Before it was shut down in 2016 and its creators arrested, the now defunct unrest-tracking blog project of Lu Yuyu and Li Tingyu recorded at least a few strikes and protests by medical workers every month.[45] In 2015, the last full year of their meticulously collected data, there were 43 such events. They also recorded dozens of "medical treatment [protest] incidents" each month, led by family members of patients, with 368 recorded in 2015.

Under such conditions of massive public divestment from the healthcare system, it's no surprise that COVID-19 took hold so easily. Combined with the fact that new communicable diseases emerge in China at a rate of one every one to two years, conditions seem primed for such epidemics to continue. As in the case of the Spanish Flu, the generally poor conditions of public health among the proletarian population have helped the virus to both gain footing and, from there, to rapidly spread. But, again, it's not just a question of distribution. We have to also understand how the virus itself was produced.

41. China Labour Bulletin, "Focus on Hospital Violence Obscures Basic Problems of Pay and Working Conditions," Dec. 30, 2019.

42. Ni Dandan, "Beijing Doctor Brutally Killed by Patient's Son," *Sixth Tone*, Dec. 28, 2019.

43. "Chinese Turn to US Doctors amid Distrust in Health Service," *South China Morning Post*, Jan. 29, 2018.

44. Ibid.

45. Archived at *https://newsworthknowingcn.blogspot.com*. See also Chuang, "Picking Quarrels."

There is No Wilderness

In the case of the most recent outbreak, the story is less straightforward than the cases of swine or avian influenza, which are so clearly associated with the core of the agro-industrial system. Despite initial speculation about the involvement of other animal vectors, the virus is now clearly identified as having originated in bats, which are usually harvested from the wild (although the particular path from bats to humans is as of yet uncertain). One reason why this origin was not immediately clear, however, was precisely because the wet market in Wuhan where the first transmission to humans occurred trafficked in a number of species, including both domesticated animals like pigs and various wild animals also known to be host to coronaviruses (such as pangolins or various bird species). Even here there is a relationship, however, since the decline in the availability and safety of pork due to the African Swine Fever outbreak has meant that meat prices rose, which led to a boost in the harvest of wild game and in the farming of other species, including those sold in wet markets as "wild" game meat. But without the direct factory farming connection, can the same economic processes really be said to bear any complicity in this particular outbreak?

The answer is yes, but in a different way. Again, Wallace and his numerous collaborators point to not one but two major routes by which capitalism helps to gestate and unleash ever more deadly epidemics: The first, outlined above, is the directly industrial case, in which viruses are gestated within industrial environments that have been fully subsumed within capitalist logic. But the second is the indirect case, which takes place via capitalist expansion and extraction in the hinterland, where previously unknown viruses are essentially harvested from wild populations and distributed along global capital circuits. The two are not entirely separate, of course, but it seems to be the second case that best describes the emergence of the current epidemic.[46] In this instance,

46. In their own way, these two paths of pandemic production mirror what Marx calls "real" and "formal" subsumption in the sphere of production proper. In real subsumption, the actual process of production itself is modified via the introduction of new technologies capable of intensifying the pace and magnitude of output—similar to how the industrial environment has changed the basic conditions of viral evolution such that new mutations are produced at a greater pace and with greater virility. In formal subsumption,

the increased demand for the bodies of wild animals for consumption, medical use, or (as in the case of camels and the MERS outbreak in 2012) a variety of culturally-significant functions builds new global commodity chains in "wild" goods. In others, pre-existing agro-ecological value chains simply extend into previously "wild" spheres, changing local ecologies and modifying the interface between the human and nonhuman.[47]

Wallace is himself clear about this, explaining several dynamics that create worse diseases despite the viruses themselves already existing in "natural" environments.[48] The expansion of industrial production itself "may push increasingly capitalized wild foods deeper into the last of the primary landscape, dredging out a wider variety of potentially proto-pandemic pathogens." In other words, as capital accumulation subsumes new territories, animals will be pushed into less accessible areas where they will come into contact with previously isolated disease strains, all while these animals themselves are becoming targets for commodification as "even the wildest subsistence species are being roped into ag value chains." Similarly, this expansion pushes humans closer to these animals and these environments, which "may increase the interface (and spillover) between wild nonhuman populations and newly urbanized rurality." This gives the virus more opportunity and resources to mutate in a way that allows it to infect humans, pushing up the probability of biological spillover. The geography of industry itself is never quite so cleanly urban or rural anyways, just as monopolized industrial agriculture makes use of both large-scale and smallholder farms: "on a [factory farm] contractor's smallholding along the forest edge, a food animal may catch a pathogen before being shipped back to a processing plant on the outer ring of a major city."

---

which precedes real subsumption, these new technologies are not yet implemented. Instead, previously existing forms of production are simply brought together into new locations that have some interface with the global market, as in the case of hand-loom workers being placed into a workshop that sells their product for a profit—and this is similar to the way in which viruses produced in "natural" settings are brought out from the wild population and introduced into domestic populations via the global market.

47. For an accessible overview drawing in part from Wallace's work, see: Laura Spinney, "Is factory farming to blame for coronavirus?" *The Guardian*, March 28, 2020.

48. Rob Wallace, "Notes on a Novel Coronavirus," *MR Online*, Jan. 29, 2020.

The fact is that the "natural" sphere is already subsumed under a fully global capitalist system that has succeeded in changing baseline climatic conditions and devasting so many pre-capitalist ecosystems that the remainder no longer function as they might have in the past.[49] Here lies yet another causative factor, since, according to Wallace, all these processes of ecological devastation reduce "the kind of environmental complexity with which the forest disrupts transmission chains." The reality, then, is that it's a misnomer to think of such areas as the natural "periphery" of a capitalist system. Capitalism is already global, and already totalizing. It no longer has an edge or border with some natural, non-capitalist sphere beyond it, and there is therefore no great chain of development in which "backward" countries follow those ahead of them on their way up the value chain, nor any true wilderness capable of being preserved in some sort of pure, untouched condition. Instead, capital merely has a subordinated hinterland, itself fully subsumed within global value chains. The resulting social systems—including everything from supposed "tribalism" to renewals of anti-modern fundamentalist religions—are wholly contemporary products, and are almost always *de facto* plugged into global markets, often quite directly. The same can be said of the resulting biological-ecological systems, since "wild" areas are actually immanent to this global economy in both the abstract sense of dependence on the climate and related ecosystems and in the direct sense of being plugged into those same global value chains.

This fact produces the conditions necessary for the transformation of "wild" viral strains into global pandemics. But COVID-19 is hardly the worst of these. An ideal illustration of the basic principle—and the global danger—can be found instead in Ebola.[50] The Ebola virus is a clear case of an existing viral reservoir spilling out into the human population. Current evidence suggests that its origin hosts are several species of bats native to West and Central Africa, which act as carriers but are not themselves affected by the virus. The same is not true for the other wild

49. It's a mistake to equate these ecosystems with the "pre-human" however. China is a perfect example, since many of its seemingly "primeval" natural landscapes were, in fact, the product of much older periods of human expansion which wiped out species that were previously common on the East Asian mainland, such as Elephants.

50. Ebola is a blanket term for 5 or so distinct viruses, the most deadly of which is itself simply named Ebola virus, formerly Zaire virus.

mammals, such as primates and duikers, which periodically contract the virus and suffer rapid, high-fatality outbreaks. Ebola has a particularly aggressive lifecycle beyond its reservoir species. Through contact with any of these wild hosts, humans can also be infected, with devastating results. Several major epidemics have occurred, and the fatality rate for the majority has been extremely high, almost always greater than 50%. The largest recorded outbreak, which continued sporadically from 2013 to 2016 across several West African countries, saw 11,000 deaths.[51] The fatality rate for patients hospitalized in this outbreak was in the range of 57–59%, and much higher for those with no access to hospitals. In recent years, several vaccines have been developed by private companies, but slow approval mechanisms and stringent intellectual property rights have combined with the widespread lack of a health infrastructure to produce a situation in which vaccines have done little to stop the most recent epidemic, centered in the Democratic Republic of Congo (DRC) and now the longest lasting outbreak.[52]

The disease is often presented as if it were something like a natural disaster—at best random, at worst blamed on the "unclean" cultural practices of the forest-dwelling poor. But the timing of these two major outbreaks (2013–16 in West Africa and 2018–present in the DRC) is not a coincidence. Both have occurred precisely when the expansion of primary industries has been further displacing forest-dwelling peoples and disrupting local ecosystems. In fact, this appears to be true for more than the most recent cases, since, as Wallace explains, "every Ebola outbreak appears connected to capital-driven shifts in land use, including back to the first outbreak in Nzara, Sudan in 1976, where a British-financed factory spun and wove local cotton."[53] Similarly, the outbreaks in 2013 in Guinea occurred right after a new government had begun to open the country to global markets and sell off large tracts of land to international agribusiness conglomerates. The palm oil industry, notorious for its role in deforestation and ecological destruction worldwide, seems to have been particularly culpable, since its monocultures both devastate

---

51. "Ebola Situation Reports," *World Health Organization*.

52. Doctors Without Borders–USA, "Ebola Response Failing Communities in DRC as Epidemic Continues," March 7, 2019.

53. Rob Wallace, "Neoliberal Ebola: The Agroeconomic Origins of the Ebola Outbreak," *CounterPunch.org*, July 29, 2015.

the robust ecological redundancies that help to interrupt transmission chains and at the same time literally attract the bat species that serve as a natural reservoir for the virus.[54]

As with the spread of influenza in China, rapid urbanization in West Africa is also at the heart of the issue. And just as elsewhere, urbanization in Africa has led to a growing demand for animal protein. But in the context of general underdevelopment conditioned by a history of colonization and imperialism, the same resources leading to "livestock revolutions" in more heavily-industrialized regions meant that the process would take on a unique character. In West Africa, animal protein had principally come from ocean fishing. Beginning in the 1970s, however, large industrial fishing fleets, many from Europe but also other parts of the world, began to out-compete smaller local fleets, dramatically depleting fish supplies. Fish stocks off the coast of West Africa had fallen by half by the late 1970s. Absent the industrial base or reserves of investment required to facilitate the same livestock concentrations that emerged elsewhere, but still abutting large forests with large animal populations, the demand for animal protein within these new urban complexes induced a spike in the hunting industry and a heavier reliance on what is often called "bushmeat." Alongside, it encouraged smaller landholders to raise more livestock at the margins of these forests, facilitating further potential for spillover between wild and domestic animals.[55]

54. For the West African case specifically, see: Rob Wallace et al., "Did Neoliberalizing West African Forests Produce a New Niche for Ebola," *International Journal of Health Services*, Vol. 46, No. 1 (2016); and for a broader overview of the connection between economic conditions and Ebola as such, see: Robert G Wallace and Rodrick Wallace (Eds) "Neoliberal Ebola: Modelling Disease Emergence from Finance to Forest and Farm," *Springer*, 2016; And for the most direct statement of the case, albeit a less scholarly one, see Wallace's article, cited above: "Neoliberal Ebola: the Agroeconomic Origins of the Ebola Outbreak."

55. J. S. Brashares, et al, "Bushmeat Hunting, Wildlife Declines, and Fish Supply in West Africa," *Science*, Vol. 306, no. 5699, Nov. 12, 2004, pp. 1180–83. Ahmed S. Khan and Sanie SS Sesay, "Seafood Insecurity, Bush Meat Consumption, and Public Health Emergency in West Africa: Did We Miss the Early Warning Signs of an Ebola Epidemic?" *Maritime Studies*, Vol. 14, no. 1, Mar. 11, 2015. Dyhia Belhabib, "Over-Fishing Is Strangling a Key Protein Source for West Africans," *The Conversation*, Sep. 20, 2016. "Reduced Fish Stocks Linked to Increased Bushmeat Trade, Wildlife Declines in W. Africa," *Science Daily*, Dec. 3, 2004.

The sale of large tracts of land to commercial agroforestry companies also entailed both the dispossession of forest-dwelling locals and
the disruption of their ecosystem-dependent local forms of production
and harvest. This often leaves the rural poor with no choice but to push
further into the forest at the same time that their traditional relationship
with that ecosystem has been disrupted. The result is that the survival of
the rural population itself increasingly depends on the hunting of wild
game or harvesting of local flora and timber for sale on global markets.
Such populations then become the stand-ins for the ire of global envi-
ronmentalist organizations, who decry them as "poachers" and "illegal
loggers" responsible for the very deforestation and ecological destruction that pushed them to such trades in the first place. Often, the process
then takes a much darker turn, as in Guatemala, where anti-communist
paramilitaries leftover from the country's civil war were transformed
into "green" security forces, tasked with "protecting" the forest from the
illegal logging, hunting and narcotrafficking that were the only trades
available to its indigenous residents—who had been pushed to such
activities precisely because of the violent repression they had faced from
those same paramilitaries during the war.[56] The pattern has since been
reproduced all over the world, cheered on by social media posts in high
income countries celebrating the (often literally caught-on-camera)
execution of "poachers" by supposedly "green" security forces.[57]

All of this becomes immediately relevant when inquiring into the
origins of SARS-COV-2. The original SARS virus was first seen in humans
in late 2002 in the Pearl River Delta region of China. In March 2003,
a team of scientists from Hong Kong identified the cause of SARS as a
coronavirus, now known as SARS-COV-1, and scientists quickly set out
to find its reservoir host and infection path. This process was difficult.

56. See Megan Ybarra, *Green Wars: Conservation and Decolonization in the Maya
Forest*, University of California Press, 2017.

57. It would certainly be incorrect to imply that all poaching is conducted by the
local rural poor population, or that all ranger forces in different countries' national forests
operate in the same fashion as former anti-communist paramilitaries, but the most violent
confrontations and the most aggressive cases of forestland militarization all seem to essentially follow this pattern. For a wide-ranging overview of the phenomenon, see the special
2016 issue of *Geoforum* (69) devoted to the topic. The preface can be found here: Alice
B. Kelly and Megan Ybarra, "Introduction to themed issue: 'Green security in protected
areas,'" *Geoforum*, Vol. 69, 2016, pp. 171–175.

Early suspicion cast attention on the civet cat, a wild mammal eaten in South China and sold at "wet markets." Authorities banned the sale of civets for a period of time, slaughtering over ten thousand animals due to be sold in live animal markets. After the outbreak died down, however, it was realized that civet themselves were not the ultimate reservoir host, but rather an intermediate amplifying host that facilitated the transmission of the virus to humans. Testing of wild civets turned up none that had the virus. In 2005, they found that bats were instead the most likely reservoir host of the SARS virus.

In fact, bats in South and Central China carried a large number of SARS-like coronaviruses, all evolving and changing in the bat reservoir host. The version of the virus that infected humans in 2002, however, was not directly found among bats, and studies have suggested that the virus evolved in infected civets in a way that they could infect humans, similar to the way that influenza strains pass from birds to pigs and from pigs to humans. Because of the specific role of civets in this transmission chain, the wild animal trade was blamed for the spread of the virus. But this ignores the changing structure of agriculture in China and draws too harsh a divide between "domestic" and "wild" sources of protein. While the civet trade did begin as a wild animal trade—in part an outgrowth of the deforestation of areas within which they lived—civets had been increasingly raised in captive breeding (in other words: farmed) leading up to the SARS outbreak. The testing of the animals on farms that sold most of the civets to the infected market, however, did not find antibodies to SARS. This means that the most likely place in which the infection of civets occurred was not on the farms but instead within the overcrowded trading networks, at some stage of transit preceding their introduction to the wet markets where they were ultimately sold. While the wet markets themselves were the likely venue through which humans were infected with C, the farmed civets were probably infected during transportation or storage on the way to market, most likely by ingesting the droppings of infected bats that may have also entered the same market supply chain. In the end, the SARS-COV-I virus infected over 8000 people worldwide, of which around 900 died.[58]

58. L. F. Wang and B. T. Eaton, "Bats, Civets and the Emergence of SARS," *Wildlife and Emerging Zoonotic Diseases: The Biology, Circumstances and Consequences of*

Containment as an Exercise in Statecraft

With 2.4 million total deaths worldwide within the first year of the pandemic, it now seems natural that the virus should have garnered such media attention.[59] But in the early months of the outbreak, this attention seemed less about the virus itself and more about the spectacular scale of the response, resulting in equally spectacular images of emptied-out megacities that stand in stark contrast to the normal media image of China as over-crowded and over-polluted. At a deeper level, though, what seems most fascinating about the Chinese state's response is the way in which it has been performed, via the media, as a sort of melodramatic dress rehearsal for the full mobilization of domestic counterinsurgency. This gives us real insights into the repressive capacity of the Chinese state, but it also emphasizes the deeper incapacity of that state, revealed by its need to rely so heavily on a combination of total propaganda measures deployed through every facet of the media and the good-will mobilizations of locals otherwise under no material obligation to comply. Both Chinese and Western propaganda have emphasized the real repressive capacity of the quarantine, the former narrating it as a case of effective government intervention in an emergency and the latter as yet another case of totalitarian overreach on the part of the dystopian Chinese state. The unspoken truth, however, is that the very aggression of the clampdown signifies a deeper level of state incapacity.

This itself gives us a window into the nature of the Chinese state, which is still very much under construction. The clampdown presented an opportunity to develop new techniques of social control and crisis response capable of being deployed even in conditions where basic state machinery is sparse or non-existent. Such conditions, meanwhile, offer an interesting (albeit more speculative) picture of how the ruling class in any given country might respond when widespread crisis and active

Cross-Species Transmission, No. 315, 2007, pp. 325–44 and Quammen, *Spillover*.

59. Nsikan Akpan and Kennedy Elliott, "How Coronavirus Compares to Flu, Ebola, and Other Major Outbreaks," *National Geographic*, Feb. 7, 2020. Though coronavirus technically has the lowest case mortality rate of all the diseases mentioned here, its high death toll has largely been the result of its rapid spread to a large number of human hosts, resulting in an elevated absolute death toll despite having a very low fatality rate. As is now clear in the American case, the final effect can be devastating regardless, especially when the response strains medical systems beyond their capacity.

insurrection cause similar breakdowns in even the most robust states. The viral outbreak was in every respect assisted by poor connections between levels of the government: repression of "whistleblower" doctors by local officials (contra the interests of the central government,) ineffective hospital reporting mechanisms and extremely poor provision of basic healthcare are just a few examples. Meanwhile, different local governments have returned to normal at different paces, largely beyond the control of the central state (except in Hubei, the epicenter). At the time of writing, it seems almost entirely random which ports are operational and which locales have restarted production. This bricolage quarantine has meant that long-distance city-to-city logistics networks remain disrupted, since any local government appears able to simply prevent trains or freight trucks from passing through its borders. And this base level incapacity of the Chinese government has forced it to deal with the virus as if it were an insurgency, roleplaying civil war against an invisible enemy.

The national state machinery really started to roll on January 22nd, when authorities upgraded the emergency response measures in all of Hubei province, and told the public they had the legal authority to set up quarantine facilities, as well as to "collect" any personnel, vehicles, and facilities necessary to the containment of the disease, or to set up blockades and control traffic (thereby rubberstamping a phenomenon it knew would occur regardless).[60] In other words, the full deployment of state resources actually began with a call for volunteer efforts on behalf of locals. On the one hand, such a massive disaster will strain any state's capacity (see, for instance, hurricane response in the US). But, on the other, this repeats a common pattern in Chinese statecraft whereby the central state, lacking efficient formal and enforceable command structures that extend all the way down to the local level, must instead rely on a combination of widely-publicized calls for local officials and local citizens to mobilize and a series of after-the-fact punishments meted out to the worst responders (framed as crackdowns on corruption). The only truly efficient response is to be found in specific areas where the central state focuses the bulk of its power and attention—in this case,

60. State Council of the PRC, "国新办举行新型冠状病毒感染的肺炎防控工作新闻发布会," Jan. 1, 2020.

Hubei generally and Wuhan specifically. By the morning of January 24th, the city was already in an effective full lock down, with no trains in or out nearly one month after the new strain of the coronavirus was first detected. National health officials have declared that health authorities have the ability to examine and quarantine anyone at their discretion. Beyond the major cities of Hubei, dozens of other cities across China, including Beijing, Guangzhou, Nanjing and Shanghai, have launched lockdowns of varying severity on flows of people and goods in and out of their borders.[61]

In response to the central state's call to mobilize, some localities have taken their own strange and severe initiatives. The most frightening of these are to be found in four cities in Zhejiang province, where thirty million people have been issued local passports, allowing only one person per household to leave home once every two days.[62] Cities like Shenzhen and Chengdu have ordered that each neighborhood be locked down, and allowed entire apartment buildings to be quarantined for 14 days if a single confirmed case of the virus is found within.[63] Meanwhile, hundreds have been detained or fined for "spreading rumors" about the disease,[64] and some who have fled quarantine have been arrested and sentenced to lengthy jail time[65]—and the jails themselves are now experiencing a severe outbreak, due to officials' incapacity to isolate sick individuals even in an environment literally designed for easy isolation.[66] These sorts of desperate, aggressive measures mirror those of extreme cases of counterinsurgency, most clearly recalling the actions of military-colonial occupation in places like Algeria, or, more recently, Palestine. Never before have they been conducted at this scale, nor in megacities

---

61. France Médias Monde, "武汉肺炎 27 城遭封 半个中国半封闭 下一个遭封大城会是谁?" Jun. 2, 2020.

62. Viola Zhou, "Zhejiang Province next to Shanghai Adopts Draconian Quarantine Measures," *South China Morning Post*, Feb. 6, 2020.

63. See the additional articles and interviews printed in this volume for more accurate, updated detail on exactly what measures were taken in the midst of the lockdown and how they relate to larger trends in the development of local organs of government.

64. "China: Protect Human Rights While Combatting Coronavirus Outbreak," *Chinese Human Rights Defenders*, Jan. 31, 2020.

65. "男子从疫情发生地到湛江不隔离，还隐瞒孙子等人行踪！被立案侦查," *Sohu*, Feb. 8, 2020.

66. Linda Lew and Kinling Lo, "China Sends in Top Investigators after Coronavirus Erupts in Jails," *South China Morning Post*, Feb. 21, 2020.

of this kind that house much of the world's population. The conduct of the clampdown then offers a strange sort of lesson for those concerned with the question of global revolution, since it is, essentially, a dry run of state-led reaction.

Incapacity

This particular clampdown benefits from its seemingly humanitarian character, with the Chinese state able to mobilize greater numbers of locals to help in what is, essentially, the noble cause of strangling the spread of the virus. But, as is to be expected, such clampdowns always also backfire. Counterinsurgency is, after all, a desperate sort of war conducted only when more robust forms of conquest, appeasement and economic incorporation have become impossible. It is an expensive, inefficient and rearguard action, betraying the deeper incapacity of whatever power is tasked with deploying it—be they French colonial interests, the waning American imperium, or others. The result of the clampdown is almost always a second insurgency, bloodied by the crushing of the first and made even more desperate. Here, the quarantine will hardly mirror the reality of civil war and counterinsurgency. But even in this case, the clampdown has backfired in its own ways. With so much of the state's effort focused on control of information and constant propaganda deployed via every possible media apparatus, unrest has expressed itself largely within the same platforms.

The death of Dr. Li Wenliang, an early whistleblower on the dangers of the virus, on February 7th shook citizens cooped up in their homes across the country.[67] Li was one of eight doctors rounded up by police for spreading "false information" in early January, before later contracting the virus himself. His death triggered anger from netizens and a statement of regret from the Wuhan government.[68] People were beginning to see that the state is made up of bumbling officials and bureaucrats who have no idea what to do but still put on a strong face.[69] This fact

67. Tom Daly and Min Zhang, "American Dies of Coronavirus in China; Five Britons Infected in French Alps," *Reuters*, Feb. 10, 2020.
68. Laurie Chen, "Mourners Pay Tribute to Chinese Doctor Who Blew Whistle on Coronavirus," *South China Morning Post*, Feb. 7, 2020.
69. In a podcast interview, Au Loong Yu, citing friends in the mainland, said that

was essentially revealed when the mayor of Wuhan, Zhou Xianwang, was forced to admit on state television that his government had delayed releasing critical information about the virus after an outbreak had occurred. The very tension caused by the outbreak, combined with that induced by the state's total mobilization, has begun to reveal to the general populace the deep fissures that lie behind the paper-thin portrait that the government paints of itself. In other words, conditions such as these have exposed the fundamental incapacities of the Chinese state to growing numbers of people who previously would have taken the government's propaganda at face value.

If a single symbol could be found to express the basic character of the state's response, it would be something like a popular video which began to circulate shortly after the outbreak began, shot by a local in Wuhan and shared with the Western internet via Twitter in Hong Kong.[70] This video shows a number of people who appear to be doctors or first-responders of some sort outfitted in full protective gear taking a picture with the Chinese flag. The person shooting explains that they're outside that building every day for various photo ops. The video then follows the men as they take off the protective gear and stand around chatting and smoking, even using one of the suits to clean off their car. Before driving off, one of the men unceremoniously dumps the protective suit into a nearby trash can, not even bothering to stuff it to the bottom where it won't be seen. Videos such as this one have spread rapidly before being censored—small tears in the thin veil of the state-sanctioned spectacle.

At a more fundamental level, the quarantine led to deep economic reverberations in people's personal lives. The macroeconomic side of this has been widely reported, with a massive decrease in Chinese growth leading to a new global recession, especially when matched with

---

the Wuhan government is effectively paralyzed by the epidemic. Au suggested that the crisis was not only tearing apart the fabric of society, but also the bureaucratic machine of the CCP, which would only intensify as the virus spreads and becomes an intensifying crisis for other local governments across the country. The interview is by Daniel Denvir of *The Dig*, published Feb. 7, 2020.

70. The video itself is authentic, but it is worth noting that Hong Kong has been a particular hotbed of racist attitudes and conspiracy theories directed toward mainlanders and the CCP, so much of what gets shared on social media by Hong Kongers about the virus should be carefully fact-checked.

continuing stagnation in Europe[71] and GDP in the US declining over three percent for the year.[72] As the pandemic spread across the globe Chinese firms and those fundamentally dependent on Chinese production networks began looking into their "force majeure" clauses, which allow for delays or cancellation of the responsibilities entailed by both parties in a business contract when that contract becomes "impossible" to perform.[73] The mere prospect caused a cascade of demands for production to be restored across the country. When the revival of industry did occur, it happened in a patchwork fashion, marked by severe labor shortages and then immediately hobbled by sharp declines in demand from foreign markets (although demand for PPE and other goods increased) as lockdowns began to cascade across the globe.

But other effects have been less visible, though arguably far more important. Many migrant workers, including those who had stayed in their work cities for Spring Festival or were able to return prior to various lockdowns being implemented, were stuck in a dangerous limbo. In Shenzhen, where the vast majority of the population are migrants, locals reported that the number of homeless people increased. Even as of January 2021, cities across the country are now running winter homelessness clean-up drives to clear out those sleeping under bridges, hanging out around train stations, etc. Not only major cities like Beijing, Shanghai and Qingdao, but also third and fourth tier cities like Hengshui and Huainan have sent out teams from "rescue centers" that are less homeless shelters and more corrals for those living on the streets.[74] The goal of these centers, in fact, is to send the homeless "home" to their place of household registration far outside the city where they are found (often a distant rural area or minor city), getting them off the books of the local government and making them someone else's bureaucratic problem. Despite the relative recovery in output, the aftershocks of the pandemic's effect on the labor market are still being experienced. Maybe the most

71. Michael Roberts, "From Amber to Red," *The Next Recession*, Jan. 15, 2019.

72. "The Conference Board Economic Forecast for the US Economy," *The Conference Board*, Dec. 9, 2020.

73. Osborne Clarke, "Coronavirus: Force Majeure, Supply Chains and Contractual Performance," *Lexology*, Feb. 17, 2020.

74. "青岛拉网排查寒夜救助露宿人员 4名流浪人员被接回救助站," *Bandao*, Dec. 30, 2020; "衡水市救助管理站为流浪乞讨人员寒冬送暖," *HebNews*, Jan. 4, 2020; 淮南深入开展 "寒冬送温暖" 专项行动, *HnNews*, Jan. 4, 2020.

stark example of this phenomenon was the fact that the new people appearing on the streets in the late winter and early spring of 2020 were not long-term homeless, instead having the appearance of literally just being dumped there with nowhere else to go—still wearing relatively nice clothes, unfamiliar with where best to sleep rough or to obtain food. Various buildings in the city saw an increase in petty theft during the year, mostly of food delivered to the doorstep of residents who were staying home for the quarantine. Across the board, workers lost wages as production stalled and those that were able to return have since been working overtime nonstop to make up for the loss. The best case scenarios during work stoppages were dorm-quarantines like that imposed at the Shenzhen Foxconn plant, where new returnees were confined to their quarters for a week or two, paid about a third of their normal wages and then allowed to return to the production line.[75] Poorer firms had no such option, and the government's attempt to offer new lines of cheap credit to smaller businesses probably did little in the long run.[76]

The Surreal War

Meanwhile, the clumsy early response to the virus, the state's reliance on particularly punitive and repressive measures to control it, and the central government's inability to effectively coordinate across localities to juggle production and quarantine simultaneously all indicate that a deep incapacity remains at the heart of the state machinery. If, as our friend Lao Xie argues, the emphasis of the Xi administration has been on "state-building," it would appear that much work in that regard remains to be done.[77] At the same time, if the campaign against COVID-19 can also be read as a dry run against insurgency, it is notable that the central government only had the capacity to provide effective coordination in the Hubei epicenter and that its responses in other provinces—even wealthy and well-regarded places like Hangzhou—remained largely

75. Adam Rogan, "Foxconn Production in China below Normal Operations Because of Coronavirus," *Journal Times*, Feb. 20, 2020.

76. Lulu Chen, Jinshan Hong, and Bloomberg, "Coronavirus Hits China's Workers as Businesses Say They Can't Pay Wages Now," *Fortune*, Feb. 19, 2020.

77. Chuang, "A State Adequate to the Task: Conversations with Lao Xie," *Chuang Journal*, Issue 2: Frontiers, 2019.

uncoordinated and desperate. We can take this in two ways: first, as a lesson on the weakness underlying the hard edges of state power, and second as a caution on the threat that is still posed by uncoordinated and irrational local responses when the central state machinery is overwhelmed.

These are important lessons for an era when the destruction wrought by unending accumulation has extended both upward into the global climatic system and downward into the microbiological substrata of life on Earth. Such crises will only become more common. As the secular crisis of capitalism takes on a seemingly non-economic character, new epidemics, famines, floods and other "natural" disasters will be used as a justification for the extension of state control, and the response to these crises will increasingly function as an opportunity to exercise new and untested tools for counterinsurgency. A coherent communist politics must grasp both of these facts together. At a theoretical level, this means understanding that the critique of capitalism is impoverished whenever it is severed from the hard sciences. But at the practical level, it also implies that the only possible political project today is one able to orient itself within a terrain defined by widespread ecological and microbiological disaster, and to operate in this perpetual state of crisis and atomization.

In a quarantined China, we began to glimpse such a landscape, at least in its outlines: empty late-winter streets dusted by the slightest film of undisturbed snow, phone-lit faces peering out of windows, happenstance barricades staffed by a few spare nurses or police or volunteers or simply paid actors tasked with hoisting flags and telling you to put your mask on and go back home. The contagion is social. So, it should come as no real surprise that the only way to combat it at such a late stage is to wage a surreal sort of war on society itself. Don't gather together, don't cause chaos. But chaos can build in isolation, too. As the furnaces in all the foundries cooled to softly crackling embers and then to snow-cold ash, the many minor desperations cannot help but leak out of their quarantine to gently cascade together into a greater chaos that might one day, like this social contagion, prove too difficult to contain.

2.
Worker Organizing under the Pandemic

Below is our translation of an anonymous Chinese article from the mainland left blog Worker Study Room, originally published in May 2020, along with a postscript from December 2020.[1] It is the only attempt that we're aware of to provide a systematic overview of workers' lives and job conditions, labor struggles and related activism in China during the first few months of the COVID-19 pandemic—although there have been accounts of individual cases, some of which are cited here. The piece is a product of what we consider to be the most fruitful left-wing current in contemporary China, which concerns itself primarily with worker inquiry and the transmission of proletarian stories among workplaces. It not only succeeds in framing the overall dynamic across regions and beyond individual struggles, but also hints at the potentials hidden in some of the pandemic organizing that extended outside the workplace.

1. "Some Observations and Thoughts on Worker Issues in the Pandemic" [疫情下工人问题的一些观察和思考], *Worker Study Room* [工人自习室], May 25, 2020.

Most striking here are a few of the telling contrasts with conditions in Europe and, in particular, the United States. In almost every respect, the Chinese situation seems to be an inversion of that in the US, where the shutdown helped to spur the largest, most assertive mass rebellion in recent history, including a steady simmer of labor unrest that has gone relatively unnoticed beneath the more spectacular riots against the police. In China, however, despite a recent history of worker organizing, struggles have remained muted, with the late 2020 uptick in some sectors and regions (described in the authors' postscript) still moderate compared not only with the explosions abroad but also with previous Chinese waves of industrial unrest from the late 1990s through the mid-2010s. In part, this contrast may be due to another, identical inversion: the fact that China readily contained the pandemic while the US has still brutally failed to do so.

But there is also a more telling inversion hinted at in the text below, relating to the question of exactly how China was able to successfully contain the initial outbreak. It remains evident that Chinese state capacity, while in the ascent, is nonetheless lower than that seen elsewhere (in, say, Taiwan, South Korea or any continental European nation). Meanwhile, the American state seems powerful and rich in expertise, even if it is clearly in decline. How, then, was China able to mobilize the resources to contain the outbreak in such a large population? China's relative success appears to have been driven by an effective recognition of the limited capacity of the state, and a subsequent devolution of power not only to local governments (who were given wide-ranging authority for containment) but also to numerous ad hoc mutual aid groups of the type outlined in the text below.

It was largely the activity of regular Chinese people that helped to contain the virus—many of whom (especially medical workers) put in immense work and took serious personal risks. Containment was emphatically not the product of the quasi-magical powers of an authoritarian state, as many media accounts would have us believe. The difference in the US, of course, is the absence of a similar mass mobilization around containment of the virus, with this task being deferred to the supposedly competent state authorities, who have proved themselves anything but. The US government has demonstrated that it does, indeed, still have an immense capacity for coordination and the allocation of resources—but this capacity has been directed almost exclusively into the hands of the police state and away from any real social functions. Such a shift is clearly indicative of a once capacious state in the throes of a decades-long decay.

Overall, then, the piece translated here gives one of the best windows into the average Chinese worker's experience under the pandemic, while also giving some illustration of the broader social organizing that helped to contain the outbreak. It also acts as an example of some of the more interesting practical analysis offered by the contemporary Chinese left.

— Chuang

WORKER ORGANIZING UNDER THE PANDEMIC

This article focuses on workers' organizing and actions in China during the pandemic, particularly within the Pearl River Delta (PRD). The article aims to bring together some useful information and make an initial analysis of the situation.

— *Worker Study Room, May 2020*

Self-Organization among Ordinary People

The unprecedented health crisis of COVID-19 witnessed the rapid emergence of self-organized mutual aid among residents and students. These included localized organizational efforts by residents of Wuhan and other parts of Hubei, people elsewhere organizing from a distance to provide support for healthcare workers and patients in the province, as well as similar local self-organization in other cities and regions.

There also emerged some temporary organizations and actions related more directly to the interests of workers as such. The most noticeable of these were the "face mask supply groups" providing masks and equipment to sanitation workers such as street-sweepers. The main participants in these groups were students, who investigated the poor safety conditions of the sanitation industry and decided to provide the workers with PPE such as masks and gloves, as well as with educational materials about how to protect oneself during the pandemic.

The formation of the face mask supply groups across the various regions was not the result of any plan made in advance. Instead, these were initiatives seeded online in response to the immediate situation that then bloomed rapidly across the country. The process by which such groups formed in each place thus had a character unique to that location. In some places they formed out of university student groups that were already concerned with social issues, elsewhere they evolved from the aforementioned groups initially focused on sanitation workers, while in still other places groups formed with the involvement of explicitly left-wing students.

The organizational practices of these groups were relatively open. Those who initiated their formation did not exercise absolute authority over the groups within a hierarchical system, and the planning of events and division of labor were decided through discussion among participants. Many of the founders did not have any experience with social or community work, and some were not even in the locale where the team would be operating but were instead participating online. The groups worked through the democratic, egalitarian participation of all, with enthusiastic volunteers collecting and sharing information day and night.[2]

The face mask supply groups mainly operated online, the whole process was transparent and open, and their activities were not politically sensitive: they did not pull back the dark curtain (exposing secrets of state malfeasance) or provoke negative public opinion. They thus played a supplementary role to the state's counter-pandemic work rather than an antagonistic one. The groups also consciously adopted a cautious approach. For example, when it came to fundraising, the volunteer groups paid close heed to the new Charity Law's strict regulations about what types of entities are allowed to raise funds.[3] Some dealt with this obstacle by affiliating themselves with more established foundations. All of the groups working in this area were highly cognizant of the domestic political situation and avoided unnecessary risks. Even though some of those involved in establishing these groups were known to have been under surveillance by the authorities, the groups were not prevented from functioning.

Online Organizing

Since face-to-face communication had largely ceased during the pandemic, an array of online activities emerged. Based on our own observations, numerous new groups focused on worker issues have formed. These

2. For example, see: "How the Mask Volunteer Actions of High School Students in Shenzhen Spread to Beijing, Shanghai and Guangzhou" [深圳高中生的口罩志愿行动，如何席卷北上广等城市].

3. *Translators*: The Charity Law, meant to curb the influence of threats such as foreign powers and domestic dissidents on civil society in China, is introduced here: Ashwin Kaja and Timothy P. Stratford, "China Implements New Charity Law," *Global Policy Watch*, Nov. 1, 2016.

include: groups that are calling for, organizing and conducting online polls to press the government to extend the Spring Festival holiday; groups that formed to protect worker rights when they resume work; and other groups to share information about trends in the pandemic, protective measures against the virus and policy information. The founders and participants in these groups have some relationship with pre-existing student groups focused on social issues, have been in worker organizations and include some left-wing activists. The workers in these online groups are from different factories and they are often from different places, meaning that they were not familiar with each other prior to the pandemic.

It was easy for people to participate in groups such as those that were mobilizing to extend the Spring Festival break. This is largely because the goals were clear, the timeframe for action was short, there was not much need to establish deep connections between people involved and it was easy to see a result through online activity. But for groups like those organizing to protect workers' rights and wages when they resume work, it's only through the workers taking action in their own workplaces that they can resolve the issue. For online organizing, where participants are not familiar with each other and are dispersed, it's difficult to take meaningful action. And this is without even considering the extra difficulties and risks posed by state surveillance. As a result, at this point such groups are primarily involved with providing advice, outlining the situation that workers are facing, and providing a forum for communication.

These groups also play a role in educating and circulating analyses of the unfolding events. The conditions of the pandemic have pushed workers to focus on wider issues than those of their wages and income. Since so many long-standing social crises have now become evident within the more general catastrophe, the tricks of the ruling class have also been made plain for all to see. While ordinarily workers sometimes avoid thinking about the impact of current events on their lives, it is impossible not to consider the impact of the pandemic on society and on oneself. For example, people are now driven to ask questions like: where did the outbreak come from, and how did it spread? Meanwhile, they begin to contemplate the importance of social security and wonder what a safe return to work might look like.

Activities of Pearl River Delta Workers during the Pandemic

For the sake of making this narrative clearer, the analysis of the period from January 23 until the time of writing will be split into three parts more or less corresponding to distinct phases of the pandemic:

1. START OF THE PANDEMIC
   Late January to Early February

2. FIRST STAGE OF THE RETURN TO WORK
   Mid-February to Early March

3. LATER STAGE OF THE RETURN TO WORK
   After Mid-March

START OF THE PANDEMIC
Late January to Early February

Industrial workers in the PRD appeared calm during the relief operations at the beginning of the outbreak. At the time of the initial outbreak, workers had already left their workplaces for the Spring Festival holidays to visit their hometowns and were therefore dispersed across the country. Thus, most were monitored by their respective neighborhoods or villages, which operated through a program of family-based prevention. Workers who had already had difficulty linking up in an effective way while in the factory were now further torn apart by the sudden onset of the pandemic. Moreover, many ordinary workers found it too difficult to obtain the prophylactic medical resources they needed and to coordinate online. It is therefore not surprising that workers in general appeared to be passive and silent.

Sanitation workers, who have been the focus of much attention during this pandemic, have not undertaken any significant collective action that we know of, despite their working throughout the whole period. Even in areas where there has been a tradition of resistance in the past, the response from sanitation workers has been muted, and other workers who remained working during the Spring Festival, such as those in transportation and logistics, including delivery workers, have not carried out any significant action aimed at raising protection requirements. Some possible reasons for this might be: When Wuhan was sealed off and news of the pandemic first came out, most people did not have a clear idea of the severity of the new coronavirus and were unaware of the danger. Later, as news of the outbreak spread nationwide through official and private channels, and quarantine control measures were strengthened everywhere, the pandemic did not break out on a large scale outside Hubei. Therefore, the workers who remained working didn't feel very threatened by the disease. This is different from many countries across Europe and the Americas where workers from various industries working in life-threatening situations during the spread of the pandemic went on strike in order to demand protective measures.

Beyond this, sanitation workers in non-infected areas were already in normal times facing occupational health and safety issues such as non-compliance with protective measures. These pre-existing problems only become prominent during outbreaks of infectious diseases, which finally brought them more widespread attention through the work of such volunteers. For sanitation workers (and similarly for other workers), occupational health and safety issues, while directly related to their own health, are of more concern than wage issues. Before the workers felt their health was really in danger they generally treated the problem with a somewhat lackadaisical attitude, hoping that dumb luck would protect them (侥幸心理). Overall, the issue of occupational health and safety is also more complex than the issue of wages since it requires that workers grasp more information. This is why systematically organized education efforts are needed for workers to be able to achieve an improvement in this field. The activity of the volunteer face mask supply groups was one such "external" effort directed towards the sanitation workers, providing them with donated equipment and information about personal protection. Meanwhile, these student volunteers also had an opportunity to step out of their lives, previously focused solely on school, and come into contact with a social group from a very different background. All this is of course still a long way from bringing about a collective action by workers.

A Small Number of Spontaneous Actions

A senior employee of a private company in Shenzhen who had already experienced SARS was, upon hearing news about the pandemic in early January, conscientious enough to take the initiative of ordering face masks to protect his coworkers. Because the company was unresponsive, he set up an awareness-raising group for protection measures among his coworkers and started stocking up on masks. When the company restarted operations and demanded workers return to their posts, he again made an appeal to his colleagues to collectively demand that they continue working from home. He reminded the young audience listening to his presentation that: "Our present is your future. Most of the people who graduate will go on to work for someone else. Making money is the only thing bosses care about, not the health of their employees. For us it's a matter of life and death."

There were also frontline workers who used the group to post information about where to locally buy affordable protective equipment and helping others in the community to obtain these goods at a reasonable price.

Other than this, there were, according to our knowledge and China Labour Bulletin statistics, only a few wage demands made in this period.[4]

FIRST STAGE OF THE RETURN TO WORK
Mid-February to Early March

For various reasons, the State Council extended the Spring Festival holiday to February 2nd, with each province setting its own exact time for the resumption of work. Most provinces implemented a gradual return to work beginning no earlier than February 10th (day 17 of the first

---

4. *Translators*: This refers to data from the China Labour Bulletin (CLB) Strike Map: https://maps.clb.org.hk. While the left-liberal CLB is often criticized for receiving money from Western governments, capitalist foundations and labor unions, and its data reflects only the small portion of labor struggles whose reports the staff occasionally collects from Chinese media, it is currently the only publicly available source that is updated regularly, so it is widely used by labor activists and researchers of all political stripes.

lunar month), but, because of the pandemic, certain provinces and
municipalities postponed the resumption of operations in construction
and other industries to a later date.[5] This partial postponement was an
official government policy in the form of an executive order that was
publicly announced via lower-level government departments. It is
unclear how the policy was drawn up, since the process of its formulation was not transparent. However, when coupled with a series of stringent control measures, it did actually help to stem a new outbreak of the
pandemic after the return to work, which meant that people returned
to work without undue fear and panic over the risks of being infected.
Consequently, with the exception of online groups calling for a more
general postponement of the return to work, workers' resistance at the
beginning of this period was rather weak and there are no reports of large-
scale incidents over issues of protective equipment or health policies
in the companies that had resumed production.

To restart work, companies had to comply with protective measures
and submit to a series of audits conducted by the local government.[6]
If new cases appeared in any company or factory, they were to immediately stop operations and isolate the whole company or even the whole
building.[7] In the initial return to work period, neighborhoods and
factories were imposing stringent quarantine measures for workers. For
example, factories with dormitories demanded that employees remain
inside dorm rooms under a lock-down regime. In factories with canteens, the dining tables were slightly modified by adding screens to guarantee separation for individuals sitting down to eat. In factories without
canteens, employees were required to eat their meals while scattered
outdoors. As a result, most people were not overly concerned about

5. "Schedule for national provinces to restart work and production! 28 provinces
and cities make adjustments, 35 national and provincial level documents enclosed!"
[全国各省复工复产时间表！28个省市做了调整, 附35份国家、省份文件！];
"More delayed return-to-work notices issued across the country again! Updated resumption of work in the provinces and cities, extended to March 16 at the latest!" [全国各地
再次发布延迟复工通知！各省市更新复工时间, 最晚延至3月16日！].
6. "Return to work by province and city" [全国各省市复工复岗时间].
7. "Measures taken in Shenzhen and Chengdu: all neighborhoods are on lock-down!
In case of positive results whole building sealed off for 14 days" [深圳、成都出手了：
所有小区封闭管理！有确诊整个单元楼隔离14天]; "Company quarantined due to
coronavirus case discovered in an office building in Guangzhou" [广州一写字楼出现新
冠肺炎确诊病例 全公司被隔离].

getting infected upon returning to work. On top of this, there were punitive measures for firms that didn't follow the rules: if some small companies restarted work in violation of the policy, workers would complain to the subdistrict office or to the management of the industrial park and the company would be penalized and instructed to rectify the situation. There were occasional reports in the media of factories, training schools, places of entertainment and similar enterprises which had restarted production early, and in such cases the persons in charge were put under "administrative detention" (行政拘留).[8] The government, whether central or local, adopted stringent measures in order to more tightly control potential new outbreaks, and there were many channels for complaints. In particular, people could use WeChat to directly reach relevant departments and log complaints on any manner of incident related to the pandemic.[9] To resolve issues pertaining to the revival of production, workers could now (in contrast with the normal situation) more easily complain when factories violated regulations. The result was that collective actions became less likely.

In this period the main conflicts were to be found in the necessity of simultaneously controlling the pandemic and restarting production. There were only a limited number of companies truly capable of realizing an all-round return to work. Besides strict control measures and complicated return to work procedures, the temporary shutdown of public transport in Hubei, Henan, Liaoning, Shandong, Hebei and other provinces as well as certain cities also significantly hindered the flow of workers back to the factories. Many cities and provinces simply imposed a two week self-quarantine period before returning workers could go back to work.[10] On top of this, many workers were afraid of getting infected on their journey to work or in the factory itself and so refused to return. This meant that many companies were unable to fully restart their operations even after being officially allowed to do so. In order

8. *Translators*: "Administrative detention" is contrasted with "criminal detention" depending on the classification of the crime, roughly corresponding to the distinction between civil and criminal law in some other countries. In China, however, the difference is often more political, with suspected dissidents usually placed under criminal detention

9. "Businesses illegally return to work early during pandemic prevention and control period, check!" [疫情防控期间企业违规提前复工，查！].

10. "Which cities and provinces are currently implementing a two week isolation period before returning to work" [目前哪些省市返工返岗需要隔离14天].

to both control the pandemic and address the sudden labor shortage, many localities did all they could to make sure that factories got a sufficient supply of labor power and chartered transport to bring workers from labor-exporting localities to factories in the PRD and the Yangtze Delta.[11] At the same time factories increased their drive for new staff through methods like giving rewards to recruiters. Enterprises like the Shenzhen Foxconn plant even adopted recruitment strategies like the "I want to hire" (我要聘) campaign, during which they promised every newcomer that came into the company before the 31st of March a record high bonus of up to 7,110 yuan.[12]

LATER STAGE OF THE RETURN TO WORK
After Mid-March

Outstanding Wage Disputes

Wages have been the principal concern of the class struggle between labor and capital. As soon as the phased-in return to work policy was announced, then, the calculation of wages became the focal point for everyone involved, with all kinds of lawyers swarming online to decipher the policy. Even though the Ministry of Human Resources and Social Security immediately released a clearer explanation of the official document—in particular clarifying the expectations in regard to workers who fall sick and receive pay during periods of isolation—this didn't prevent companies from passing the costs of pandemic-related work stoppages and isolation onto their workers, with a number of small enterprises using particularly bizarre methods to suppress workers' gains.

In March, as workers obtained their February salaries one after the other, inquiries about wages began to increase, as did online lectures about how exactly to calculate them. A few relatively large-scale enterprises

---

11. "China's major labor exporting provinces and cities open special trains to help migrant workers return to work across provinces" [中国多个劳务输出大省市开通专车专列帮助农民工跨省返岗].

12. "Apple's anxiety behind the 300 yuan-a-day recruitment rush" [300 元一天的抢人大战背后，是苹果的焦虑].

that were already in line with regulations correctly understood the situation and kept their wage calculations more or less in line with the official legislation, leaving their employees little legal room to challenge them. That said, there's also been news of some workers' demands pushing beyond the provisions laid out in the law. For example, workers at Foxconn in Shenzhen made formal complaints through their [official ACFTU] union in order to change the company's policy of forcing employees to use their yearly vacation time to cover their period of isolation.[13] By contrast, those small enterprises that were already violating regulations on a day-to-day basis prior to the pandemic continued as usual, confiscating wages and generally leaving workers' pay in a state of disarray. Wage arrears, lowered pay during the extended isolation period, or even treating the isolation period for migrants returning to work from outside the area as if it were a leave of absence for a personal matter— these were the main issues being discussed and reported by workers.

The continued blockage of roads prevented many workers registered in Hubei from returning to work elsewhere, making the problem of severe wage arrears and reduced pay even more widespread. Three such workers employed at an underwear factory in Shenzhen didn't receive their back wages after returning to work and were instead told that they needed to apply for personal leave for February and March. Similar allegations spread through online media, where it was claimed that some large-scale enterprises in Shenzhen were excessively docking the wages of Hubei-registered workers who had spent their two months of isolation in their hometowns, with the lowest only being paid a mere 600 yuan. As one worker lamented, "The pandemic has already caused such suffering for us Hubei people, this wage issue is isolation only adding oil to the fire!" The companies then played further tricks, not even sending the reduced wages to workers who were in quarantine in Hubei or asking other employees to "donate" to support their coworkers. Certainly, many enterprises suffered serious losses due to the shutdown, but how much could they really recoup by docking wages? In reality, the situation is summarized well by one worker, in a report made to the labor bureau complaining of a firm not in line with regulations:

---

13. Long Xiaodong, "Under Worker Pressure, Foxconn Provides Restitution for Lost Vacation Pay" [迫于员工压力，富士康返还年休假], Feb. 29, 2020.

"It's not that the company is not turning a profit, just that it's making less than before."

On the 20th of March, workers at the electric car firm BYD — which had just received a 2.3 billion yuan subsidy from the government—made headlines for unfurling a protest banner. As one employee explained: "Our bonuses were all cut: bonuses for productivity, for working time and for performance points.[14] Then the one week of doubled salary that we'd originally promised was cancelled on the 16th of March, making everybody angry."[15] Although BYD officials have declared that the version of events reported online is untrue, this and other grievances from BYD employees continue to be posted on Baidu forums and elsewhere.

Throughout March, dissatisfaction among workers generalized due to declining incomes. But the actions ignited by this dissatisfaction don't actually appear to have been very aggressive. While there are, for example, reports of a thousand workers at an electronics factory in Shenzhen protesting the reduction in pandemic pay by collectively requesting a leave of absence or simply skipping work, it has been far more common for workers to seek formal legal advice, file official complaints, or make allegations online.[16] Some possible reasons for this are that, for the most part, the issues only really applied to income for a short period of time, and that everyone could see the losses being taken by enterprises under the pandemic with their own eyes. The result was that neither expectations nor motivation were particularly high.

In addition to this, the Labor Bureau was already prepared for battle, ready to prevent and control such disputes between capital and

14. *Translators*: Many Chinese companies' wage systems are fairly complicated and localized to that particular company. Often, various "points" systems are used to calculate workers' final wages in addition to their base salary. This is similar to a productivity or performance "bonus" being added, but with the "bonus" often being a substantial portion of their final income. Conceptually, it's most similar to working on a commission system in sales or relying on tips in the service industry, but translated into the factory production context.

15. "Investigating the 'Rights Abuse' at BYD: Employees' wages for February are a mere 300 yuan, while the company just received a 2.3 billion stimulus" [比亚迪"维权事件"调查：员工2月到手工资或不足300元 公司刚收到23亿补贴], *ifeng*, March 24, 2020.

16. Long Xiaodong, "After protests at several electronics factories in Longhua: What is the result?" [龙华某大型电子厂派遣工抗议过后，得到了什么？], March 20, 2020.

labor at every level of government, from the central state down to local administration. As conflicts arose, they all coordinated to release a series of guidelines and measures to be used in managing industrial relations.[17] At the same time, the lowest-level government agencies strengthened the forces they'd deployed to resolve such disputes, or even broke new ground by setting up online platforms for mediation or having local officials mediate directly in order to ease the tension between capital and labor.[18] This was all particularly effective in dissolving workers' shared grievances into an array of individual complaints, thereby reducing the potential for collective action.

The High Tide of Lost Work and Halted Production

The severe scarcity of work experienced in February continued into the first third of March. As the virus spread to Europe and the US, the automobile, clothing and electronics industries were greatly impacted, and the effects were worst for companies engaged in export processing and foreign trade.[19] Gradually, the common practice of working regular overtime became rarer, hiring paused, and then production. Within workers' groups on social media, it became common to see reports about several months of time off being circulated.[20] Rumors emerged online that, due to the steep decline in Apple sales, Foxconn workers would be

---

17. "Ministry of Human Resources and Social Security's best practices in the workplace with regard to the novel coronavirus epidemic" [力资源社会保障部办公厅关于人力资源和社会保障系统做好新型冠状病毒感染的肺炎疫情防控有关工作的通知], *Ministry of Human Resources and Social Security of the People's Republic of China*, Jan. 23, 2020.

18. "Ningbo Comprehensive Plan for Prevention and Control: Guaranteeing Harmonious and Stable Labor Relations during the Pandemic" [各省市人社部门官网均有相应报道。例：宁波市综合施策主动防控　确保疫情期间劳动关系和谐稳定], *Zhejiang Province Human Resources and Social Security Department*, March 17, 2020.

19. "Key overseas parts suppliers halt production, revealing the Chinese auto industry's long-standing bottleneck" [海外核心零部件因疫情停产才发现中国汽车业早已被「卡住脖子」], *Baidu*, May 11, 2020; Jia Linwei and Huang Shan, "With foreign orders dropping precipitously, what can bosses in the clothing sector do aside from halting production and laying off workers?" [外贸订单被大量取消 服装厂老板除了停产裁员还能做些什么], *Sina*, April 2, 2020.

20. "Notice: Because of declining orders due to the pandemic situation, work and production will be halted for 6–9 months!" [通知：受国外疫情影响已无订单，停工停产，预计6–9个月！], *Kuaibao*, March 29, 2020.

asked to take four months off starting in May. Foxconn's official response to these rumors was that "the factory districts of mainland China are currently all operating as usual, and there simply isn't a situation of mass layoffs or forced vacations." But regardless, large portions of the country had stopped hiring new workers, and the decline in overtime was an undeniable fact.[21]

Aside from compulsory leave, some companies also used other methods to cut down on labor costs during the production stoppage, including encouraging workers to resign or to request an unpaid absence. Thus, questions of pay during the shutdown, alongside both overt and covert layoffs, ensured that wage demands would once again become prominent. At one technology firm in Guangzhou, employees alleged that the company requested every department place 15–20% of its staff on 6 months leave until orders began coming in again, at which point they'd be expected to return to work. Meanwhile, the company planned to immediately deduct the 6 months from the workers' social insurance funds in advance for the time they'd be on "vacation."[22] This made the workers placed on leave absolutely indignant. On the one hand, they felt that it was simply unfair, but on the other, it was more than unfair, since the company was making cuts to their social insurance at the same time that their income had been reduced to an unsustainable level. Some workers complained to the Labor Bureau, but they were simply told that the company was within its rights to arrange time off, and all that could ultimately be done was to strive for regular social insurance deductions, as opposed to the advance deductions announced by the company.

In the midst of all this there were also workers who were still on the job, but even they didn't have it easy. Employers used every method to reduce their official staff numbers, leaving those who remained with heavier burdens. The remaining work intensified, and workers grew dissatisfied even as they went along with it. Complaints arose in every

21. "Foxconn: Mandatory Overtime, Reduced Salaries and No More Overtime" [传富士康：强制放假、降薪，暂停招工！], *QQ News*, May 7, 2020.
22. According to the relevant law, social insurance taxes are supposed to be withheld from an employee's pay each month and transferred to the Social Insurance Department. Moreover, if the employee's wages are lowered upon their return from time off, the amount they pay in social insurance taxes should be lowered to a comparable degree.

industry. Those heard in manufacturing were a mirror image of those heard in food service: the bosses said that business was not good and therefore they had to cut staff, but, in reality, the amount of work for those left never actually decreased that much. They didn't get any days off, and they didn't get paid for overtime either. If anyone asked for more money, the bosses would just say, "Get the damn work done or go home—there are tons of people out there waiting to take your place."

Meanwhile, news of numerous bankruptcies began to arise. It was reported that the Fantastic Toys (泛达) factory, which had been in operation in Dongguan for 30 years, began to see its cash flow fragment.[23] Early on in the pandemic, the boss had briefly disappeared, becoming difficult to contact. He finally reappeared on the 24th of March, only to announce that the factory was shutting down. Negotiations between workers owed backpay and the district labor bureau ended with no results, and when they went to file a complaint with the Dongguan city Labor Bureau they were met by attackers of unknown origin (maybe thugs hired by the company, possibly cops out of uniform), clashed with them and were dispersed, some suffering injuries.[24] Nor was this an isolated example. According to the National Enterprise Bankruptcy Disclosure Platform, from January 1st to March 15th of this year, there were already 8,243 cases of bankruptcy. In the corresponding time period for 2019, there had been 4,895 and for the same period in 2018, only 2,078.[25]

23. *Translators*: The original Chinese reads 资金链断裂. The implication here is that the company was dependent on a complicated chain of financial transactions, and when one link in that chain shattered, it broke the company's overall cash flow. Reading the sources cited here, and other related stories about the factory closure, it appears that this Hong Kong-owned firm would use its regular big orders received from Europe as collateral to secure loans to fund production, many of which used the local government (not that of Dongguan city, it seems, but the even more local government of Chashan Town, within the city) as the ultimate guarantor of the loan. This is one reason that the municipal authorities got involved so early and directly in the case. In general, this is also a good example of the fragile financial character and generally low profitability of many firms such as this, a typical old-style Pearl River Delta factory, financed from Hong Kong and clearly reliant on collusion with local government officials who may have originally had some sort of family ties to the original investors.

24. "Well-known old toy factory in Dongguan goes out of business, the employees seek payment and are assaulted" [东莞老牌玩具厂倒闭，员工讨薪被打], Ctoy.com.cn [中外玩具网], March 25, 2020.

25. For a summary, see "Well-Known Firms going Bankrupt due to the Pandemic!"

Confronted with the rapidly changing situation in these first few months—which saw declining overtime, work stoppages and layoffs, all resulting in lowered income—it seems that workers were still in a period of adaptation, so the forms of struggle that emerged were largely defensive in character. According to statistics gathered by the China Labour Bulletin, collective actions by workers from January to April of 2020 were fewer than those seen in the same time period in 2019. As in the past, it may be that there have been some more limited collective actions on the part of workers at certain enterprises that have not yet been picked up by the news and have therefore been difficult to hear about. But it may also simply be that, up to this point, no large or sustained collective actions have taken shape. For most workers who've suddenly become unemployed or been asked to take compulsory time off, the normal response has been to find temporary work of some sort in order to supplement their income or to return to rural hometowns in order to reduce their cost of living, all the while waiting for the situation to improve before they begin looking for work again.

Comparing the Current Crisis with that of 2008–2009

There are many comparisons being made between the present crisis and that of 2008–09. During that crisis, many industries made cuts to workers' conditions and wages, factories ceased production, and there was a wave of closures across the Pearl River Delta. At that time workers were also dissatisfied with their situation, but most chose to put up with it and worker protests went into a lull. However, as the economy picked up again, workers started a new cycle of actions.

So, how does the current situation compare? If we analyze the conditions of employment, wages, commodity prices and other elements related to workers' lives, we find at least the following points: In 2009, while there was also a significant number of workers who lost their jobs and returned to their hometowns and villages, many of those workers would have had some amount of savings. And following the subsequent and substantial state investment in infrastructure, the renewed stimulus for domestic demand, and the recovery of the global economy, it wasn't

[因疫情破产的知名企业！], *CBF Trade Focus*, May 13, 2020.

long before workers could find a job again. But the economic prospects for the PRD today are far less hopeful. After all, at that time the Chinese economy was still in a period of growth and development. But since 2014 the domestic economy has entered a weaker "new normal," characterized by declining growth rates. The impact of the pandemic has already caused a sizable reduction in income and we are seeing the beginning of widespread bankruptcy of businesses large and small. At this point it is unclear when these conditions will ease.

As a result, it seems that the unemployment situation in the PRD (and we might even say for the Chinese economy as a whole) is far more serious this time around. Even though the national unemployment rate for March 2020 was only 5.9%, this represents an increase of 0.7 percentage points on the March reading for 2019. But according to a report by Zhongtai Securities, in reality the number of unemployed has already surpassed 70 million people, in which case the unemployment rate would be 20.5%.[26] The latter figure is more in accordance with what is generally understood about the current situation.

Coupled with the already widespread condition of temporary and insecure employment, it will be a long time before many workers find stable and secure work again. This condition is not limited to common workers either, but also includes technical workers and some managers. During the crisis 10 years ago, it was only a few months after these workers had to leave their jobs that they could return and find some kind of work to make a living. But it seems very unlikely we will see a recurrence of this type of situation.

As the pandemic brings all these pressures to bear upon workers' lives, they also face shrinking wages and wildly increasing prices for everyday goods. It is worth comparing again to 2009. In February of that year, the national consumer price index (CPI) fell 1.6% year-on-year, and continued to fall until October 2009. At the same time, workers' income (based on the minimum wage), had been increasing since 2005. However, in 2019 the CPI was already increasing, and in February 2020 the national year-on-year CPI had increased by 5.2%. In that same period

26. "How high is China's unemployment rate?" [中国失业率有多高?], *Macroeconomic Policy Report* [宏观策略专题报告], Zhongtai Securities [中泰证券], April 24, 2020.

the price of food had risen even more dramatically, up by 21.9% year-on-year. While there was a slight decline during March and April, we still find an increase of 18.9% and 14.3% respectively.[27] Based on the perspectives of manufacturing workers (especially frontline workers) who we've been in touch with, real incomes have not been increasing for the past 4–5 years due to declining pay conditions and reductions in overtime. But as we have seen the CPI has soared since 2019, especially the price of food. These conditions have put even further strain on the already stressed pockets of workers.

In sum, the impact of job losses and declining real incomes on workers' lives is much greater than before. Each of these factors has increased the hesitancy and concern of workers to act and has repressed the beginning of a renewed period of struggle. However, the willingness of Chinese workers to resist has not changed—particularly among those in the PRD who have fought directly before. Viewed from another perspective, given the seriousness of the conditions and the caution that workers will take in planning collective actions, the result will likely be that their resistance becomes better organized.

POSTSCRIPT
December 2020

Amid the state's bold announcements about China taking the lead in the world's economic recovery, those who have borne the greatest costs of that recovery have been frontline workers, who are facing longer working hours, harder work, less security, more precarious employment options and even lower income.

This can be seen not only among workers in manufacturing and services—even urban white-collar workers are not doing much better. According to data from Zhaopin, 37.3 percent of white-collar employees experienced pay cuts in the first half of 2020, and one third of those surveyed reported layoffs at their workplaces.[28] Many were willing to accept

27. National Bureau of Statistics [国家统计局官网].
28. Zhaopin [智联招聘], "Report on 2020 Trends in Employment Relations" [2020

pay cuts as the cost of maintaining their "rice bowls," with nearly one-fifth indicating their desire for the future as "I just don't want to be unemployed." 69.2 percent reported that their companies had proposed new employment requirements, including an increase in workload, stricter performance assessments, and an expansion of the types of work to be done for the job.

In July, the State Council, the National Development and Reform Commission, and the Ministry of Human Resources and Social Security all issued statements calling for an increase in various forms of "flexible employment" and "shared employment" (共享用工), to be supported at the state level.[29]

Overall, both enterprises and the government have taken advantage of the pandemic to strengthen the attack on workers' interests. Informal, precarious forms of employment have become even more prevalent than before, and the environment for labor struggles is objectively worse. But does this mean that workers' resolve to fight back has weakened? Not at all.

While courts and arbitration agencies were closed until April due to the pandemic, in the first half of 2020 the official number of labor dispute cases throughout China still surpassed that of 2018.[30] In Shenzhen, the nation's historic front line of labor disputes since the 1990s, such cases saw a 14 and 20 percent increase over last year during the second and third quarters of 2020—resuming the annual rise in cases that had begun back in 2018.[31] The pandemic merely put this trend on hold, rather than changing it.

Workers are continuing to fight. The question is how to bring these struggles together.

雇佣关系趋势报告], Aug. 31, 2020.

29. "Shared employment" refers essentially to informal hiring, without an employment contract, as permitted in the *Ministry of Human Resources and Social Security Circular on Implementing Shared Employment Guidance and Service* [人力资源社会保障部办公厅关于做好共享用工指导和服务的通知].

30. Data from the Ministry of Human Resources and Social Security's report on *The Handling of Employment Disputes in the First Half of 2020* [2020年上半年全国劳动人事争议处理情况], Sept. 22, 2020.

31. Data from the Shenzhen Bureau of Human Resources and Social Security.

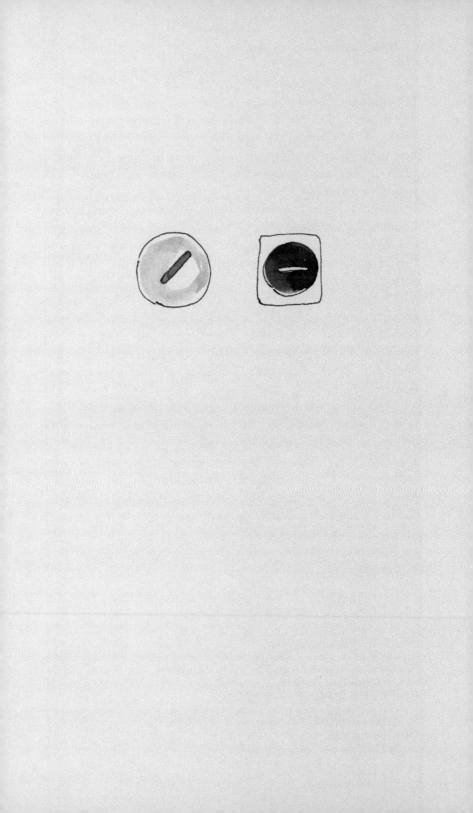

3.
As Soon as There's a Fire, We Run: An Interview with Friends in Wuhan

The interview transcribed and translated here was conducted online in late 2020, following conversations over the previous months. The interviewees, X, Z, and W, belong to a collective based in the outskirts of Wuhan.[1] They produced a series of illustrated stories about their experiences called *Wuhan Diaries* (武汉日记), which were published separately in various media outlets, including the March 2020 edition of the *Black Book Assembly* newsletter. Their collective project involves a space for musicians to practice and perform, lodging for travellers, and "a copyshop and risograph printing studio convenient for the neighbourhood but also for the sharing of knowledge, movement and DIY culture as a means to initiate and explore the possibilities of new alliances." All three participants are in their thirties and have been living in Wuhan for at least ten years, on and off. X is originally from Wuhan, where she currently works as a freelance writer and translator while learning to farm and make clothes, also earning a small income from the printshop (along with Z). Z and W both moved from their homes in Guangxi to attend school in Wuhan before deciding to stay, with Z moving away for a few years before returning in 2018. Z works as a freelance illustrator while W works as a day laborer in the construction and renovation industries.

---

1. We use pseudonyms throughout to protect the identity of the interviewees and their contacts. W only appears in the last session below. The quotation about the collective is from their website, whose details we omit for security reasons.

I

Chuang: The first question is about the period immediately before
the lockdown in December and January. Were you both in Wuhan
at that time?

Z and X: Yes.

C   How did you first hear about the outbreak, and what did you
think was going to happen?

Z   In late December I saw people reposting information about the
outbreak, and then in the next few days you started to see state ref-
utations claiming the rumors were false (辟谣). It must have been
early January when I saw a post from a friend whose family lives in
Shuiguohu, the compound for the Hubei Provincial Government,
they're civil servants. He posted photos of people in HAZMAT
suits spraying disinfectant at the Huanan Seafood Market, along
with a note clearing up rumors.

   Then on January 12th and 14th I received messages from
our friends E in Hong Kong and XC in Japan, saying that they
had heard about this virus in Wuhan so we should be careful.
They had read about it in the news. Even though we were the ones
in Wuhan, we weren't as clear about what was happening here as
they were.

   Then on the 19th our friend TC came from Shanghai to visit,
and that was the first time we really became aware of the danger,
because he was taking all these precautions like wearing facemasks.

C   How is it that people in Shanghai knew more about it than you
in Wuhan?

X   I think because the media in Shanghai was paying more attention
to it there [whereas here the media wasn't allowed to report on it].
He was actually just passing through on his way back to Hunan
and was trying to decide whether it was worth the risk. He spoke
of Wuhan as if it were a war zone, whereas most people here
didn't take it seriously.

C   It's surprising that there can be such a disconnect of information between these two cities in this era of social media. Even with state censorship, can't you access the same information here as you could in Shanghai?

X   I think there were stricter controls on social media in Wuhan at the time because of the "Two Sessions" [meetings of the metropolitan and provincial governments from January 6th to 17th, in preparation for which the authorities censored reports on the outbreak and silenced whistleblowers like Li Wenliang]. Also I heard that someone had taken a sample of COVID-19 to a lab in Shanghai, so there was more media attention there in particular.

Z   In addition, I think a lot of people in Wuhan had the attitude that maybe there was some truth in the rumors, but the government would take care of things and we didn't need to worry too much about trying to figure out exactly what the truth was.

C   So, when your friend came to visit from Shanghai, that was when you started to take those rumors seriously?

X   Yes. I remember we took the bus together and that was the first time we put on facemasks. That night I went online and ordered a bunch of masks—good thing too, because a few days later they would be sold out! Because I think it was just the next day, on January 20th, when Zhong Nanshan announced on CCTV that COVID-19 could be transmitted from human to human. So then everyone started snatching up all the PPE they could find, and soon it was impossible to get masks in Wuhan.

Z   I remember after that announcement the three of us debated its significance, about how serious the outbreak would be.

C   What was your thinking at that time?

X   I was already thinking it was going to be serious, because on the 19th we noticed lots of other people suddenly starting to wear facemasks, maybe one third of the people on the bus. This was even before the CCTV announcement, but some people had access to information. For example, my extended family has a [WeChat] group, and some of my cousins have kids, so they're especially concerned about public health. All the way back on December 30th, my cousin had sent a screenshot of the post by Dr. Li Wenliang saying that cases of SARS had been discovered in Wuhan. That was when we had first heard of it.

X After Li's post another doctor, Liu Wen, responded that at Wuhan's Number Two Hospital a case of contagious pneumonia had been linked to a type of coronavirus, that it was basically confirmed to be SARS, so he recommended medical staff to be careful.

C Between December 30th and January 20th, were there no official statements from state authorities about this?

Z I remember that a few days before January 20th there was a refutation (辟谣) circulating, saying that although there was a virus it wasn't SARS, that you couldn't catch it from humans, and that those earlier messages were just rumors.

C In the two days between the January 20th announcement about human-to-human transmission and the total lockdown of Wuhan on the 23rd, did the authorities recommend any protective measures, like telling people to stay home or wear masks?

X As far as I know, the only announcements in those days were about the number of new cases being confirmed. I don't think any protective measures were announced before the lockdown.

C How did you find out the city was being locked down, and what did the popular sentiment seem to be at the time?

Z We found out [a day before the lockdown was announced] on the morning of the 22nd when TC went back to Hunan. He had originally planned to take the train but then got worried that would be too dangerous, so he found someone to ride with in a car. But as soon as they tried to get on the highway they discovered that many of the on-ramps were already being closed.

X Also, in my family's [WeChat] group people posted messages about this, and about traffic jams as people started frantically rushing to escape the city.

C   Why were people trying to escape? Was information about the impending lockdown leaked from the government?

X   I think so, or from hospitals. Then finally at 2 am it was finally announced what was happening: that Wuhan has being locked down and no one would be allowed to leave the city after 10 am.

C   Did the government send out an announcement via SMS?

X   Not about the lockdown, just about the highway controls (高速管制). The lockdown was announced in the press that morning.

C   And then when people woke up to that news, they just had a couple hours to leave? That must have been crazy!

X   Yes! I know two people who were just visiting Wuhan for the Chinese New Year and had to rush to make it out that morning. The whole process was pretty chaotic.

C   What was the popular sentiment at the time?

X   In the days leading up to the lockdown, there was an atmosphere of growing worry about the virus itself, but on the 23rd that turned into surprise and nervousness about the lockdown. Because no one had expected that, it was announced so suddenly, and we had no idea what was going to happen. The thought never crossed my mind that we should try to escape, but there was a sense that we had been cast aside (抛弃).

Z   I was excited! I felt like, "Fuck, I can't believe this is happening!"

X   Yeah, it felt like we had become caught up in a historical event (破天荒). Excitement combined with nervousness.

C   How was it historical?

X   For example the 23rd was the day before New Year's Eve (除夕), and it quickly occurred to everyone that this would be the first time in our lives that family gatherings would be canceled and we'd have to stay at home by ourselves.

C   And you said it felt like you had been cast aside—do you mean by the government?

X   Yes, because they had just gone from [denying everything the
    doctors had been saying for weeks], to finally acknowledging that
    this might actually be something to worry about, to then sud-
    denly closing down the city three days later. It really felt like a...
    disaster! [*Laughs.*]

C   Did you feel like the people of Wuhan were being sacrificed?

X   At the time we hadn't started to use that word "sacrifice" yet, but
    there was a sense that someone had been ridiculously irresponsible.
    [*They both laugh.*] It was like, "Are you kidding me? How is this
    even possible?"

Z   I actually felt like we were watching a drama unfold. Luckily
    we had gone ahead and stocked up on groceries on the 22nd, so we
    weren't too worried about running out of supplies any time soon.
    As long as we just stayed in the village [on the outskirts of Wuhan]
    we would be alright. I was actually looking forward to seeing
    what kind of mess the government had gotten itself into.

X   It felt like the government was revealing its true nature. Like this
    is how it had been all along, and now everyone could see it.
    It had created this mess and now the only help it could offer for
    ensuring people's survival was to shut everything down, with
    no way for people to get anything they needed to live.

Z   It felt like we were just a piece on the national chessboard. All they
    cared about was preventing the virus from spreading outside
    of Wuhan, but not about how those of us stuck in Wuhan could
    survive.

C   This is what you and your friends were thinking, but how wide-
    spread do you think this kind of sentiment was? Did most people
    believe the government would take care of them and had their
    best interests at heart?

X   In those first days the main people I talked to were my relatives
    online, because of the New Year, and I got the sense that cousins
    of my generation did not have much faith in what the government
    had been doing—from its contradictory announcements to the

lockdown of the city. Everybody felt like there was a huge lack of transparency, and we had no idea what might happen next. But at first people were just surprised, and everything seemed absurd. It wasn't until later that people started to look back and appraise what had happened.

Z   In those first days of the lockdown, every morning I had to get up and walk the dog, and the village would be empty except for a few vehicles parked along the road. Of course, the dog would want to pee on the tires, but I was worried the cars might have brought the virus back from the city with them. This is just an example of the sort of hysterical feeling that pervaded the atmosphere at the time.

Another example is about our landlord. She's a farmer, so she has one of those machines for spraying pesticide on the crops. In February, the village authorities distributed bleach powder (84漂白粉) to the villagers and told them to disinfect everything, so she put bleach in the pump and walked around spraying everything. Before long her skin started breaking out and turning red, and for the next few weeks she hid inside her house, afraid to come out. She was afraid to come into direct contact with other people, as well as dogs and cats. Also, she was angry at the village committee about the bleach.

C   Did the village committee come up with this idea on their own, or was it an order from a higher level of government?

X   Our village belongs to QL *shequ* ("community"), the local branch of government for this area. That's the entity that distributed the bleach and other supplies like facemasks and rubbing alcohol, along with directions about how to use them. But it didn't do this until a few weeks after the lockdown had begun. During the first couple weeks the government didn't take any concrete measures to help people. A couple days into the lockdown the [Wuhan Municipal] government set up something called the Novel Pneumonia Prevention and Control Center (武汉新型肺炎防控指挥部), which then released a series of ordinances (条例). A month later, these ordinances finally provided some explanation about how things would operate during the lockdown, things like how people could get food if the markets were closed. Prior to that, the government had just ordered everything to be closed with no apparent concern for these problems. I remember the first ordinance was about transportation, simply saying that all mass transit had to close, and that private automobiles had some restrictions.

C   When was that first ordinance released?

X   That one came out right away in the first couple days of the lockdown, like January 25th.

C   And you said earlier that in those first few days nothing else was officially required to close—neither businesses nor housing complexes, so people could move around freely, it's just that the buses weren't running. When were the markets forced to close?

X   Well first there was the Huanan Seafood Market. That was closed and disinfected back in late December or early January when Li Wenliang traced the virus there. Then right before the lockdown [on January 22nd] when we went to our local market, the vendors there said it would be closed the next day [the 23rd] to disinfect the place. Later we found out that this would happen throughout Wuhan. At the time it didn't seem like a big deal, because New Year was coming up, so everyone was stocking up on food as usual, and most vendors wouldn't show up to run their stalls anyway.

C   But New Year's Eve wasn't until January 24th, right? Wouldn't a lot of people plan on shopping on the 23rd? I wonder if a lot of people got stuck without enough food.

X   No. Most people start shopping like a month in advance, and they're already stocked up a week or two before New Year's Eve.

C   Oh, so this was a really convenient time to start the lockdown. People had already stocked up on supplies, and most were on vacation anyway so wouldn't think it was too strange or inconvenient to have to stay at home in those first days. If it were at any other time of the year, this could have been a huge problem.

Z   Absolutely! There would have been a major panic.

X   At first the only way to get around was on foot, and most of the supermarkets were closed, so if people hadn't stocked up large amounts of food for the holiday they would definitely have run out of food.

C   When did the markets reopen?

X   They never reopened [until the whole city reopened in April]. A few big supermarket chains stayed open: Zhongbai, which is the main supermarket chain in Wuhan; and the big online supermarkets: Hema [owned by Alibaba] and JD.com. Zhongbai stayed open throughout most of the lockdown, but eventually you couldn't go inside—instead you had to order food through "Community Shopping" (社区采购) [i.e. through the government].

C   How did "Community Shopping" work? When did that start?

X   It started when the housing complexes were sealed off, because you couldn't go out to buy anything, so you had to make a list and send it to the director (负责人) of your *shequ*'s residents committee (居委会), or to whichever volunteers were in charge of that service.

Z   I think that started in late February.

C   So individual housing complexes weren't sealed off until a month after the city as a whole went on lockdown?

Z   They were closed off earlier in the urban core, but our village wasn't sealed until later because it's in the outskirts of the city.

X   Yeah, everything was freer and took longer to implement here, and the authorities' "regulatory consciousness" (管理意识) wasn't as strong here, for one because the village isn't a walled compound, so it's harder to close off, and people aren't used to living like that.

C   Why was Zhongbai allowed to stay open when all the other brick and mortar stores had to close? Is it a state-owned enterprise?

X   I think it's a municipal enterprise (城市企业).

Z   I think the idea was that it would be easier to manage than the smaller businesses. Also a lot of the smaller business are run by people who aren't from Wuhan, and they went back to their home towns for the New Year. We went out on January 26th and every-thing was closed except for Zhongbai and two pharmacies.

C   Had the government ordered all those businesses to close, or had they just stayed home out of fear of infection?

Z   I think they had just stayed home out of fear.

X   I remember people talking about how the government had not yet announced any clear rules about whether businesses could operate.[2] In our area, only those two pharmacies were open, but they didn't have any facemasks or other PPE. My mom had the same problem in the city: I searched online for businesses in her area and found a convenience store that was open, but they were sold out of PPE. Everything had been bought up already in the first days of the lockdown.

Housing complexes weren't all sealed off at once. The press would announce which *shequ* had been shut down. And I have a note from February 23rd saying that the press had criticized our *shequ* for failing to shut down the villages here properly, so it was only after this that many of the entrances to the village were actually closed off, and that a checkpoint (执行点) was set up at the main entrance. Based on memory I think the urban *shequ* were shut down about two weeks before that, in early February.

---

2. Later X looked this up and found that on February 16th the Wuhan government had announced (in Circular Thirteen [13号通告]) that certain types of "public venues" (those related to "culture, sports and tourism," including cinemas, internet cafés, mah-jong parlors, swimming pools and museums) were not allowed to operate, and that others (including hotels and supermarkets) could operate if everyone who went there registered with the new "health code" system and were confirmed there as low-risk. However, these regulations were not well publicized (and people couldn't keep up with the frequently changing rules), so when businesses began reopening in the spring, it was not until police came and explained the rules that both owners and customers learned about them, by which time they had changed. Also, the health QR code system was not yet fully operational at the time of the February 16th announcement. (The interviewees did not encounter a situ-ation where they needed to register with the system until they tried to take a bus after the lockdown was lifted in April.)

C   So in late January all that was officially shut down within the city
     were the markets and the buses? What about private automobiles?

X   The rules about private automobiles kept changing. At the time
     people made fun of them because they were so contradictory and
     full of loopholes. Like one said that if you didn't receive an SMS
     message from the Transportation Department stating that you
     were prohibited from driving, then it was OK to drive, and no one
     in the city seemed to receive any such messages, so that meant
     everyone could drive as usual. Later they changed it to say you were
     only allowed to drive if you got a pass (通行证) from your *shequ*'s
     residents committee. At that point the traffic police set up check-
     points throughout the city, where they would stop people
     and check their passes.
        By then the responsibility of quarantining housing complexes
     had been assigned to the residents' committees. All shopping,
     medical care, etc., had to be arranged by the committee. If you
     needed to drive somewhere you also had to contact the committee
     and get a pass. For example, if you had to go to work, or if someone
     was sick and had to go to the hospital, you had to get a pass.
        Later the government provided a vehicle to each *shequ*'s
     residents committee, and if anyone in the *shequ* needed to drive
     somewhere, they could apply to use that, and at that point it
     became much harder to get a pass for driving your own vehicle.

Z   Wuhan has eleven districts, and each district was supposed to
     get twenty vehicles, but our district only got 8 vehicles because it
     has a lower population size.

C   I heard that these vehicles were provided by taxi companies, com-
     plete with drivers, is that right?

X   Yes, the government requisitioned vehicles from taxi companies
     and hired some taxi drivers to work as "volunteers" (志愿者).

C   They were paid, right?

Z   Yeah, I heard they were paid a lot more than they would have nor-
     mally made as taxi drivers. Also the other "community volunteers"
     were paid wages (工资).

X   They weren't paid wages, they were just given stipends (补贴).

C   So in the early days of the lockdown, even though housing complexes weren't under quarantine, most people didn't go out— both because the buses weren't running, and because they were afraid of infection?

X   Yes. People had already stocked up on food, and everyone was afraid, because they had just heard there was this disease but didn't have any clear information about it, so they just stayed at home to wait and see what would happen, looking online to try to get more information. So most people didn't go out. A lot of firsthand information was coming out of the hospitals—a lot of videos. For example, when people got sick and went to the emergency room, they would take scary videos of deathly ill people waiting in packed rooms or standing in line outside. Then after the buses stopped running, there were a lot of people who still needed to get to work, including doctors and nurses, who couldn't get to work. At that point a lot of people volunteered to drive them to work. These were ordinary citizens who spontaneously volunteered to do this without compensation.

C   This is an example of the mutual aid networks you mentioned [when we spoke previously]?

X   Yes, the earliest mutual aid networks emerged to solve transportation problems, because the government had shut down the buses but hadn't yet provided any other way for essential workers like medical staff to get to work.

C   At that point these volunteers could drive freely without needing passes. Did they run into trouble getting passes later on?

X   I know someone from one of these groups who was able to get a pass and continue volunteering throughout the lockdown. They would deliver PPE and drive medical staff to and from work. They could get passes if they were in a carpool group (车队). It became harder if you were just trying to do it by yourself, later on. For example, if someone in your family got sick, you couldn't just get a pass to drive them, you had to apply for your *shequ*'s residents committee to arrange a vehicle for you. Also, if you got sick, especially if it was some kind of respiratory illness like a cold, the residents committee would not allow you to go to the hospital on your own. If you had any suspicious (疑似) symptoms, you had to go register (登记) with the committee, which would arrange for you to get a nucleic acid test, and while you were in line waiting to get the test, you weren't allowed to go to the hospital on your own. Then after the results came out, the committee would either transfer you to a quarantine site (隔离点) or take you to the hospital.

Z   When was it that LN came to visit? She had managed to get a driving pass.

X   That was late February, but the restrictions on private cars weren't very strict yet. Because when housing complexes started closing down in early February, it happened gradually—it wasn't like all the complexes in the city were closed off at one time. At first it was just those near Huanan Seafood Market and other places with serious outbreaks (高发地). Hankou [one of the three cities that make up Wuhan] went into lockdown before Wuchang. Also some older complexes – because implementation depended on the work situation of each *shequ*'s residents committee, and if it was an older complex, normally the residents committee didn't pay any attention (管) to them, and often those complexes didn't have property management authorities (物业) [for the Committee to coordinate with], so they couldn't be sealed off (封不起来). If it was a new complex, or one that the residents committee cared more about, it would be sealed off earlier and more strictly (严格). I remember when talking to friends in early February, people would always ask "has your complex been sealed off?" "Are you allowed to go outside?" So it was a gradual process.

C   Can you talk about some other examples of mutual aid?

X   About a week after the city went on lockdown, several major hospitals started running out of supplies, and they began calling

for help from society. This was unprecedented, for hospitals to
directly ask society for help. After these calls went out, ordinary
people began forming volunteer groups to look for PPE and
donate them to hospitals—on top of the volunteer carpool groups
that had started forming earlier. I got involved because my friend
D, she's in the music industry and had already been pretty active in
her work, networking with all kinds of people—kind of like a gang-
ster (大姐大) [laughs]—she organized a group called the Masked
Angels (蒙面天使救援队). She just happened to live in the same
building as my mom, which is close to a lot of the big hospitals.
The group was divided into several teams—one looked for facemasks, one was in charge of transport and D's team was in charge
of communicating with hospitals to find out where the PPE was
most needed. And I have an aunt who is a head nurse at [one
of the big hospitals], so she knew which departments were short
on what type of supplies, so I put her in touch with D, and
they were able to set up a supply chain.

In the first month after Wuhan went into lockdown, the government hadn't yet started the residents committees' intervention
(介入), they hadn't assumed control over (接管) unofficial activities supplying materials to hospitals, so the volunteer groups had
to find the materials and transport them to the hospitals themselves. But about a month into the lockdown, more and more hospitals began running out of supplies and followed the initial ones
in calling for outside support from people in general. Meanwhile, more and more people from all over China were sending supplies to Wuhan, and the volunteer groups didn't have any central
directors, they acted independently at a local level, or in the network of people they had contacts with, so it became hard for them
to deal with the vast quantity of supplies that were coming into
Wuhan. And I remember that at that time the government started
requesting (要求) that all donations go through (对接) one of
two [registered NGOs]: the Red Cross and the Charity Center
(慈善总会). From that moment, the government started imposing limits on volunteer groups' activities and access to supplies.
For example, they contacted D and told her to stop doing PPE
supply work, so the Masked Angels switched to other activities.

For example, they started delivering food to healthcare workers. Because the hospital cafeterias were closed, and the restaurants were closed, so they couldn't get anything to eat.

C   Then how did they eat in the whole month before that?

Z   A lot of them just had instant noodles and cold food.

C   Why did the hospital cafeterias close?

X   I think because the cafeteria staff couldn't get to work. My aunt would either bring food with her or go home to eat during lunch break. So the Masked Angels set up their own kitchen (食堂) and delivered food to healthcare workers. Actually, a month before the lockdown they had already started delivering instant food, like ramen noodles and bread, but later, when the government took over the supplying of PPE, the Angels redirected their resources to specializing in food provision, setting up the kitchen and delivering hot food to the workers, as well as to people who had gotten trapped in Wuhan without a place to live, sleeping under bridges and whatnot. They would donate hot food to them as well.

But I had stopped participating by the time they shifted their focus to food provision. Instead, I switched to helping people with COVID symptoms get tested and, if confirmed, get treated at a hospital, since that was something I could do online. This was another big area of volunteer activity because the residents committees were too busy to handle all the cases. Also, the committees didn't have much experience interacting with most residents on a regular basis. Besides, they didn't have enough staff, especially at the beginning. So if you got sick and went to the committee, they often didn't have time to deal with you, plus you had to wait in a long line. And while people were waiting, often their conditions got worse, so they went online, on WeChat and Weibo, and sent out calls for help. Sometimes they just needed to get a nucleic acid test, because only if you tested positive could you be admitted to a hospital or a quarantine site. So a lot of volunteer activity was helping these people.

Z   Why don't you tell them about the LML Mutual Aid Group?

X   It was a group of musicians based in LML that did some volunteer
    activities, driving healthcare workers and organizing the donation
    of facemasks.

Z   That group was interesting because it started out as just an
    informal network of people who met by going to see live music
    performances together, and then after the outbreak they began
    raising funds to buy PPE and donate them to hospitals. Then
    when the government restricted such work to the Red Cross
    and the Charity Center, the group discontinued their activities,
    worried they would get in trouble if they continued.

C   Why did they worry they would get in trouble?

X   I think the government decided it would be hard to manage these
    small, independent groups.

C   Did the government ever explicitly prohibit independent volun-
    teer activities, or ask the volunteers to work together with the
    Red Cross somehow?

X   Ms. D from the Masked Angels said that a residents committee
    they had been in communication with approached them telling
    them to discontinue their PPE donation and delivery activities.

Z   Also, there was the transportation issue: if you wanted to get
    the driving pass necessary for volunteer activities, you had to ob-
    tain approval from the residents committee.

C   That brings us back to the question of the changing role of the
    residents' committees. You mentioned that at first, they didn't have
    enough personnel to deal with problems like the need for testing
    and getting people to hospitals, and volunteer groups helped
    to make up for this shortage. When the government moved to
    take over these activities, did most of the volunteer groups just
    dissolve, or did they get incorporated somehow?

X   As far as I know, the only volunteer activity the government com-
    pletely took over was the donation and delivery of PPE. As far as
    helping residents to get tested and treated, that was still too much

work for the residents committees, so they didn't prevent the volunteer groups from continuing with those activities, along with the provision of food.

C   Did everyone have to pay full rent throughout the lockdown? I heard some people got rent reductions.

Z   In most cases, yes. For example our landlord lives right next door, so we had to pay in full every month. But with some businesses, they rent spaces owned by some government entity, and the government announced that rent could be reduced in these cases. But if your landlord is a private entity, then you just have to negotiate with them.

C   Is it common for people to rent from the government?

X   Not very common. But we do know someone who runs a shop in a space rented from the government, and they got a waiver for the first three months of rent, then only had to pay half for the next three.

C   Well that's good for them. As for negotiating with private landlords, I've heard that throughout China there was a popular sentiment that pressured landlords into waiving rent or providing discounts, and that if a landlord evicted someone for failure to pay, they would meet with some pretty intense criticism. Have you heard of any cases like that?

X   I think it was pretty rare for landlords to reduce the rent. The landlord of [the livehouse venue] WP waived one month's rent for the three months of lockdown, but that was the only case of private rent reduction that I've heard of. It was common for landlords to let you wait a couple months to pay, but outright reduction was rare. More common was for businesses to just close down and leave after a couple months.

C   This brings us to the topic of protests and struggles. Negotiation and postponement of payment might be considered a weak form of resistance, but do you know of any collective resistance to rent or eviction?

X   No collective resistance to evictions that I can think of, but there
    were some collective actions around food.

Z   What were those?

X   In one housing complex, a woman complained about the food that
    the residents committee was providing for them, saying it was
    too expensive, that the committee was doing a bad job of coordi-
    nating with the residents. So in the [WeChat] group for that *shequ*,
    she criticized the committee, and then screenshots of her com-
    ments went viral, because other people agreed with her. Before
    the government had taken over, the residents of the complex had
    been cooperating among themselves to contact food suppliers
    and buy their food together. They had already set up their own
    system of bulk buying, and it felt like the residents committee had
    usurped (篡夺) that system and weren't doing as good a job. Plus
    the prices had gone up, and residents suspected the committee was
    skimming off the top.

II

Chuang: Did [your collective] host any events related to the pandemic? You mentioned a fundraising party by friends in Japan that you attended online.

Z   Our role in that was just to contact friends in Wuhan and invite them to attend. They raised 5,000 yuan to help our friends at the livehouse pay rent during the lockdown.

C   Had the government already prohibited bars and restaurants from operating at that time [shortly after the city was closed off in late January]?

Z   No, it's just that everyone was afraid of infection so they stayed at home. No clear rules were publicized until weeks later. Some friends would meet up at the livehouse and drink but not open it to the public, because the booze was going to expire and they didn't want to waste it.

C   That sounds really different from the situation in some other countries, where there have been lots of disputes between business owners who wanted to continue operating, and governments that called for people to "shelter in place." Yesterday a friend in the UK told me that bars keep operating illegally, because all the government can do is fine them, but the fines are lower than the income they would lose from staying closed. Of course this is after many months of the economy being ravaged by the pandemic, but this sort of thing was already happening from the beginning back in March. And I'm sure you've heard of the protests in various countries demanding that governments lift their lockdown restrictions. But from all you've said, it sounds like in Wuhan most businesses closed down in January and February just because everyone was staying at home voluntarily, long before the government had proposed any regulations. Is that right?

Z   Yes. Things started to change in April. I remember that at the time, if restaurants or bars reopened, sometimes the police would come.

X   But even then there were still no clear government regulations about this, as far as I know.[3]

C   What did the police do when they came? Did they fine the owners and force them to shut down? Did anyone refuse to shut down?

X   Sometimes they would shut them down, or just say that the clientele had to sit outside. When our friends' livehouse reopened [in May], the police came and took one of the owners to the station, but they just told him that there were new rules in place saying that people had to sit outside.

C   Did this apply to all kinds of businesses? Doesn't the *chengguan* (Urban Management Force) normally come and shut businesses down that set up tables on the sidewalk?

X   Ha! Yes, but around that time the central government started advocating the promotion of a "street stall economy" (地摊经济), so the local news started running stories about high-end hotels setting up dining tables on the sidewalk. This never really took off in Wuhan, but in some other cities like Chongqing it became really widespread, with all kinds of businesses setting up shop on the sidewalk. At first [local governments] encouraged the "street stall economy," but before long they changed their minds and went back to prohibiting it.

C   Yeah, I heard that in Guangzhou it never took off. After the central announcement, a bunch of people went out and set up stalls, but immediately the *chengguan* came in and shut them down as usual. Can you talk about what happened after Wuhan's lockdown was lifted in April? You've mentioned that businesses reopened but the police told them they could only operate outdoors. What about transportation?

Z   City buses resumed operation at that time, only now you had to register a "green code" [i.e. an account in the QR "health code"

---

3. As noted above, the Wuhan government actually did release a set of regulations on February 16th, but they were so little known that many people didn't learn about them until businesses began reopening in the spring, when police came and explained them (sometimes after shutting them down and taking the owners away).

system on one of several platforms, such as WeChat and Alipay].[4] The one on WeChat includes more information, tracking all the places you've been to, but the one on Alipay seems to be less invasive, so we chose the one on Alipay.

X   The lockdown was lifted on April 8th, and I think buses resumed the next day.

C   I remember you clarifying back then that it was only movement in and out of Wuhan that was reopened at first, and that within the city a lot of restrictions remained in place.

X   Actually, people had been allowed to enter Wuhan before that, it was just that they couldn't leave. So "lifting the lockdown" (解封) really just meant that people were finally allowed to leave the city [and, over the following weeks and months, restrictions on movement within the city were gradually loosened].

C   And within the city you say you didn't start using the health codes until buses resumed service in April. Before that, didn't you use them to go in and out of residential areas? In *Wuhan Diaries* you mention that your village was closed off when two cases of COVID-19 were confirmed there in February, and no one could leave after that, but surely people could still leave under certain circumstances. Weren't the health codes used for that?

Z   No. You were only allowed to leave for certain jobs [or medical reasons] and for that you needed a work permit (工作证明) and your ID, and then they would take your temperature when you got to your destination.

C   Did anyone come and check your temperature if you didn't need to leave the compound?

X   At some point the government issued a notification that *shequ* staff

4. The interviewees refer to these codes as "green codes" (率码), but in most places they were called "health codes" (健康码), with "green" status indicating that you were not at risk." These were basically designed to be track-and-trace systems to help with the containment of the outbreak, but often didn't work as intended. See the final chapter in this book for more detail on how the system operated.

would start going from door to door on a regular basis to check everyone's temperature, but later they realized that they didn't have enough personnel to do this, and also that doing so would actually increase the opportunities for spreading the virus. So they stopped, instead telling everyone to report their own temperatures every day via WeChat. And everything happens later in our village, so we never went through the phase of people knocking on doors—we just self-reported our temperatures. Of course most people didn't have thermometers, so everyone just said their temperatures were regular unless they really felt like they had a fever and wanted to see a doctor.

C   Yeah that's what everyone did at my workplace in [another Chinese city]. What would happen if you actually reported a fever?

X   You had to report it to the *shequ* [residents committee] and they would send you to a quarantine site (隔离点). They would get a vehicle to take you there.

C   They wouldn't take you to the hospital?

Z   No, the government had a rule saying you couldn't go straight to the hospital. First they had to take your temperature again to confirm you had a fever, then they sent you to a quarantine site.

X   Every *shequ* had its own quarantine site, usually a hotel that had been taken over for this purpose. And there you had to wait [several days] while [the residents committee] applied for you to get a nucleic acid test. When your turn came up, they would take you to the hospital to take the test, and then take you back to the quarantine site to await your results [for a few days]. If the result was positive, then they would take you back to the hospital for treatment, or one of those temporary facilities (方舱医院).

C   A lot of this is already well-known, so let's move back to the question of people's attitudes about all of this, such as how the government was handling everything: whether they thought it

should have been done differently—both among your friends and
the wider public. Also I'd like to hear more about how people's
more critical attitudes at the beginning changed to not only praise
for the government but even the strengthening of patriotism
and xenophobia, including conspiracy theories about the virus being intentionally unleashed on China by foreign powers.

X I think it had a lot to do with the influence of the media. Everyone
could feel the media relaxing at first and then tightening up,
and the shift of public opinion was closely related to this. Within
the first month of the lockdown, major news outlets like *Caixin*
and *Southern Metropolis Daily* ran a series of reports tracking the
origins of the virus, its spread and the responses to it, including Li
Wenliang's discovery in late December, constructing a timeline
of events. Actually, the media traced it further back to cases
appearing in early December. And in the timeline they would
correlate the "Two Sessions" [January 6th to 17th] with a period
of decline in the public awareness about the outbreak and safety
measures that had started to grow before that, and you can see
how cases began skyrocketing right afterwards [when reporting
on them was allowed to resume]. So everyone could see the connection. Then when the central authorities came down and investigated, everyone felt like we were watching a performance (看戏),
as central and local authorities tried to push the blame onto each
other. No one wanted to take responsibility for what had happened. Throughout the first month of the lockdown, the media
was full of reports like this.

C What did ordinary people think about all this?

Z Two examples come to mind. One was on the evening after Li
Wenliang died [on February 7th], everyone was reposting the news
about it. Even many friends and relatives who normally didn't care
about politics at all were sending out really indignant (愤慨)
messages. You could tell they were furious. The other was when
I went out to a little shop nearby, the owner said [the government]
would be handing out money soon. She said everyone in Wuhan
would get 3,000 yuan. Messages were circulating about this. I don't

know if they were based on any official announcement, but in the
end no one ever got any money.[5]

X   That's the same woman who said that the virus was brought from
    the US [by athletes from the US Army who visited Wuhan in
    October 2019 for the Military World Games]. Because at that time
    [in early March, Zhao Lijian, spokesperson of China's] Ministry
    of Foreign Affairs had claimed that. That's an example of how close-
    ly public opinion followed shifts in the mass media.

C   Was [Zhao's statement] an important turning point in popular
    attitudes—from anger at the local government to the renewal
    of patriotism and the redirection of blame toward other countries?

X   I think you can say it marked a shift in the attitudes of middle-
    aged and elderly people. But I think it was different among young-
    er people.

C   What did younger people think?

Z   They could be divided into different points [of focus]: Some were
    more concerned with where the virus came from, others with
    who should take responsibility, still others with how to avoid infec-
    tion. But as far as attitudes toward the government, some were
    more radical (激烈) while others were more moderate.

C   Several friends and I have heard people in [other cities] express that
    China's rapid assertion of control over the outbreak, in contrast
    with the ongoing disasters in other countries, has vindicated
    China's political system. Some people go so far as to say things like
    "other countries are too democratic" or "too free," that freedom
    and democracy are to blame for their terrible handling of the pan-
    demic, so "our system is better" (还是我们中国的制度比较好).

---

5. Later W clarified that this was not merely a rumor: migrants (people who were not
registered as residents of Wuhan) were eligible to apply for such one-off relief money from
the Wuhan government, if they met certain requirements, and he knows of a few people
who received it. (Wuhan residents were not eligible for any form of relief money.) Z & X
explained that their intention in mentioning this and the following story was that a number
of rumors began circulating in February that redirected blame for the pandemic onto
foreign powers, and cast the local and national governments in a more positive light.

Have many people in Wuhan expressed different attitudes, considering their experience in January, and the pandemic's more severe effects on people's livelihood there?

X   One of my aunts is a low-level civil servant (基层公务员), and another is a nurse. Both of them have expressed criticism of the local government for its initial handling of the outbreak, but overall I think they've followed the media in seeing that as a problem of a few individual officials rather of the political system. This seems to be a common attitude, especially among older people.

C   What about economic issues, such as the lack of support for people who haven't been able to work?

X   People do complain about that. One of my aunts mentioned that she heard people in other countries were getting relief funds, but it would be impossible for that to happen here.

Z   That aunt also complained that she's now having to work six days a week to make up for the months under lockdown. In our area, a lot of shops never reopened after the lockdown. Most of the owners were from other parts of Hubei, and during the lockdown they moved their businesses to other cities.

X   At a gallery where I worked for a few months there was a girl from rural Hubei, and her parents used to work at a supermarket here in Wuhan, but after the lockdown was lifted they weren't able to find work here, so the whole family moved to Guangzhou to work for a logistics company. Because even after the lockdown was lifted a lot of businesses didn't reopen here. An old classmate of mine is an accountant at a big local chain of hotels and they didn't go back to work until the summer. They laid off a lot of employees. She was lucky enough to keep her job, but only made one-third of her salary during those months.

Z   In the construction and renovation industries, no one was allowed to work on privately-owned sites until the summer. Only state-owned sites were open. Our friend W does day-labor in those industries, and he wasn't able to work until then.

C   With so many people out of work for at least half the year, what
     kind of impact did that have on the economy and life in Wuhan?
     How did all these people get by? If they couldn't afford rent
     did they move in with relatives?

X   Most of the people I know have places to live in Wuhan, and like
     my friend at the hotel company, some of them were able to get
     like one-third of their salary even when they weren't going to work.
     As for people from other parts of Hubei, I think they mostly just
     moved to other cities, or went back to the countryside. That
     musician who used to live with us is from [another province].
     He went back there during the lockdown, and after it was lifted he
     didn't come back right away because music venues weren't allowed
     to open for a few more months, so he wouldn't have been able
     to play here. Instead, he got a job as a shop clerk in [another city].
     Finally he found a gig at a bar in [yet another city]. And a local
     friend who worked in music went back to his old job at an
     insurance company.

C   Last time we talked about mutual aid in transporting people
     and supplies to hospitals, but do you know any examples of eco-
     nomic mutual aid to help people get through these months
     of reduced income?

X   Not that I can think of regarding unemployment or lodging, but
     another example during the lockdown was that some people
     teamed up to raise money for purchasing women's sanitary prod-
     ucts and delivering them to female healthcare workers.

Z   I can't think of any other economic mutual aid, but another exam-
     ple was related to mental health. An artist set up a bunch of on-
     line groups for people throughout China to make friends with
     people in Wuhan, since a lot of people here were suffering from
     isolation and trauma and needed someone to talk to. I'm not sure
     how far that developed, but it was an effort to use art to build
     mutual aid networks for supporting people's mental health.

III

Chuang: What were people's first impressions of the health code system? You mentioned that the government's announcement on February 16th required it when anyone visited public venues, but that many people didn't actually start using it until April, when you needed it to get on the bus.

Z I think we first came in contact with green codes in mid-March, when we went out to work on the land that we rent from one of the villagers [for gardening]. We met up with him out at the field to pay the rent, and he had a photograph of his green code with him, because he didn't have a smart phone. Someone had prepared it for him so he could scan it to leave and re-enter the village.

C So already at that time people had to scan their health code to enter and leave? How did you get out of the village without it?

Z We took a side path. The village boundaries weren't monitored very strictly at that time.

C Had the *shequ* residents committee stationed someone at the village entrance to register people in the system and scan their codes?

Z It was mainly "volunteers" from the village who were hired by the committee [for 200 to 300 yuan per day].

C I thought in March people were still not allowed to leave their residential complexes except for certain essential jobs. Were villagers allowed to go out for farming?

X Yes, it must have been around that time that the village started allowing people to go out for farm work, because the weather was getting warmer and it was time to plant. If they had waited any longer it would have been too late. And some villagers had this problem, because they had moved to the city and their complexes wouldn't let them come out to access their land until after the [citywide] lockdown was lifted in April.

C   As far as leaving the complex for medical treatment, you said
that everyone with a fever was moved to a quarantine site, where
they had to wait until they could get a nucleic acid test, and
then again until the results came out. If positive, then they would
be sent to a hospital. But what if the tests were negative? Were
they sent to different hospitals for other illnesses? And were they
able to get treatment during all this time of waiting for test results?

X   Generally not, as far as I know, because it was considered a risk
for medical personnel to enter housing complexes and quarantine
sites, so they just had to wait. Sometimes they could get some
medication delivered. And yes, some people with other illnesses
were sent to special hospitals, but a lot of people were not able
to get treatment, because regular hospital facilities were converted
to specialize in COVID-19 care. I'm sure a lot of people died for
that reason.

Z   For example, [activist filmmaker] Ai Xiaoming's father died at that
time from another illness because he wasn't able to get treatment.
This also happened to someone in my friend's family.

C   To some extent this was probably unavoidable, simply due to
the large number of cases overwhelming the medical resources
available in Wuhan, but do you think any of these problems could
have been avoided if things had been done differently?

Z   I think the system wasn't prepared at all. Actually you can see this
sort of problem in normal times as well, just at a smaller scale.
The government doesn't normally do anything useful, then when
anything unexpected arises and higher-level officials come down
to investigate, or when ordinary people start asking questions, all
of a sudden the government mobilizes lots of resources in an effort
to patch things up. For example, with the East Lake incident,
when [the Wuhan government signed a deal with a developer to]
fill in part of the lake [and convert the ecological preserve into a set
of commercial projects],[6] you could see how these government

6. The 2010 protest movement against this development project is recounted in our
article: "Gleaning the Welfare Fields," *Chuang Journal*, Issue 1: Dead Generations, 2016.

officials don't normally do anything. But then when you go and
demand that they release information—like the blueprints
[for the project], the location of drainage outlets—suddenly they
can get all that information within a couple days' time. When
they deem it necessary to shut you up, suddenly they can mobilize
resources from multiple departments to get what they need.

X   I think the government's behavior felt like a joke, when they
suddenly decided to close down the city after weeks of inaction,
without providing any information about the virus or how to deal
with the crisis—and worse, propagating misinformation. At that
time people were wondering whether the government was giving
up on (放弃) Wuhan, and our trust in the authorities was shattered,
so we felt that we could only rely on ourselves to get whatever we
would need to survive, be it food or healthcare. When the city was
first locked down, a lot of people rushed to the hospital to check
and see if they had COVID—people with any kind of symptom.
Lots of videos circulated of people crowded into the hospital
corridors, many without facemasks, terrified that they might have
the disease. It was like a run on a bank (挤兑). Later we learned
that a lot of transmission occurred at that time, in the hospitals.
Many otherwise healthy people with common colds went to see if
they had COVID, and then they got infected. This state of panic
continued for weeks after the lockdown began. Nobody knew
what to do, so they just depended on their own judgment and
rushed to the hospital [if they could get there], because they knew
the hospitals were running out of resources, so they were afraid
if they waited it might be too late. Before the lockdown, [the gov-
ernment] just tried to suppress information, then afterwards it still
didn't provide much practical assistance, including basic information about how people should deal with this kind of crisis.

C   So during the first couple months of the outbreak, not only
in January but even through February, it sounds like people were
mainly coping with the crisis on their own through mutual aid,
not so much in cooperation with the government but more
in spite of its initial suppression of information, and then its sudden imposition of severe restrictions on movement—which at

first stimulated a panic that made matters worse. The mainstream explanation of China's relative success in quickly bringing the outbreak under control, in contrast with most other countries, is basically that the government was able to react in a more draconian manner, with many people here now saying that this vindicates the political system. But what you're saying suggests an alternative explanation: that if you can call Wuhan a success, this was due especially to the responses of ordinary people in spite of the government's reactions. This is consistent with another discourse circulating in China, that people here have responded more effectively than in other countries, starting with initial news of the virus in December, due in part to their greater experience with previous pandemics such as SARS in 2003. What do you think?

Z　That sounds about right.

X　I think the experience of SARS in 2003 was important, but for my cousins who have children, for example, they belong to [WeChat] groups with other parents [that shared information about the virus starting in December], and in normal times they're always discussing the latest scares over things like food safety, problems in the schools, etc. Parents devote a lot of energy to concern for the health of their children, including the transmission of infectious diseases, because when a disease breaks out, the government's response will be merely remedial (补救性的施政), just making a show of responsiveness to satisfy public opinion after it's too late and a lot of people have already been affected. Parents don't want to take a risk of waiting for that, so in these groups they often discuss preventative measures, how to protect themselves against things like epidemics before the schools and the government [take action]. Just to ensure basic health and safety, you have to expend a lot of effort to form your own social groups, like these parent groups. You have to do it yourself, rather than leaving it up to the schools or the government, otherwise your child may be at great risk. Remember the incident at RYB Kindergarten in Beijing, where the teachers sexually assaulted the children [and the

police helped them destroy the evidence]?[7] There have been
a lot of things like that, and it scares parents into forming these
groups.

C   Do you think people here trust authorities like schools and the
government less than in other countries?

X   I don't know about other countries but Wuhan could be contrasted with some other Chinese cities like Shanghai or Hangzhou,
where people seem to trust the government more. Here people are
less likely to turn to the government for help, because they know
nothing will come of it.

Z   Some people say that after Xi came to power he got rid of a lot of
people who were technically qualified to deal with issues like
this health crisis, replacing them with his political cronies. Early on
in the pandemic some people talked about that as an explanation
for what went wrong.

X   For example [in early January] when the Chinese Center for
Disease Control sent people to Wuhan to investigate, they should
have been able to identify that an epidemic was emerging, but
still they didn't do anything about it. People say that the scientific
experts have been marginalized for political reasons.

C   [*Laughs*] That sounds like the US! Among other countries.
But the fact remains that China managed to bring the outbreak
under control much more quickly than most other countries,
so I'm wondering whether that should be attributed mainly to the
political system (which you say actually made the problem worse
at first), or to popular initiatives, or something else?

Z   I agree with the idea that popular initiatives played a big role, and
I think this is partly because people here have long been in the
habit of distrusting the government, so they have to take matters
into their own hands.

X   I think people in Wuhan distrust the government, even more so

7. "Another Kindergarten Abuse Case: Beijing's RYB Education Branch Accused
of Drugging and Molesting Children," *What's On Weibo*, Nov. 23, 2017.

than people in some other cities, as I was saying. One example that comes to mind is the incident in Hangzhou a couple years ago, where a nanny set fire to her employer's apartment. The employer and her kids might have survived if they had run away down the staircase, but instead they just called the fire department and sat around waiting for them to come until it was too late.[8] In Wuhan, as soon as there's a fire, we run. As soon as something happens, we try to save ourselves—we don't trust state agencies enough to rely on them.

C   What do you think about the idea that China's efforts to control the outbreak domestically was a success, in contrast with other countries?

X   I think that's true in some respects, but in others, I think ordinary people had to pay too high a price for it. Especially looking at things from a longer-term perspective. For example, the way the government has used the pandemic as an opportunity to push forward its "grid-style social management" (网格化管理).[9] The pandemic has provided not only a new excuse for implementing this system, but also a way for us to become accustomed to its logic and technologies. I think this is terrible. Not only is your personal information exposed, they also monitor your specific location at all times. For example, after a few new cases of COVID

8. Yuan Suwen, Yu Lu and Li Rongde, "Are Prosecutors Concealing Firefighter, Property Management Negligence in Nanny Arson Case?" *Caixin*, February 2, 2018. In this case, the fire department and the property management company each blamed one another for their fatal delay in rescuing the nanny's employer and three children.

9. This system (inspired by a surveillance system in London) was piloted in Beijing in the 2000s and then expanded to other experimental zones throughout China starting in 2015 (including Wuhan). It employs minimally trained civilians as "grid managers" (网格员) to collect data on everyone living within a certain area, including by knocking on doors to check on residents and, now (starting a couple years ago in the largest cities), to have them register their phones in the grid system by scanning a QR code that the managers attach to everyone's door. It's related to the process of experimentation with grid-style administrative subdivision which ultimately established the *shequ* as the lowest level of urban governance. It's currently unclear how effectively the "grid manager" system or cellphone registration has been or whether it is beginning to be rolled out nationwide. Currently, it is operational only in central areas of the most important cities. For an overview of the system in its pilot form, see: Wu Qiang, "Urban Grid Management and Police State in China: A Brief Overview," *China Change*, Aug. 12, 2014.

recently emerged in Beijing and Dalian, our village's grid manager kept sending messages in our village's [WeChat] group reminding anyone who had been to those places to go register with the authorities.

Z   In the past we never felt so controlled (管制) in the village.

X   They had already started up the grid system throughout Wuhan over the past couple years. We saw signs designating that a given area belonged to a certain zone in the grid, and who the grid manager was for that area. But it wasn't until after the lockdown that we actually came into contact with the managers. If a case of coronavirus emerges in a given zone, it is the responsibility of the grid manager for that zone. So the managers go around making sure that everyone implements policy directives to the letter.

Z   In *Wuhan Diaries*, there's a story about Yulin where the system is represented visually as a grid pattern with the people and build-ings in it.[10] After one of my relatives tested positive for COVID-19, [the grid managers] looked up all their information and sent the entire family [of ten] to quarantine at the hospital, then they sealed off the area around my house, trapping everyone inside for two weeks and delivering food every day. They also posted my relatives' personal information publicly on WeChat, where it was shared by people throughout the city.

C   What did grid managers do, exactly, during the lockdown? Would they knock on your doors?

Z   Yes, they would knock on the door and get everyone registered in the system. They were also responsible for making sure every-thing got disinfected regularly.

C   I thought that was the responsibility of the *shequ* residents committee.

X   Yes, but there seems to be an overlap in their responsibilities. The grid manager seems to be the person who gets blamed if there

---

10. "News from Yulin," *Wuhan Diaries*, Part Three, Jan. 31 – Feb. 16, 2020.

is a problem. But the grid managers work more closely with
the Public Security system [i.e. the police]. If there's a problem,
they can immediately send information, including the precise
location, to the Public Security authorities (公安). In fact anyone
can scan the QR code on the stickers [that grid managers affix
to everyone's doors] and directly alert the police of an incident.

IV

Chuang: Let me ask you the same question I asked X and Z last time: how do you feel things have changed in Wuhan since the pandemic began a year ago? For example in everyday life, the economy, people's attitudes toward the government, or anything else that comes to mind.

W   Well one big thing for me is that there was no work for several months, from the start of the lockdown last January until after it was lifted in April [and really not until the summer]. There were no regular jobs in renovation or construction. Some factories were able to get a Work Resumption Permit (复工证明) at that time. But there were no construction jobs during the lockdown, except for building hospitals.

C   Why didn't you go work on the hospital projects?

W   I didn't have the guts. [*Laughs.*]

X   But you could have gone if you wanted, right? I remember someone offered you a job on a hospital [during the lockdown].

W   Yeah, they did, but I was too scared!

C   You mean afraid of being infected?

W   Of course! Who isn't afraid [of COVID-19]?

C   And you say factories reopened first—when was that, exactly?

W   Already during the lockdown I went to work in a [motorcycle seat] factory for a few days. They hadn't completely reopened, I just [went there with the owner and his son to do some machine repair work for a few days]. There was also a [flooring project] near our village where I worked [for about a week] during the lockdown. It had already started before the lockdown but took a break for the Chinese New Year, when the workers went back to their hometowns. The boss knew I was in Wuhan, so he asked me to come help [finish it up in March]. We couldn't get food delivered, nothing was open, so every morning the boss brought a rice cooker, and at noon he would cook rice right there on the site, while his wife went home and cooked a few dishes for us. We didn't dare order take-out, we were too scared. Besides, nothing was open.

C   How many workers were there?

W   Just four or five plus the boss and his wife.

C   But throughout Wuhan you say factories opened earlier than construction sites. Why was that?

W   Because a lot of the construction workers hadn't come back to Wuhan yet. Also it was harder to meet the safety requirements necessary to get a Work Resumption Permit for construction sites than for factories.

Z   I heard there was a factory in Jiangxia [District of Wuhan], making something like screens for cellphones, and it never stopped operating throughout the lockdown. The workers got stuck there [they couldn't leave Wuhan to return to their hometowns during the lockdown] so they just stayed at the factory the whole time and kept working.

C   But most factories had to shut down during the lockdown and then gradually reopened starting in April, followed by construction sites? And last time Z said state-owned construction projects were able to reopen a few months earlier than privately owned ones—is that right, W?

W   Yes.

C   Why? Did private companies have more trouble getting the permits?

W   For the sort of small renovation projects I normally do, they just couldn't find enough workers [because everyone had left Wuhan and it took a few months for them to start coming back].

C   Why were state-owned companies able to find workers then? Do they hire more local people?

W   Let me give an example. Right now I'm working on a renovation
      project at a hotel, and the contractor says that last year he got
      a bunch of permits for all kinds of work. And he's not a big com-
      pany, he just has connections. For state-owned companies, it's
      even easier.

C   Then why didn't you get a job on a state-owned site, instead of
      waiting until the summer for private sites to reopen?

W   I was afraid. Even by the summer I still had mixed feelings [about
      taking the risk of going out to work]. Because the people who
      worked on those hospitals [during the lockdown] had to be
      quarantined after they finished. Also, I live together with Z and X,
      and I didn't want to risk bringing the virus back to them. So
      my thinking was that I should just wait as long as possible before
      going back out to work.

C   So you could have gotten a job at a state-owned site if you had
      wanted to?

W   Well you couldn't just show up at the site and get a job—you
      had to know someone there who could introduce you. [Also] you
      would need to have a license for a lot of the technical jobs,
      such as electrician or welder, [whereas you don't always need those
      for private sector jobs].

C   Although you were afraid to work until the summer, were there
      a lot of other people who wanted to work but couldn't find jobs in
      those months? How did they survive? Did they have to borrow
      money from relatives?

W   Yes, there were lots of people like that, not just in Wuhan but all
      over China, because construction sites closed down in those
      months throughout the country. Most people went back to their
      hometowns and lived on their savings. Some people with land
      went back to farming. But I know there were a few people who
      got stuck in Wuhan, and they just got by however they could.
      Usually there was somebody in the family with a source of income
      they could fall back on for the time being.

C   Now that things have gone back to normal, more or less,
    have there been any changes in the industry compared with before
    the pandemic? Like are wages lower, or have they gone back to
    the same rates as before?

W   In the first few months when people started coming back to
    Wuhan [around the summer and fall], you couldn't find any high-
    paying construction jobs, they all paid less than in the past.
    Even the bosses [i.e. contractors] had it rough. Everyone had
    gone for several months without any income, so they were des-
    per-ate for anything, there was no room to bargain. But this
    situation didn't last very long. After things stabilized and every-
    thing reopened, the wages got better.

C   Are they now the same as last year?

W   They weren't affected much.

C   How much do you make?

W   I mainly work for bosses I'm already familiar with, and they pay
    me the same as in the past. If I went out to work for someone
    I was just meeting for the first time, someone I had found online,
    they post rates online for certain jobs, saying what type of work
    they need.

C   Your type of work is called "common laborer" (杂工), right?

W   Yes.

C   What is the market rate for that, and how much do you normally
    get paid working for the bosses you're already familiar with?

W   A little more [than the market rate]. I've been doing this longer
    [than most people], I'm more skilled, like I know how to use
    all kinds of power tools.

C   So you're not really a typical common laborer. But do you know
    what the market rate is for ordinary laborers in Wuhan now?

W   180, 200... No one gets paid less than 160 [yuan per day].

C   And you make a little more, since you have some skills and the
    bosses know you.

W   Yeah they pay me 240 or 260.

C   How many hours do you normally work in a day?

W   That depends on the season. It won't be more than eight or nine
    hours.

C   Have there been any other changes in the industry since last year?

W   There's less work. For example, some people had planned to
    renovate their homes, but because of this year's hardships, they de-
    cided to postpone those plans. Lots of people have done that,
    so there's less work available.

C   So in addition to losing several months of income in the first
    half of the year, would you say that even now monthly income is
    lower than last year for most construction workers?

W   Yes, monthly income is definitely lower than before [even though
    daily wage rates are about the same as before]. When I talk to
    skilled workers (师傅), many of them say they used to make sixty
    or seventy thousand yuan a year, but this year they just hope
    to make enough to cover their living expenses. They've lowered
    their expectations and just hope to cross over into next year
    safe and sound (求个平安). A lot of people I used to work with
    have gone to the Northeast to work this year. They waited until
    July or August to leave their hometowns, thinking "It will be
    enough if we just make it through the year safe and sound, if
    the situation is still so complicated [i.e. if the risk of infection is
    still high], then we'll just stay at home and not make any money
    this year."

C   Do most of the workers you know have land at home? And do
    they know how to farm?

W   Yes, the people I'm talking about do.

C   Do you think they've chosen to devote more time to farming this
    year as an alternative source of income?

W   Yes, if it weren't for [the pandemic] they would have already come
    out to make money, but now that they've run into this situation,
    they're just staying at home, taking care of the work that needs
    to be done at home [i.e. farming].

C   Are there any other things that have happened in the past year that
    you'd like to talk about? Anything that surprised you?

W   One thing that stood out is that after I started working again, a
    lot of produce markets were being completely renovated, especially
    those that sell seafood. There were a lot of projects like that—
    not just one or two, but throughout all of Wuhan. We worked on
    some of them. Some were multi-story buildings that were com-
    pletely dismantled and renovated.

C   Was the idea to disinfect the markets or to change their structure?

W   Both, but it was mainly to rebuild the drainage systems, because
    the old ones were just for show, they didn't actually work. Dirty
    water would just collect next to the stalls, and it was up to the
    vendors to mop it up. If they didn't, it would just stand there indef-
    initely. So we dug up the whole floor and installed a system where
    the water would actually drain away.

C   Have you noticed any changes in people's attitudes—toward the
    government, for example, or toward the economy?

W   Yes, there have been some changes. Let me tell you a little story
    about that. [Around about August] I was injured and had to take
    a break from work for a while, so I was hanging out at a game
    stall near the village, where you could play Chinese chess. It was
    mainly older people, but there was a guy there in his twenties, a
    guy from out of town playing chess with an old man, and I over-
    heard their conversation. The young guy had returned to his home
    before the New Year and he was asking the old man what it was
    like here during the lockdown. The young guy had read some
    things in the news, like about people standing in line at the hospi-
    tal. He criticized the government for covering up the outbreak at
    the beginning, and the old man just said, "Yeah, but it's even worse
    overseas now. Looking back at what happened in our country

compared with what's happening overseas, if you just look at the end results, you can see that what our country did was effective."

So a lot of people have mixed feelings, including myself. We ordinary people didn't learn about the outbreak until too late, after it had already grown into an epidemic. People outside of Wuhan found out about it before us because the information was blocked. On that point, I think that shouldn't have happened. But after that, the measures that were taken, like sealing off the city, they came suddenly, and after the lockdown started, there was no concrete preparation, and that caused a lot of inconveniences in our lives. It was really hard. But if you look at the end results, they were effective. And the other older people sitting around criticized the young guy, saying "You should be happy! You should be content with your lot (知足)." They mentioned that the government had paid for the treatment of everyone who had gotten sick, and so on.

C Do you think this conversation was representative of a broader divide between young and old people in their attitudes?

W I don't know. I think people of all ages have mixed feelings about all this.

C What do you think accounts for the difference between how people have responded to the outbreak here and in those countries where it has gotten worse?

W I think a big part of it has been people's awareness of the need to protect themselves (自我保护意识). The lockdown of Wuhan was an important measure in its own right, and I'm sure that helped prevent the spread, but at least as important was the way everyone reacted to news of the lockdown throughout the country. When they heard about it, everybody suddenly started to take the virus seriously and stay home. Like those workers I mentioned— they could have gone back out to look for a job much earlier, but they decided to stay home as long as they could, because they were afraid.

4.
Plague Illuminates the Great Unity of All Under Heaven: On the Coming State

Introduction: In the Shadows

Plague literature is rarely about the plague. It is, instead, a drama simultaneously social and microbial. As existential ruminations condense in isolation and seep outward, these tributaries slowly sculpt the terrain of a popular culture now faced with a type of catastrophe that can no longer be denied out of convenience. The exemplars of the genre see in the plague a more monstrous return of class conflict, scorning its long denial. In these cases—for example Poe's "Masque of the Red Death" or Bruno Jasieński's *I Burn Paris*,[1] which, in a chilling echo of the present, envisions an insurrection occurring in the midst of a plague in 1920s France—the drama mobilizes the plague as a form of class warfare

---

1. See: Benjamin Noys, "Microbial Communism," *Mute Magazine*, Sept. 24, 2013. *I Burn Paris* is less well-known in the anglophone world but was once among the best-selling books of communist fiction—so popular that it succeeded in getting its author expelled from Poland and the book banned.

severed from political agency altogether, since political agency has failed it. Instead, the conflict is transposed onto the more fundamental substratum of biology where it becomes less concerned with the ethics and consequence of revolutionary bloodletting. In such fantasies class is not overturned, but unbound in a great, uninhibited violence unleashed by the unknowing hand of the plague itself, a barely veiled metaphor of overspilling vengeance. The genre is nihilist and apocalyptic, but also preternaturally political—as if those desperate, hopeful, wrathful slogans scrawled across Hong Kong in 2019 just months before the pandemic had levered themselves out of the concrete and crawled into the blood: "if we burn, you burn with us," "I'd rather be ashes than dust."

But the more common cultural current is conservative, defined by a recognition of the catastrophe without the ability to delineate its cause. At its most reactionary, this manifests as a pure substitution: tens of thousands of people for whom politics is nothing but endless paranoia deny the existence of the virus outright, seeing in it nothing but an excuse for the overreach of the state. Others take an equally reactionary but opposite position. They vigorously amplify the myths that states craft for themselves by pointing to the relative success of various East Asian governments in containing the outbreak (and conveniently ignoring their failures that facilitated it).[2] Whether rallying around the state or rallying against it, these are a concise expression of an almost universal approach to the question of the plague, ranging from the party propagandist, to the paranoid anti-masker, and from there all the way up to the ivy-league philosopher. The thematic core is this: the plague is not the plague but is instead simply one face of the totalizing state. The state here acts as a sort of final threshold of ideology. This is the limit-point beyond which one has no other option but to gaze upon contours of the beast we call capitalism. At this threshold, the rule is to speak of the plague without speaking of its origins, to speak of society without speaking of the social and to speak of the pandemic as a purely administrative matter conducted by those at the helm of the state. In short, the most common way that the pandemic is spoken of today is not to discuss it at all and to discuss the state in its place.

2. This is true not only for China but also South Korea, for example.

The shadow of the state is dark and cloaks all that lies beneath. What should be a deeper lesson in the microbiological and macroecological devastation that necessarily accompanies production for the sake of never-ending accumulation is thereby disguised as a stereotypical drama of the "man versus society" archetype, as taught in high school English departments and here retaining all the depth of a teenager's essay on Orwell. The cliché is played out not only in news media but also in what is the most representative form of the genre today: the plague diary, serialized over social media. These diaries first began to appear in Wuhan in the midst of the Chinese lockdown. They circulated on the grey market of not-yet-banned Weibo and WeChat posts, where they were discussed between friends and (sometimes) archived outside the reach of the censors. Once banned domestically, they began to recirculate outside the country, often in translation. The best of these were simply personal records, detailing the surreal, existential experience of life under lockdown, but the most widely distributed have been those that emphasize the melodramatic conflict between individual expression and the authoritarian state. The latter produce consumable clichés that direct public ire away from the social and economic system governing our everyday lives and instead toward the politically proper focal point: a government simultaneously too near and too distant.

The most famous and familiar narrative of the recent plague literature, then, is certainly *Wuhan Diary*, a collection of social media entries penned by the award-winning author Fang Fang during the lockdown in Hubei.[3] Since it was written by an already well-known celebrity with millions of Weibo followers, it quickly garnered the attention of the foreign press. Meanwhile, given its generic liberal undertones and lack of any real political position aside from constantly bemoaning media censorship and decrying the government's opaque, deadly mismanagement of the early stages of the outbreak, it matched the ideological predilections of the foreign publishing industry. The account was therefore translated into English and German at breakneck speed and released by

---

3. Fang Fang is the penname of the fiction author Wang Fang. She was the recipient of the Lu Xun Literary Prize in 2010, one of the country's most prestigious awards for novelists. Though better known in Chinese, several of her major works have been translated into English. None, however, have seen the same success as the rapid translation of *Wuhan Diary* in 2020.

major publishers via Amazon in both languages a mere two weeks after the final installment of the Chinese version was published (on April 8th, the day that the lockdown ended). This is the *Wuhan Diary* most visible to the outside world, firmly planted in a naïve liberalism stretching from the first entry in January to the preface written for its translation in April, where the author offers nothing more than the clichéd kumbaya solution of the fleece-wearing intelligentsia: "The only way we can conquer this virus is for all members of humankind to work together."[4]

In fact, this sentence is Fang Fang's hedge against the realization that her work had been actively mobilized by those seeking political gain through the attribution of the pandemic to the mismanagement of the Chinese state. But the virus was not caused, as she claims, by the "arrogance" of "humankind."[5] Moreover, the deployment of her diary in ongoing geopolitical conflicts was hardly incidental. In her very first entries from late January, she characterizes the outbreak in the language of American conservatism:

> When the world of officialdom skips over the natural process
> of competition, it leads to disaster; empty talk about political
> correctness without seeking truth from facts also leads to
> disaster; prohibiting people from speaking the truth and the
> media from reporting the truth leads to disaster; and now we
> are tasting the fruits of these disasters, one by one.[6]

Similar statements are sprinkled throughout *Wuhan Diary*. The supposed political neutrality and well-meaning invocations of the shared lesson that the virus has taught to humankind disguise a fundamentally conservative logic where competition is "natural" and authoritarian censorship in the name of politics is the real cause of the disaster, rather

---

4. Fang Fang, "Introduction: The Virus is the Common Enemy of Humankind, Section V," *Wuhan Diary*, New York: Harper Collins, 2020.

5. Ibid.

6. The quote is from the entry of Jan. 26, 2020. It needs to be noted here that "political correctness" (政治正确) in Chinese denotes the practice of aligning one's public statements and policies with the current language used in the government's official media pronouncements. The book's English translator, however, does not make this clear, purposefully conflating the conservative use of the term in English with this more specific usage in Chinese.

than the pandemic's actual origin in profit-driven factory farms and widespread ecological destruction.[7]

When confronted with the reality of such a catastrophe, critics who hold to the fundamental inalienability of capitalism will always turn their attention instead to the state, which is, after all, the supposed nexus of representation for "the public." And this elision is the real point of interest in today's plague literature: Why does the state play this substitutionist role at every level of inquiry? In other words, why do people end up talking about the state when they set out to talk about the plague?

In these accounts, the totalizing state and its pervasive, panoptic power seems to be the prime mover in a paranoid conspiracy that flips Hobbes's *Leviathan* on its head. This sort of sovereignty has no material origin. In this conception, the state becomes little more than an ancient, amorphous specter haunting humankind. This is the state's own myth of itself, the final reification disguising the fact that the state today cannot be understood separate from its functions under capitalism—just as, historically, states are inseparable from questions of class and production. Capitalist imperatives are the foundation of the state and conflicts arise from the fact that disjointed processes of state building and state decay exist side by side within a single global economy. This material conception of the state requires an understanding of it in its specificity—that is, in relation to civilization as a whole and to particular modes of production—rather than as some exaggerated, paranoiac Leviathan haunting humanity from the moment the first grains were cast into the soil. Here, otherwise incidental factors of history, geography and culture can be adapted into integral elements of statecraft, so long as they can be mobilized to effectively serve fundamental capitalist imperatives.

The pandemic cannot be primarily explained through the behavior of the state. At the same time, the response to the outbreak has illuminated both the state-building process underway in China and the general decay of public institutions in the United States and Europe. Neither of these processes can be understood as distinct from one another, since

---

7. Rob Wallace, *Dead Epidemiologists: On the Origins of COVID-19*, NYU Press, 2020. This general argument is made in "Social Contagion" above.

each is shaped by the same industrial conflict between different factions of capitalists who have divergent interests defined by their investment in competing trade blocs. This does, however, raise deeper questions about the nature of the state under capitalism and its attendant concepts. Included here are the questions of how much the institutional structure of the Chinese state necessarily needs to emulate its Western counterparts to fulfill its capitalist imperatives and, symmetrically, how much latitude it has to develop in a different direction. This latter point is especially relevant, given that the last two decades have seen influential intellectuals and high-level political leadership both intentionally and openly place more and more emphasis on a different logic of statecraft rooted in a different genealogy, even while they contribute to the construction of a state that fundamentally serves capitalist imperatives. In this regard, the Chinese literary and philosophical tradition exerts an evident influence (especially via its living interlocutors) on the potential shape of the state currently being constructed—even if this state absolutely cannot be reduced to its cultural features nor understood in a purely or even primarily cultural fashion.[8] In other words, the key questions are: how much must the Chinese state resemble the capitalist states that have preceded it, how much latitude is there for adaptive experimentation and what intellectual environment might provide the resources for such adaptation?

Answering these questions requires a concrete analysis of the mechanics on the ground — how power is actually developed and deployed—rather than a purely discursive approach detailing how the state speaks of itself and articulates its power to the populace. These pragmatic features are what we emphasize below. At the same time, the deployment of power does not occur in a vacuum. We might echo a truism here and say that the mode of production (mostly, but not exclusively,

---

8. Throughout, we refer to a "Chinese" philosophical and literary tradition. This is not to imply that a "Chinese" state or even a single coherent "Chinese" civilization has actually existed in East Asia for millennia—this claim is relatively recent and is largely a product of the 20th-century nation-building project. Instead, the reference is to the fact that Chinese characters were the universal writing system across the region, allowing for authors speaking mutually unintelligible spoken languages to have their ideas rendered in a mutually intelligible fashion. This enabled the growth of a single Chinese-language canon of literature, history and philosophy to form which would be a shared reference across dynasties.

its ruling class) makes its own states, but it does not make them as it pleases. Instead, it crafts them under circumstances given and transmitted from the past, with materials salvaged from the contingencies of culture and geography. These materials are assembled within a given intellectual context, through which they are made available to those with the power to shape wide-ranging transformations in governance.[9] Today, this intellectual context is global, but not homogenous. Similarly, the globalization of European practices of statecraft—and the influence thereby exerted by capitalist imperatives on their evolution—has been an incidental outcome attending imperialism and colonization, not a logical necessity. Given the different material challenges faced by capitalism today and a different intellectual genealogy from which to draw, there is every reason to expect that the state currently being constructed in China will, in certain respects, be without precedent *even while its fundamental function remains the same.*

In what follows, then, we begin by exploring previously invisible intricacies of state construction illuminated by the sudden catastrophe: how the party mobilized its local organs of authority in response to the pandemic and how this mobilization was itself insufficient, demonstrating a persistent incapacity that could only be overcome through the participation of millions of volunteers. All these mechanisms—identified through a series of original interviews, in our own personal experiences and via secondary accounts of the quarantine—compose the actual deployment of power on the part of the state.[10] They are, therefore, the

9. The process from here is experimental and evolutionary: reforms in governance are piloted in certain areas (often developing as a makeshift response to some local problem) and only extended elsewhere if and when they prove functional in maintaining the baseline conditions of accumulation or in overcoming limits to continuing growth. Even then, there is no guarantee that any given adaptation will be taken up elsewhere, since selection between multiple equally adequate options then depends on numerous contingencies.

10. The primary material collected from interviews and personal experience is almost all urban, though it was supplemented by secondary information about rural areas. It covers experiences in Wuhan itself and in several other major cities of China (all large and most coastal) and includes roughly equal representation between Chinese and foreign respondents—with a disproportionate number from Wuhan. This means that any biases in the sample population will skew in the opposite direction of our fundamental thesis that the response was haphazard and displayed a deep incapacity on the part of the state: containment was conducted most thoroughly in Wuhan and Beijing, more strictly in major cities and most severely for foreigners and those from Wuhan. Had more respondents from rural areas and small cities been included, it's likely that the inconsistencies

material from which we can theorize the progress and character of the state-building project in China today. We will first explore the history of experimental reforms that led to the current distribution of power at the local level and illustrate the role of all the major institutions mobilized in response to the pandemic. After this, we systematically anatomize the various forms of volunteer self-organization that were the real means by which the outbreak was contained. This is followed by an overview of the policies implemented in the lockdown and their deeply fragmented nature, mirroring the fragmentation of the state more generally. Overall, it becomes apparent that the supposed success of the Chinese government in containing the virus was really evidence of a deeper weakness. In conclusion, we offer a few speculations on the likely future direction of the state-building project at the local level. Throughout, we periodically return to more theoretical concerns about the nature of the state under capitalism, the characteristic institutional structures that have prevailed in the region historically, and the philosophy of statecraft that informs those in power today.

Ships in a Storm

The first stage is marked by a sudden divergence in the flow of information. Rumors originating in medical circles had begun to circulate about some new sort of flu. The official response was that these rumors were overblown—specifically, that there was a virus, but it wasn't a SARS variant, and it wasn't transmitted from human to human—but locals began to suspect evidence to the contrary as the Huanan Seafood Market was shut down and Wuhan's hospitals began to feel the influx. Those who knew better (specifically doctors and other workers in the medical sector) began to share warnings to friends and family, as a quiet run on PPE began. Stores began to empty of masks, gloves and hand sanitizer long before the lockdown. Of course, behind the scenes there was a multilateral struggle occurring within the state itself. Local officials denied everything, and local police admonished doctor Li Wenliang and other early whistleblowers. At the same time that the local state was

---

and inefficiencies of the containment effort would have only been further emphasized.

cracking down on "rumor mongers," the central authorities had been alerted by the Chinese Center for Disease Control and Prevention that a new, unidentified flu (suspected to be SARS) was spreading in the city. Beijing sent experts to Wuhan as early as January 1, 2020, and a corona-virus was identified as the cause on January 8. Rather than attempting to cover up the outbreak to the rest of the world (as had occurred during the SARS epidemic), the central state assisted the release of the virus's genetic sequence in record time and didn't make any attempt to officially deny the early foreign reporting on the epidemic. It did, how-ever, condone and support local officials' early attempts to constrain the spread of information in Wuhan and Hubei more generally. Thus, a strange situation emerged in which many in Wuhan often got the most authoritative news of the virus not from local health officials but instead from relatives and acquaintances elsewhere in China or even from overseas. Before the lockdown of any physical space came an omi-nous sequestration of information, signaling the fragmented command structure of the state.

In many ways, this was a textbook example of state incapacity. Even while the core epidemiological infrastructure operated with relative ef-ficiency in identifying the virus, tracing its geographic origins and roll-ing out widespread testing in record time, the social infrastructure of pandemic control ran up against the fissured nature of the Chinese state. The central government appears to have continued to defer administra-tive responsibilities to the municipal and provincial governments in the normal fashion throughout most of January, despite its own scientists identifying a new coronavirus circulating in the city early in the month. Following standard practice, it initially backed up the pronouncements of its local administrators by repeating these positions in the official national media outlets. In Hubei, officials constrained local information at precisely the time that public access to such information would have done the most to prevent further infection. Then, something appears to have shifted toward the end of January. The speed of the shutdown and the fact that so few expected it seems to hint that some protocol was triggered at the central level. As our respondents remark in Chapter three, the lockdown announcement was released at 2 AM on the 23rd of January, with no one allowed to leave after 10 AM on the same day— apparently, however, on-ramps were already being closed as early as

January 22, albeit with no formal notice of the fact. Later, the CCP had to reverse prior positions and exonerate whistleblowers who had originally been admonished by the local authorities, such as Dr. Li Wenliang (who had since died from the disease), with authorities even offering a "solemn apology" to his relatives. Throughout the early response to the pandemic, the fragmentation of information itself reflected the deeper fragmentation within the actual mechanisms of the state.

With the experience of the first SARS outbreak in mind, the central authorities clearly had at least a rough playbook for how to deal with an epidemic that had such a clear geographic center. Despite the shock and fear in Wuhan itself, the fact that a single point of origin was so quickly identified was ultimately a blessing for the management of the pandemic: it ensured that, so long as thorough attention was paid to Wuhan and Hubei (as well as anyone who had recently travelled there), the quarantine as a whole wouldn't fail, even if its implementation elsewhere was inconsistent. Similarly, it was a serendipitous fact that the outbreak occurred prior to the Chinese New Year and its massive movement of population. Due to the upcoming holiday, most people had already prepared for normal shop closures by stocking up on food, and most companies had already planned to close for the week. The sudden Wuhan lockdown represented the central state's clear realization that these two bits of luck were quickly running out. The spread outward from Hubei was well underway, and New Year travel threatened to accelerate it beyond all hope of containment. Though it's still unclear exactly what command mechanisms were mobilized, the lockdown appears to mark the point at which the central government unequivocally stepped in. This not only ensured that the lockdown would be enforced in Wuhan— first and foremost through travel restrictions in and out of the city, which were implemented ahead of anything else, and second through various forms of internal restrictions on commerce and movement within the city—but also that the example would communicate the sort of policies expected of lower-level officials elsewhere, since the state had no capacity to ensure consistent application in the countryside.

This was the first-ever quarantine of this scale in human history. The conduct of the quarantine certainly gives some insights into the nature of the state's response to the pandemics caused by the very economic system that it cultivates. But the function of such lockdowns is not to preserve health for its own sake. Instead, the state treats health as an ancillary necessity for maintaining a competent laboring population and preventing insurrection. In this regard, the Chinese state (which has long practiced its ability to effectively operate from a position of weakness while slowly building capacity) proved much more capable of taking decisive action in favor of the long-term interests of the economy, even if this meant sacrificing short-term profits. This contrasts markedly with the United States, where a long hemorrhaging of state capacity coincided with the poor luck of a particularly inept administration to produce the opposite outcome: the sacrifice of the population for the short-term gain of the economy. Ironically, this divergence has now proven the American state to have been the less effective administrator of that economy's baseline conditions, since its short-game strategy has been worse for accumulation in the long run. In the immediate moment, however, all these larger questions were relegated to the backdrop. Instead, those trapped in the lockdown were faced with a more existential condition, suddenly isolated in a flash-frozen world stalked by some invisible threat.

At first everything took on a surreal dimension. Our interviewees offer nervous laughter describing those initial weeks of lockdown in Wuhan and elsewhere. Non-Chinese respondents illustrate interactions with a bureaucracy simultaneously banal and baroque. At times, the experience is laughably harmless in its inefficiency. In others, it might entail a half-month nightmare of shuttling back and forth between makeshift hospitals in a dystopia of Kafkaesque clichés. One of our friends describes it well in Chapter three: "at first people were just surprised and everything seemed absurd." The same friends write of those absurd first weeks in quarantine in their own "Wuhan Diary," printed as a sort of DIY comic book.[11] In contrast to Fang Fang's more famous version, the comic doesn't gravitate toward mundane questions of corruption and censorship but instead shows a far more intimate portrayal of the lockdown's living absurdity. Throughout, the authors use the metaphor of being stranded at sea, each apartment or housing complex its own ship

11. The diary was printed as a comic strip in Chinese in various outlets and in both Chinese and English by a left-wing newsletter put together by the Black Book Assembly in Hong Kong.

stuck in the eye of the storm:

> From the ship I look out of a small window, and through
> its yellowing glass and the layers of fog, there are people wav-
> ing flags trying to tell us something [...] Many friends also
> send messages to us (in a bottle) along the tidal waves, asking
> us what our situation is.

These messages to and from distant friends and family are invariably mundane—stories about the health of the family dog and pictures of the meals prepared in lockdown—but somehow this fact makes them more valuable, each presented with the care of an archeologist unearthing spare records of lives otherwise scoured from history.

One of the first, most salient effects of the lockdown was the way in which this isolation engendered an alien experience of mundane surroundings and one's own body—not quite dissociation so much as an unmooring from the many minor rituals that compose the everyday practice of embodiment. In this absurd, atomized inversion of the mass strike, the same suspension of quotidian economic life was realized but also severed from its automatically communal dimension. At first, the inverted strike manifested as a series of surreal encounters with various commodities populating the narrative. As the denials dissipated and lockdown began, news poured in of highway checkpoints and rolling closures of all shops and pharmacies, which led to hundreds of thousands rushing to evacuate and a complete shortage of PPE. The temperature dropped and the battery on one of the authors' iPhones began to expand, causing the phone to "swell up like a real apple." At the more general level, commodity circulation itself exhibited an equally indeterminate logic. Simply obtaining cooking gas became an eerie bureaucratic hurdle where even the local authorities half-jokingly assured everyone waiting out in the cold that, in the worst case, they could all just loot the delivery truck. Local markets began going to the different neighborhoods, inverting the active and passive roles in the economic relationship as commodities exuded the specter of the animate. In these early stages of wintry isolation, surrealism seeped into every facet of consciousness. One author saw "a video of a wild pig fleeing on the Second Ring Road" and ruminated on an abandoned idea "for a novel where all of humanity would enter a 100 year-long sleep mode and nature would slowly recover." Meanwhile, other ships passed silently in the night. The storm expanded beyond the wall of fog.

The Floating State

Over time, the surreal strike was forced to turn to practical questions. These took two forms, with some overlap: First were **questions of basic survival**—dealt with largely within the reproductive sphere of the household and within the village and community/neighborhood (社区 —*shequ*). The latter two locales have parallel formal and informal reproductive infrastructures, however, since they include both the sum of households that compose the locality as well as specific base-level government agencies with affiliated local-level state and party organs. Often, informal cooperation between households fused with formal initiatives led by the central state as delegated to these organs. Similar issues were confronted in the workplace. Labor organizing was limited during the lockdown and muted in its immediate aftermath. But several months after the reopening, the strain placed on logistics workers finally culminated in a series of strikes.

Second were **questions relating to the pandemic itself**. These were dealt with through various makeshift organizations which sometimes overlapped with local governmental agencies (by staffing government initiatives with volunteers, for instance) and sometimes did not. In general, these forms of self-organization can be characterized as far exceeding the capacity of the state in many places, by both outperforming the state in provision of essential medical resources and simply in their ability to mobilize more labor than the state alone was capable of.

From afar, one could lump all the above together under the label of "mutual aid" and thereby equate these examples with what seem to be similar grassroots efforts in other countries. While this equation is wrong on multiple levels, it nonetheless hints at the essential role played by volunteer work (志愿者工作) and mutual aid (互助) in the successful effort to contain the pandemic.[12] By the same measure, though,

---

12. In general, "volunteer work" or "mutual aid" were the terms used to describe these activities at the colloquial level within China. It's essential to realize, however, that the

it also illustrates how seemingly grassroots volunteer efforts have long been integral to Chinese statecraft and remain fundamental to the current state-building process. Mass mobilization distributed through lengthy, intertwined relational networks ultimately linking back to the formal bureaucracy has always played an important role in both the political philosophy of the region and in the way that power has traditionally been deployed. This also means that "civil society," "direct democracy" and "autonomy" are already subsumed within the more general practice of governance—often in a highly formalized fashion, with terms like democracy and autonomy written into law, despite not existing in any recognizable form in everyday life—and thus, these concepts are poor registers for understanding challenges to the state. Similarly, the presumption that mutual aid work is politically empowering for those involved may not carry the same implications if this empowerment not only fails to oppose the state but, in fact, keeps it afloat. The pandemic demonstrated that categorizations dependent on a clear divide between the formal realm of government and the informal realm of governance may not accurately capture the real anatomy of the state.

In order to understand the present state-building effort and the nature of its relation to local mutual aid initiatives, some general historical context is necessary. Though the socialist developmental regime is the immediate historical precursor from which mechanisms of government were inherited, here we emphasize the nature of the state in the dynastic era, because it is precisely the "long" history of statecraft that is being actively revived in Chinese political philosophy today, taking on increasingly overt expression in official pronouncements and in the design of new administrative mechanisms. That said, *any influence exerted on the present by ancient political philosophy is nonetheless subordinate to the state's fundamental functions under capitalism.* There is a thin line between recognizing the true influence of Chinese political philosophy's discursive universe (or any other contingent, cultural-linguistic

---

term for mutual aid does not imply any separation from or opposition to the state as it does in English. In fact, it often implies the opposite due to its incorporation in the political terminology of the developmental regime (as in rural "mutual aid teams"). The term "self-organization" (自组织) began to be used later—largely by left-liberal political thinkers, though sometimes also by more radical leftists in worker organizing circles—in order to class such activities together in a way that implied greater independence from the state.

features of society) in this subordinate role and overemphasizing it such that the Chinese state becomes a sort of neo-Confucian Leviathan that overdetermines all other forms of social organization, just as spectral and mythic as its European counterpart.

This is an increasingly important distinction to make as such portrayals are today becoming only more common—promoted both by conservative philosophers and media pundits outside of China (where they're fused with an inherent anti-communism) and by the Chinese state's own invocation of itself as the inheritor of "five thousand years of civilization."[13] The CCP's bi-monthly theory periodical *Qiushi* (求是), circulated among high-level party officials, has in recent years elevated the position of "traditional culture" to the same level as "revolutionary" culture and that of "socialism with Chinese characteristics," following Xi Jinping's own frequent invocations of the CCP's civilizational mission.[14] A more telling example can be found in the aftermath of the state's crackdown on Maoist student groups involved in the 2018 Jasic Affair.[15] This crackdown saw Beijing University's Marxist Society not only dismantled (alongside counterparts at Renmin and Nanjing Universities) but also reconstituted by the university's administration in early 2019. New student leaders committed to upholding "Xi Jinping Thought" were appointed. The first lecturer invited to the reconstituted society was not a Marxist in any sense. Instead, it was Yang Lihua, a Confucian scholar, who delivered a speech "about how to be a virtuous person based on his reading of... a twelfth century Confucian text," followed by Sun Xiguo, executive dean of the School of Marxism, who lectured on the potential interpretive synthesis between Confucianism and "Marxism-Xi Jinping Thought."[16] Though it's an exaggeration to portray

13. Alison Kaufman, "China's Discourse of 'Civilization': Visions of Past, Present and Future," *ASAN Forum*, Feb. 19, 2018. Kaufman outlines the many permutations of this phrase in Chinese political discourse.

14. 求是 [Qiu Shi], "What Kind of Cultural Self-Confidence Should We Uphold?" [我们应该坚定什么样的文化自信], QStheory, June 20, 2019.

15. "Seeing through Muddied Waters, Part 1: Jasic, Strikes & Unions," *Chuang Blog*, June 10, 2019; "Seeing through Muddied Waters, Part 2: An Interview on Jasic & Maoist Labor Activism," *Chuang Blog*, July 2, 2019.

16. Some of the most earnest interpretations of contemporary right-wing Chinese philosophy come from equally right-wing "neo-traditionalist" scholars writing for an anglophone audience. Many of these individuals are today associated with "governance studies," but trace their roots to the remnants of various waves of accelerationism and bear

these facts as a wholehearted embrace of traditionalism, they do demonstrate a real revival of interest in the terms of classical political philosophy within the academy. Moreover, classical philosophy's mobilization
as part of a larger political crackdown also shows that such thought has
some patronage among major leaders. But it's important to keep in mind
here that this revival of interest, tended by high-level patronage, is also a
reinvention of the basic terms of Chinese philosophy through conversation with its Greco-German counterpart. Many of the thinkers drawing
on these concepts are, at the same time, Chinese scholars whose careers
have been built on interpreting the work of prominent European philosophers or introducing the terminology of Western schools of management and public policy into the Chinese intellectual sphere.[17] This
has meant that the revival of classical debates on Chinese statecraft has
occurred through the translation of European political philosophy for
a Chinese audience—a process in which the premiere interlocutors

---

some relation to both neo-traditionalists like Aleksandr Dugin and the late-acceleration-
ist "neoreaction/NRx" trend affiliated with thinkers such as Nick Land. Their conservatism inherently biases these sources. They tend to emphasize traditionalist elements in
contemporary Chinese philosophy above either liberal or so-called socialist thinkers. This,
however, is a useful corrective since the trend has been precisely the opposite in previous
decades. It is also precisely because of their conservatism that they are able to identify
intricate differences between various conservative thinkers. Here and throughout, we will
therefore refer periodically to such sources, but with a warning to the reader about their
bias. One of the most significant sources promoting neo-traditional Chinese thinkers has
been *Palladium*, a rightwing outlet dedicated to "Governance Futurism." The story
about the Marxist Society is told here: T.H. Jiang and Shaun O'Dwyer, "The Universal
Ambitions of China's Illiberal Confucian Scholars," *Palladium*, Sep. 26, 2019.

17. The final section of this article returns to this issue, but a brief list of such thinkers includes: Jiang Shigong, the premier translator and interpreter of Carl Schmitt; Deng
Xiaomang and Mou Zongsan, both prominent interpreters of Kant; and various members
of both more authoritarian and more liberal factions of the New Left such as Gan Yang,
Wang Shaoguang, Wang Hui and Cui Zhiyuan, who all teach at various public policy and
management schools and act as important interlocutors between the Chinese academy
and Western political science. Gan Yang was particularly important to the introduction of
Western political philosophy to China (himself influenced by Martin Heidegger, Michel
Foucault, Herbert Marcuse and in particular Leo Strauss), and leading an effort to re-
organize the liberal arts curriculum at Sun Yat-sen University to emphasize both ancient
European and Chinese thought. He is also interesting as a case study in the life cycle of
Chinese intellectuals of that era: first a liberal, then gravitating toward the New Left
and finally settling around a vaguely socialist traditionalism. See: Shi Anshu, François
Lachapelle and Matthew Galway, "The recasting of Chinese socialism: The Chinese New
Left since 2000," *China Information*, Vol. 32, No. 1, 2018, pp. 139–159.

then offer their own distinct political philosophy as a contrast with both European and Chinese precedent. The final section of this article will go into more detail on these currents, providing notes toward a deeper philosophical critique. Here, however, we begin by scaling the distinctly capitalist state in China today against the longer history of the state as such in mainland East Asia.

A useful starting point is the fact that, although used here, the term "governance" is in many ways an inadequate descriptor. On the one hand, this is because the divide between the formal rule (统治) of a government (政府) and broader notions of habitual or informal governance (治理 / 管制) or governmentality (治理性 / 治理术) is a relatively recent import derived from the influence of Western political philosophers. It rose to prominence early in the transition to capitalism and tended to be used most readily by liberals arguing that such a divide *ought to be* developed within the political system. They ascribed the absence of such a divide to the totalizing nature of the developmental regime's political project, but some influential scholars of the era pointed out that this mismatch had deeper roots. The pioneering sociologist and anthropologist Fei Xiaotong (费孝通)—whose work spanned almost the entirety of modern Chinese history and established the basic terms on which social sciences would be founded during and after the developmental regime—famously argued that kinship and the nexus of social relationships around it were integral to understanding the concentric structure of authority in the region. This was because political power existed as a two-track system split between local customary authorities and the central government's distant bureaucracy (itself intercut with informal, reciprocal social obligations). These two levels (and the informality that constituted them to different degrees) were interlinked in what he called *chaxugeju* (差序格局), or the "differential mode of association." This term's implication is essentially that one chain of social authority does not prevail in all contexts. Fei contrasts it with what he calls the "organizational mode of association" (团体格局) that forms the basis of European states, predicated on the aggregation of individuals into organizations with clear boundaries between who lies inside that organization and who lies beyond it. In contrast, the *chaxugeju* conceptualizes webs of social relations and social influence extending out from the individual, with these concentric networks thereby shaping and intercutting one another. Since this mode of association formed the basis of both local customary authority and that of the bureaucracy, the polities of mainland East Asia tended not to cultivate clear divides between public and private spheres and, therefore, between "government" as the formal deployment of authority and "governance" as an informal or habitual practice of power.[18]

Fei's work was influenced by Chinese scholarship and by the paragons of twentieth century European social science. He also led the effort to reconstruct social science in the 1980s by coordinating visits by scholars from the US, who helped to train a new generation of social scientists during the transition period. The work of foreign scholars studying China from the outside shaped Fei's own presumptions. In many respects, he clearly exaggerates certain aspects of Chinese society, sometimes by overgeneralizing an almost metaphysical East-West divide which would, if argued by a Western scholar, have long ago been dismissed for its orientalism. Regardless, Fei's influence on the social sciences and the perception of "traditional" Chinese social structures was foundational. Many of today's intellectuals passed through a Chinese academy reconstituted in line with these presumptions, which have thereby shaped contemporary political philosophy's basic perception of tradition. At the same time, later research has borne out most of Fei's fundamental observations and restated them in less essentializing terms. The *chaxugeju* as described by Fei means that the dynastic state was neither a civil sovereignty representing the interests of the populace nor an absolutist sovereignty in the style of some early-modern European monarchies.[19] Instead, the state was defined by a sort of

18. Fei Xiaotong, Chapter 4, *From the Soil: The Foundations of Chinese Society*. University of California Press, 1992.

19. Absolutism refers to both the historical dimensions of the absolute monarchies in Europe (epitomized by Louis XIV, but also including Catherine the Great and other "Enlightened" monarchs) and the school of theorists who influenced and promoted them (such as Thomas Hobbes and Jean Domat). Colloquially, it is often claimed that various dynastic states of mainland East Asia are prototypical examples of "absolutism." However, this is a remnant of Late Renaissance and Early Enlightenment European political thought within which China acted as a sort of magic mirror onto which thinkers could project their own fears and hopes. No serious historian or political philosopher today claims that these dynastic states were "absolutist" in the strict sense of the term, except for possibly the late Qing dynasty as it attempted to reform itself along European lines.

universal or civilizational sovereignty rooted in a moral cosmology.[20] The bureaucracy's rule was neither the representative government of citizens nor absolute rule over administered Cartesian subjects. Instead, it had a cosmological-moral authority over all "under heaven" (*tianxia*— 天下) upheld by the "Mandate of Heaven" (*tianming*—天命).

Though it is easy to mystify and exaggerate the role played by *tianxia* and *tianming* in the political systems of the dynastic states, we cannot ignore these essential terms for understanding the character of those states' obligations and the ways in which their material dominance was justified in a particular discourse of legitimacy. Power was defined concentrically by proximity to the imperial court, in terms of geography and nearness to integral state functions, such as waterworks projects, road-building and military activity. It therefore took the shape of a relational network of interlinked authority and social obligation wherein the formal state power of the bureaucracy emerged from and gave way to more local obligations and customary forms of authority. Horizontal, relational linkages were fundamental here. We might argue, with only the slightest bit of irony, that dynastic states were composed of a thousand plateaus: Formal, vertical command was only enabled through an overlapping of myriad, less formal, horizontal networks interpenetrated by the bureaucracy—where kinship ties, for instance, remained a central and widely acknowledged factor in all forms of appointment, despite the system being technically meritocratic—and which tended to grow in prominence the further one went from the central activities of the imperial state. But even the furthest, least formal deployment of authority at the local level, or in various tributary states, were conceived of as still being included in this civilizational conception of sovereignty. Similarly, rebellions were expressed within the same calculus as rulership itself and thus the potentially oppositional forms of authority that arose under this system of indirect government were ultimately rendered into the same logic of civilizational sovereignty.

In part, this calculus took the form of the Mandate of Heaven, which was seen to be an active practice of power gained through just and able governance. It was not an earnest religious proclamation of the

20. *See*: Yuk Hui, *The Question Concerning Technology in China: An Essay in Cosmotechnics*, Urbanomic, 2016.

emperor's absolute power nor simply a smokescreen for the material fact of class exploitation—though certainly this was part of it. Instead, it was seen to be an active practice of power gained through just and able governance. Thus, the Mandate could be forfeited by those who had once held it if their government failed to be just or lost its capacity for administration. Similarly, it could be gained by those—even of common or non-Han (夷) origins—who rebelled against or invaded an unjust state, so long as they then ruled in a just and capable fashion, perpetuating the core civilizational practices of the preceding polity.[21] In the most material sense, the Mandate was a highly mystified recognition of the fact that general disorder due to poor administration would cause rebellion. It was also an acknowledgement that challenges to the throne were strongest when they portrayed themselves as serving the common people rather than the imperial core. Even if claimed in an entirely cynical fashion, the Mandate nonetheless exerted its burden. While, in practice, the Mandate was usually taken for granted by the winner in a rebellion or any other power struggle, and not all winners then demonstrated just and able governance, it nonetheless offered any potential competitors a good and justifiable cause to rebel against the ruler.[22] The exact historical details of the Mandate and the *tianxia* concept of sovereignty are less important than the form they have taken within contemporary political philosophy and the state's own discourse.

The civilizational sovereignty of *tianxia* proved functional, in part, because it was a method for projecting power beyond the proportions of the central state itself—an ideal notion of sovereignty for an imperial court that was small and poor relative to the size of the population it administered. Similar strategies have remained relevant to recent Chinese history. The government today appears monolithic: built around an administrative system that extends down to the most local level, while also shadowed and reinforced at every level by the CCP.

21. Hui, *The Question Concerning Technology in China*. See also: Jiang Yonglin, *The Mandate of Heaven and the Great Ming Code*, University of Washington Press, 2011.

22. One example is the case of Hong Chengchou (洪承疇), a Ming general who defected to the invading Manchurian forces that would ultimately gain victory and establish the Qing Dynasty, within which he became one of the most influential politicians. After the conquest, Hong then played an important role in deescalating tensions between the Manchu rulers and the Han populace—justified in terms of upholding the Mandate for the new dynasty.

However, the reality is that China has long suffered from an inherited condition in which lower-level governmental agencies exhibit strong autonomy from the central government, even if they are also ultimately beholden to it.[23] On the one hand, this autonomy has been a necessity for a government with a budgetary base that even today ranks behind that of the United States, despite having a population five times larger. At the same time, this autonomy has long been an inherent, functional feature of states in mainland East Asia. The bureaucracy always floated atop a *de facto* local autonomy and was defined by a multi-tiered, dependent horizontalism. The form that this autonomy took under the various dynastic states was the everyday independence of the local gentry and those below them in almost all matters save taxation, participation in large public works projects, the administration of the national exam requisite for entry into the bureaucracy and wartime contributions of men and material. These local gentry held dual status as local leaders and state-endorsed scholars, at least after the Tang dynasty, but the central state had the most *de facto* control and oversight over the officials highest in its hierarchy and those geographically closest to the imperial court. Only the core territory where the court was located was directly apportioned to the central government. The bureaucracy's power spread outward from this core, geographic and figurative, in a concentric fashion, with authority delegated to major officials closer to the court and minor officials further from it.

In such conditions, the state is best imagined as a sort of structure that floats over the populace without ever sinking fully into it, like the *fuqiao* (浮桥), pontoon bridges first invented in the Zhou dynasty as one of the government's early public works projects. In this metaphor, the local gentry play an essential role as the individual pontoons beneath the bridge. These are the only portions of the structure that actually come into contact with the populace, even partially sinking into it. Atop these pontoons float the upper echelons of the bureaucratic state, culminating in the imperial court itself, a sort of superstructure atop a superstructure. The court has no regular, direct contact with the

---

23. Chuang, "Sorghum & Steel," *Chuang Journal*, Issue 1: Dead Generations, 2016. Here, in the first part of our economic history of modern China, we review how this condition arose and the form it took during the developmental regime.

common people outside of a few highly formalized conventions for petitioning the government, facilitated at every level by lower officials.
Simi-larly, the separation goes both ways, allowing for local resistance
and mobilization in the face of imperial overreach. In this structure, if
one or two pontoons sink it's no huge loss, creating at most some momentary instability while they are replaced. Local mobilization that esca-
lates into rebellions of the gentry or the population underneath them
are easily quashed without much threat to the floating superstructure
or its functionality. When widespread failures or rebellions, though,
would rupture many of those local links all at once, the dynastic state
would fragment—the bridge sundered into separate segments afloat
their separate ways, or even sunk outright into populist revolt. "The water can carry the boat and also capsize it" (水能載舟，亦能覆舟), said
Xunzi during the Warring States period.[24] The sentiment was an integral
part of ancient statecraft, conditioned by necessity. But it also took on
an intentional character beyond this necessity. Its ethical dimensions
and the details of its operation were a long-standing topic of Chinese
political philosophy, statecraft being only one specialization within a
much larger relational ontology.

Autonomy and Bureaucracy

The heritage of the floating state did not simply disappear under the
socialist developmental regime. Instead, the revolutionary government
attempted to build a new sort of state inspired in part by that of the
Soviet Union and in many ways emulating the ideal of certain schools
of ancient Chinese philosophy.[25] In this new type of state, the formal

24. In this proverb, repeated in various forms by later thinkers, the water represents
the populace and the boat the ruler.

25. See: Li Yu-ning (Ed.), *Shang Yang's Reforms and State Control in China*, Sharpe,
1977. And: Arif Dirlik, *Anarchism in the Chinese Revolution*, UC California Press, 1993.
Namely Legalism and Mohism, but also making use of numerous Daoist concepts of good
statecraft. The connection here was in some ways explicit, with the anti-Confucian campaign during the Cultural Revolution periodically accompanied by explicit endorsements
of major Legalist thinkers and with Mao himself giving Legalists more regular and favor-
able citation in his own works than other schools of thought. In fact, the earliest piece of
his recorded writing is an effusive high school essay on the Legalist Shang Yang. In other
ways, the connection was simply implicit in the ways that European anarchist and communist thought was translated and received.

bureaucratic apparatus would sink its roots into the populace and directly derive its strength from "The People." This actualized the universal character of the state's civilizational sovereignty both through the nearness and permeability of the new bureaucracy, as well as the politics of mass mobilization. Rather than a floating bridge, the new state was supposed to be something more akin to a mangrove forest—still relational with its upper echelons elevated above the populace but now also dependent on an intricate root system that sinks down into the water, tracing out a simultaneously formal and informal base among the masses. Old forms of informality, like the role of lineage groups in village politics, were suppressed here. But new forms of informality, such as kinship ties that defined inclusion in autarkic production units or the way that family history ascribed social position decades after the revolution, penetrated more directly into the bureaucracy at the smallest scale, as the sheer number of local officials proliferated, and exerted a direct influence on the bureaucracy at the largest scale, since the stormy, mass mobilizational dimension of the new politics could periodically break, uproot and even invert entire portions of this bureaucratic structure. This was, at least, how the new state was envisioned in theory.[26] In reality, the bureaucracy of the socialist developmental regime was deeply disjointed. The dynastic regime's floating bridge had been broken up into a thousand balkanized plateaus jostling one another and was not repaired nor ever truly rooted in the populace. The roots that it did begin to develop were frequently broken off by the many storms of the era, and the collapse of the developmental regime would see them retract almost entirely.

The beginning of the reform era saw not only the collapse of the developmental regime's particular political ideal of the universalized state, but also the gradual retraction of the bureaucracy's newly formed local organs of government. This retreat of the state was experienced first and most markedly in the countryside, where it was shrouded in language of local "autonomy" or "self-government" (自治). It was also paired with the parcellation of village land into family-controlled units, which could now sell excess agricultural production in resurgent rural markets. Questions of exactly how labor would be deployed and how production

26. Chuang, "Sorghum & Steel," 2016.

would be organized were also gradually devolved to localities and, from there, to individual rural enterprises or family units. This was real "autonomy" in that rural areas were no longer expected to emulate generic "models," as set out by distant planning authorities, or to participate in mass-mobilization campaigns beyond the normal workday. So long as they met their tax obligations, such areas were now ostensibly allowed enormous room for experimentation. But this experimentation occurred within *de facto* bounds set by the rollback of state resources. As the local planning mechanisms of collectivization were disassembled, no other mechanisms for coordination existed aside from the long suppressed organizing principles of kinship and the market. Since marketization was gradually being encouraged by the central authorities, the flourishing of rural trade was made the focal point of this history. But beneath this, the era also saw a massive revival of lineage groups (家族), which invoked a traditionalist and communitarian heritage in order to coordinate village activities through patriarchal, extended family structures but did so in the context of widespread marketization.

This process was codified at the administrative level as the implementation of "village autonomy" accompanied by local "democracy," including the election of members to the village committee.[27] In reality, this "democracy" ultimately amounted to direct control by those with more power in the village—usually some combination of well-connected officials, representatives from the largest lineage groups and emergent local capitalists who often already belonged to one of the former two groups, but gradually developed distinct interests. In this way "autonomy," now explicitly rendered as local self-government, came to be seen as an important component of reforming the structure of the Chinese state itself. While some saw in this a return to older practices, in which the central state ceded territory to a new generation of local gentry, the reality was that this was an administrative expedient that allowed the state to concentrate its resources elsewhere. Autonomy was never imagined to be in opposition to the state, something signaled by its codification in law. This is precisely why theorists who took the claim of

27. This process began in the 1980s and was first formalized in the Organic Law of Village Committees (村民委员会组织法), implemented in a trial form in 1987, where it had already been preceded by the *de facto* extension of such practices in numerous villages, and then adopted nationwide in 1998.

village "democracy" seriously were so baffled when no one seemed to care that village elections were most often deeply undemocratic. These theorists therefore portrayed the promise of local autonomy as perpetually unfulfilled and in need of further reforms to ensure its reality.[28] But its reality was already evident on the ground. Local elites were developing corrupt self-government. This served two necessary functions: to buffer higher authorities from popular opposition, since they could always step in to punish the most extreme cases of local overreach, and to begin to shape a coherent network of capitalists who were also capable administrators, thereby forming the skeleton of the future state that is only today in the early stages of being formalized.

In the urban sphere, the same process of administrative reform took the *shequ* (now linked to popular translations of Western texts discussing "community governance") as its focal point. Attention to both village- and *shequ*-level reforms occurred through the rehabilitation of the social sciences in the mid-1980s and the use of *shequ* as a distinct concept describing a unit of governance was very quickly adapted from sociology into a more formal usage deployed by the Ministry of Civil Affairs to describe the smallest territorial units of urban government. As the myriad social services that were provided to urbanites by their industrial work unit declined, these *shequ*-level organs were (at least in theory) supposed to take on many of these abandoned welfare functions, now rebranded as "community services" (社区服务). The result, however, was even more immaterial than the "democracy" of village elections. Almost no resources were reapportioned to serve this purpose, and devolution of social services to the community level was therefore nothing more than a well-meaning theoretical recognition of declining welfare and increasing market dependence. Behind the scenes, however, these seemingly insubstantial administrative reforms had created new paths by which the state could sink its roots into the population. After the urban rebellion of 1989, the CCP began to use these organs as the basis for a renewed party-building effort. The Ministry of Civil Affairs was tasked with formalizing and regulating the rollout of *shequ*-level

28. This was the case with numerous Chinese liberals, the populist factions of the Chinese New Left and among foreign scholars of China. The June 2000 Special Issue of *The China Quarterly* (No. 162): "Elections and Democracy in Greater China" is an example of one collection of this material.

organizations in all cities across the country. This also included the centralization of oversight in the organ of the residents committee (居委会), discussed in more detail below.[29]

None of these were "neoliberal" reforms where the state permanently gave way to the market.[30] As we've documented elsewhere, the disassembly of the planning apparatus inherited from the developmental regime was accompanied by both privatization and the exaptation of vestigial state mechanisms for new purposes.[31] We thus see again that market and state are neither separate nor opposed in a capitalist society. This is a basic, irreducible component of the communist critique of the present world. Over these decades of transition to capitalism, then, the Chinese state was not being replaced by market mechanisms, but rather being reformatted to tend to them. In fact, the particular characteristics of the contemporary Chinese bureaucratic system are an especially sound illustration of this more general theory of the state, since in China every bureaucrat[32] is also a capitalist, as are almost all members of the party who have ascended above its lowest rungs. Some Chinese capitalists certainly lie "outside the system" (体制外), having neither governmental connections nor party membership. But these tend to be smaller-scale capitalists who, aside from a few minor skirmishes, have

29. See: David Bray, "Building 'Community': New Strategies of Governance in Urban China," *Economy and Society*, 35(4), 2006. pp. 530–549. These early transformations have been well documented in both Chinese and English language academic literature.

30. In fact, this has not been a real characteristic of "neoliberal" reforms in any country. The entire postwar period has been marked instead by the growing prominence of the state at the global scale and its interpenetration with the economy's uppermost echelons. This growth has been obscured in a "neoliberal" discourse about privatization, emphasizing the mythic separation between market and state and claiming unrivalled efficiency on behalf of the market. The term was briefly useful as a descriptor for this discourse. It has since been muddied to such an extent that it is at best useless and at worst damaging in its implication that the root problem is "neoliberalism" rather than capitalism itself.

31. See: Chuang, "Red Dust," *Chuang Journal*, Issue 2: Frontiers, 2019.

32. In Chinese, the term "bureaucrat" in both its critical (官僚) and official (官员) variants refers exclusively to higher-level officials within a given ministry, party branch or government office. In English, "bureaucrat" is often assumed to refer to or at least include individuals who are minor government functionaries. But in Chinese, the latter are referred to as "civil servants" (公务员) not bureaucrats. Generally, anyone at or above the "section chief" (科长) position in a state ministry or local government office is a bureaucrat, and anyone below is a civil servant. Thus, the idea that "all bureaucrats are capitalists" in China should not be translated as: "all state employees are capitalists" but instead as: "all upper level state officials are capitalists."

been unable to pose any real challenge to the much larger and better organized elites "inside the system" (体制内). Even those capitalists who might appear to be "outside the system" due to their entrepreneurial rise through the private sector, such as Jack Ma and his Ant Group, almost always ultimately become party members subject not only to internal party discipline but also to the many conventions of "the system" as such. Among these capitalists, opposition to conventions can be punished formally, as when Ant Group's IPO application was rejected at the highest levels of the Xi government, or informally through a cascading collapse of the relational networks that provide easy access to financing, prevent legal challenge and ensure continued contact with key markets.

In other words, the Chinese state is the direct administration of society by the organized capitalist class. It is tasked with the general reproduction of existing society and acts as a mechanism for the resolution of intra-class conflicts between capitalists. This is true of all states, of course, but elsewhere there is at least an illusion of separation, attended by a specific fraction of the population who are tasked with the dirty business of roleplaying representative government, even while they still serve the direct interests of their real capitalist patrons.[33] In China there is no such separation. The state apparatus that the capitalist class tends through both direct appointment in governmental positions and indirect oversight in party positions is devoted to the maintenance of the baseline conditions for capitalist accumulation. This is the sole function of the Chinese state, as of any capitalist state, though this prime directive includes a wide variety of ancillary obligations. The most important of these is the resolution of conflicts between capitalists, which takes place almost entirely "inside the system" and, specifically, within the auspices of the single party into which all major capitalists are organized. But other ancillary obligations include the responsibility of attending to social reproduction at the macro-scale by keeping fundamental

---

33. These people are called "politicians" and, despite both the appearance to the contrary and the many characteristic brutalities of the Chinese system, the almost complete elimination of this occupation should be seen as a great historical advance—even if they were ultimately replaced by capitalists with imperial seals. In the end, the absence of true politicians (as mediators between classes) will prove to be an immense advantage in the moment of insurrection, since it will be harder for this demographic to step in and repress popular unrest by claiming to "represent" the rebelling populace.

infrastructure, such as roads, utilities, food systems, operating efficiently and in an orderly, regulated fashion, ensuring a relatively healthy and well-educated workforce and preventing social instability through the dual weapons of policing and social services. It is among these ancillary functions that we find the state's responsibility for pandemic control. Similar to the management of other extreme externalities produced by capitalist production—like widespread environmental devastation or the destruction of the labor force itself through overwork, child labor, widespread malnutrition—the containment of the plagues unleashed by capitalist production's microbiological metabolic rift requires something like a state power to step in against the short-term economic interests of individual capitalists who just want their businesses to keep operating in order to preserve the long-term interests of the capitalists as a class.

The current state-building project was in some ways inaugurated under Jiang Zemin's administration (1989–2002), which oversaw simultaneous "community building" and "party building" projects at the local level. Similarly, the Hu-Wen years (2002–2012) saw an attempt to reconsolidate the higher echelons of the state and create an apparatus for it to intervene into the financial and industrial systems with greater efficiency. All of this cleared the path for the more intensive process of state building underway today. The Xi administration, which has taken state building to be among its primary responsibilities, inherited a bureaucracy limited in scope and resources, with control rights separated among different levels of government and intercut with the private interests of the bureaucrat capitalists who staffed it. On the one hand, this was a necessary sacrifice, which has enabled local policy to be implemented, albeit with an extreme degree of flexibility. On the other, it was an advantage, since it enabled a degree of integration between the capitalist class and the state infrastructure not possible in other conditions. Essentially, this meant that the system worked as follows:

> the central government sets up goals and targets in specific
> areas and then subcontracts to the intermediate government,
> which has the right of incentive provision and actual organi-
> zation of implementation, while the central government main-
> tains the right of periodic inspection to review and evaluate
> the outcomes. Since the superior authority could cast arbitrary

power to its subordinates despite the official rules and legal-rational logic of bureaucracy, Chinese bureaucrats tend to develop informal personal relationships with their superiors to seek protection and promotion while at the same time focusing more on passively avoiding misbehavior. The state thus employs a campaign-style governance to overcome setbacks and failures of the routine power of bureaucracy, which always requires intensive mobilization of resources and attention, therefore campaigns are always partial, selective and temporary.[34]

Though this system might seem riven with inefficiencies, it has proved capable of stretching state resources while also maintaining, and in fact strengthening, the integral core of the bureaucracy and the party's unchallenged control over it. This fact would become particularly relevant when the pandemic broke out. Historically, this system also recruited new capitalists into the party, adapted old mechanisms of the bureaucracy to serve accumulation and crafted new ones that facilitated the organized leadership of the domestic capitalist class to intervene on behalf of the long-term interests of that class as a whole. Thus, the attempt to systematize governance in China should not be seen as an effort to overturn all of these features of the inherited system. These features were not simply failures of governance. Instead, they gestated a new type of governance, more suitable for maintaining the baseline conditions of accumulation into the near future.

It is in this regard that the revival of older concepts from Chinese political philosophy are becoming particularly relevant. Xi Jinping is well known for his numerous references to Chinese classics and, in particular, for his repetition of Legalist adages such as the need to "govern the state according to law" (依法治国).[35] But this is not merely a per-

34. Zhang Shiyu, "The Institutional Logic of Governance in China: An Organizational Approach," *Book Reviews—Harvard-Yenching Institute*. 2017. The quote here summarizes the main positions of Zhou Xueguang [周雪光], *The Institutional Logic of Governance in China: An Organizational Approach* [国家治理的制度逻辑：一个组织学研究], which is only available in Chinese.

35. David K. Schneider, "China's New Legalism," *The National Interest*, No. 143, May–June 2016. pp. 19–25.

sonal affect. Instead, similar terms have been increasingly utilized in both state propaganda and in more detailed political treatises by theorists as justification for the current administration's policies. For example, a recent white paper released by the State Information Council on global development cooperation programs emphasizes a number of neo-traditional moral platitudes and gives prominent mention to *tianxia* as a positive framework for China's global influence. It claims that "China's launch of international development cooperation has its origins in the Chinese philosophy of Great Harmony for All Under Heaven [天下大同]" and that "China carries forward the traditional value that 'all under heaven are one family and share one fate.'"[36] Platitudes aside, such ideas are even more thoroughly developed by prominent philosophers like Jiang Shigong (强世功), a contributor to key white papers released by the State Council in the past, a former official posted in the Hong Kong Liaison Office, and one of the best known exponents of Xi Jinping Thought.[37] Jiang is at least partially responsible for this branding itself, having produced probably the most "authoritative statement of the new political orthodoxy under Xi Jinping" in his 2018 essay "Philosophy and History."[38] Here, he argues that Xi Jinping Thought represents the "crystallization of the wisdom of the entire party," the culmination of an entire century of political philosophy and, most importantly for our purposes, "the product of the merging of Marxism with Chinese traditional culture."

Jiang himself explicitly frames this as the "Sinification of Marxism" (马克色主义中国化) and it is within this framework that he argues in another essay "Empire and World Order" for a pursuit of global power

36. 新华网 [*Xinhua*], (受权发布) 《新时代的中国国际发展合作》白皮书 ["(Official Release) Modern China's International Development Cooperation: White Paper"], 国务院新闻办公室 [*State Council Information Office*], Jan. 2021.

37. Jiang was directly influential in the decision to increase central government power over the Hong Kong political system and is widely suspected to have been the primary author of a 2014 white paper which began the process of reinterpreting the nature of the "one country, two systems" model, a process continued in recent years by increasingly open and direct intervention in Hong Kong politics.

38. The essay is available in English here, with the quote in this sentence coming from the translators' introduction and those in the following sentence coming from Jiang himself: Jiang Shigong, "Philosophy and History: Interpreting the 'Xi Jinping Era' through Xi's Report to the Nineteenth National Congress of the CCP," Trans: David Ownby and Timothy Cheek, *Reading the China Dream*, Jan. 2018.

not under the hypocritical notion of Westphalian sovereignty but instead through the cultivation of an inherently plural, civilizational "empire" distinct from and dialectically interdependent with the state.[39] Jiang is wary enough that he never explicitly claims that China is currently seeking global hegemony in an imperial fashion. He merely characterizes it as "a great world power that must look beyond its own borders [and] absorb the skills and achievements of humanity as a whole" in order to ensure "the reconstruction of Chinese civilization and the reconstruction of the world order as a mutually re-enforcing (sic) whole." Throughout, he clearly draws from older notions of civilizational, *tianxia*-style sovereignty. But he does so by referring to the material reality of party rule in China, which he defines as offering a *de facto* constitution providing continuity beneath amorphous legal changes. This concept is also formulated in conversation with various Western thinkers, the most important of which is the Nazi jurist Carl Schmitt, whose works Jiang has translated and actively introduced to Chinese intellectual circles. These facts ensure that Jiang is not as speculative in his prescriptions as other, similar thinkers. He always poses his arguments in realist terms. For example, he points out that, despite its disavowals, the United States helmed the first true "World Empire 1.0" after overtaking the British and that this global empire is now stricken by intensifying internal competition. This "single world empire" is now in the process of being torn apart by its own centrifugal forces.

Jiang is clear, however, that this is absolutely not a repetition of older conservative positions about an inevitable "clash of civilizations," which he argues are a holdover from preceding regional empires, whose geographical, cultural and linguistic features are periodically mobilized in "revolt[s] against the world empire from within." For Jiang, this separation is an illusion, since:

> henceforth, no country will be able to exist outside this system
> of global trade [...] every country, whether it wants to or not,
> will of necessity be implicated in the construction of this

---

39. The basic outlines are explained fairly well by one rightwing European philosopher, whose ultimate conclusions and points of emphasis must be treated with a critical eye: Vincent Garton, "Jiang Shigong's Chinese World Order," *Palladium*, Feb. 5, 2020.

world empire [...and thus] this competition is a competition
occurring *within* the system of world empire, a struggle to
seize economic and political leadership *after* the realization
of world empire.[40]

China is no exception here. Instead of a simple disintegration, Jiang
sees the fate of this "world empire" as integrally connected to simultaneously economic and geopolitical competition, and he seems to imply
that China may be better poised to helm a reconstituted world empire
precisely because of its own more open, civilizational concept of sovereignty.[41] More importantly, his purely theoretical vision of a coming
Chinese hegemony is both influenced by and has exerted influence
upon the official state discourse about overseas development programs
and the expansion of geopolitical power in the region. Jiang's theory is
not the secret playbook of the party. Instead, he is quite straightforward
and acknowledges that the relationship runs in the opposite direction:
he is merely synthesizing in theory a process already underway on the
ground.

---

40. Jiang Shigong, "The internal Logic of Super-Sized Political Entities: 'Empire'
and World Order," *Wenhua Zongheng* (文化纵横), Trans: David Ownby, *Reading the
China Dream*, 2019.

41. Jiang's argument is worth quoting in full: "The United States is under great pressure as it seeks to maintain its world empire, the pressure coming especially from Russian
resistance and Chinese competition. But we must acknowledge that this competition is
a competition occurring within the system of world empire, a struggle to seize economic
and political leadership after the realization of 'world empire.' In fact, we can understand
it as a struggle to become the heart of the world empire. This struggle could lead to the
collapse and disintegration of the world imperial system, or to a change in who holds the
ultimate power in the world empire, or even to the reconstruction of the system of world
empire, but what will absolutely not happen is a return to the historical period marked
by the existence of regional civilizational empires."

Local Organs of Government

Until now, this state-building project has been most visible in its extremities: the anti-corruption campaign, the repression of the recent revolt in Hong Kong and the deployment of increasingly carceral policies in Tibet and Xinjiang. In each of these instances, certain new features of governance were piloted in more extreme and experimental forms. Now, the state of emergency induced by the outbreak has unveiled similar, previously shrouded capacities in every major city. While much had been written about how the upper echelons of the state and its official public health infrastructures were reformed to be more responsive and attentive to potential outbreaks following the original SARS debacle, the exact character and efficacy of local-level state administration remained somewhat murky. The everyday function of these organs of government was often little more than rubber-stamping village/neighborhood development projects and keeping standardized residential records, or at least pretending to. If local party officials are in the news, this is usually because of some corruption scandal or new development deal. Natural disasters like the 2008 Sichuan earthquake and winter storms gave some indication of how higher authorities might mobilize these networks, but the fact that these disasters were somewhat localized meant that central resources could be funneled to just one or two regions. Thus, these instances did not demonstrate the absolute capacity of these organs at the national level or their potential differentiation by geography. Only with the pandemic do we have a clear case in which the central government called for more or less total active mobilization of its administrative organs, all the way down to the local level. This simultaneously displayed their surprising capacity and their more fundamental limits.

From our own series of interviews, alongside research into secondary reports, we have identified a handful of local administrative organs and ancillary agencies that acted as the main points of contact between the general populace and the state. Two were directly administrative: the **villager committee** (村委会) and the **resident committee** (居委会), both of which have local-level shadows in party organization. Two were police organs, including the formal apparatus represented by the **precinct-level police station** (派出所) and the informal apparatus represented by the numerous unofficial **security guards** (保安) who populate Chinese cities but are not legally police and are often on the payroll of private companies. One is related to urban residential housing complexes specifically: the **property management authority** for the complex (物业管理), which is usually a company hired by the homeowners association. In addition, foreigners, those from Wuhan and anyone who had recently travelled to a high-risk area often came into contact with the **local medical system**, and temperature-taking became standard practice when returning to work after the lockdown. Sometimes this just meant an interview and temperature check upon entry into an area, followed by periodic contact with a nurse, such as sending in a temperature. In more extreme cases—as when the temperature came back too high— this could entail involuntary quarantine at local hospital facilities. These organs of local governance were, altogether, the primary points of contact between the state in its broader definition and the population. It will be helpful, then, to give some detail on each.

The two "committees" (委会) listed above are "grassroots mass organizations for self-government" (基层群众自治组织).[42] The villager committee is the rural variant, while the resident committee is the urban variant. Both are part of nested structures with similar higher-level committees standing above them, to which they are accountable.[43] In the city, the point of contact was specifically the *shequ* residents committee, which is the smallest and most local. In both city and countryside,

42. "Self-government" here is often translated as "autonomy" and "grassroots" (基层) but is more literally translated as "base-level."
43. This nesting is still a bit uneven, but in general it looks something like this: in the countryside the village (村) lies at the 5th order, which is the level of "grassroots mass organizations for self-government" (基层群众自治组织). In the city the *shequ* or "community" (社区) residents committee sits in the same position. Above these are 4th-order organs which exist at the "township level" (乡级) and include urban subdistricts (街道), rural towns (镇), and a few other similar categories unique to particular areas. Above these are the 3rd-order organs, which exist at the "county level" (县级), though some effectively extend into 2nd-order roles. The most common of these are rural counties (县) and urban districts (区). In the centrally administered municipalities and a few other special cases, the county, district or other special units take on 2nd-order roles, but elsewhere there are specifically 2nd-order administrative organs operating at the "prefecture level" (地级), including prefectures (地区), prefecture-level cities (地级市) and sub-provincial-level cities (副省级城市). Above these lie the 1st-order units: centrally administered municipalities (直辖市, currently numbering four: Beijing, Tianjin, Shanghai and Chongqing), provinces (省) and autonomous regions (自治区). Above these lie the central government.

these committees are also shadowed by local party branches, which themselves were reformed in the same period and in a similar direction. While the party branches trace back to the socialist developmental regime, the committees have a more recent history with only a loose precedent in either the early PRC or in the dynastic states that preceded it.[44] Such organs for local autonomy were first piloted in the countryside in the reform period, leading to the explosion of literature on theories of local direct democracy mentioned above.[45] In reality, the result was that the **villager committee** and its counterpart in the local party branch were quickly dominated by local elites. These were usually either local officials who'd lost access to official resources due to the retreat of direct state power in the village in this period; heads of the local lineage groups which resurged after the collapse of the developmental regime; or nascent local capitalists who usually began as one of the former but gradually developed distinct interests.[46] Their day-to-day business is usually just the management of their own local investments, while also trying to attract outside money to the village and settling any minor disputes that arise. Periodically, this can escalate into a larger conflict

44. Technically residents committees existed during the developmental regime, overseeing the provision of welfare services to urban populations not assigned to a formal work-unit. At first, this meant that the institution was minor, overseeing a small and impermanent fraction of the urban population, such as the first migrant workers. As migration increased and the traditional work-units were dismantled, the residents committees were automatically expanded, but without many more resources being assigned to them. Thus, they remained skeletal until recent years, when they became the target of intentional reforms to bolster the local state.

45. This scholarship was popular in both English and in Chinese academic circles. For one example of the reception of such topics in English, see *The China Quarterly*'s "Special Issue: Elections and Democracy in Greater China," No. 162, June 2000. For one example from the Chinese literature, see: Wang Xu 王旭. 1997. 乡村中国的基层民主：国家与社会的权力互动 [*Grassroots Democracy of Rural China: The Interaction of Nation and Society*], 香港：二十一世纪 [Hong Kong: 21st Century]

46. There has been an enormous amount of literature produced on this phenomenon among Chinese scholars. See, e.g.: He Xuefeng 贺雪峰. 2005. 论村治模式 [Methods of Village Politics], 江西师范大学学报（哲学社会科学版）[*Jiangxi Normal University Journal, Philosophy and Social Sciences*], 2; Jin Taijun 金太军. 2002. 村庄治理中三重权力互动的政治社会学分析 [A Sociological Analysis of the Three Interacting Powers in Village Politics], 战略与管理 [*Strategy & Management*], 3; Li Changjian and Wu Wenhui 李长健、伍文辉. 2006. 建设社会主义新农村的第三种力量 ["The Third Force Building the New Socialist Countryside"], 黑龙江社会科学 [*Heilongjiang Social Sciences*], 3期.

between local capitalists who lie "outside the system" and the official bureaucracy "inside the system," as in the famous case of Wukan village. In these conflicts, local elites are often able to draw on dissatisfaction among villagers to mobilize the population against higher levels of government. But the common outcome is a reshuffling of who, exactly, sits on the village committee.[47]

The *shequ* **residents committees** have a very similar legal mandate to that of the villager committees. When villages are absorbed into neighboring cities, it seems that committees from several villages are merged into one *shequ* over time and then further subdivided as population increases, meaning that some *shequ* may actually be rural. Residents committees were never subject to the same illusions of "direct democracy" that proliferated in the academic literature on village elections. By law, the main responsibilities of the residents committee include conducting propaganda on state policy and law, settling civilian disputes, "assisting in public security" efforts and relaying public concerns to the government and police. The law also requires the committee to assist the government or police with public health and family planning. In the 1990s, the law stated that the villager committees serve communities between 100 and 700 households. In recent years, the management size of a resident committee in large cities is around 1000 homes, or between 4000 and 5000 people. Though residents committees are technically also subject to similar elections as villager committees, most places seem to have abandoned even the illusion of this process. In reality, they tend to be dominated by a particularly petty class of local elite, often themselves small landlords or business owners who then extract further rents and other minor advantages from the position. Absent an emergency, their normal duties essentially just entail advertising government programs and snitching on anyone breaking the subset of rules that the central state has deemed particularly important. In the past, for instance, they would regularly report people for having more children than allowed under the family planning policies, even while they would use their own position to break those same rules. The residents committees often worked closely with the local police precincts (派出所), and

47. Shannon Lee, "Looking Back at Wukan: A Skirmish over the Rules of Rule," *Shannon Lee's China Blog*, July 14, 2017.

in some cities there were rumors of dark local detention centers jointly controlled by the two. More recently, cities that have seen some application of the experimental "grid-style social management" (网格化管理) system with civilian "grid managers" (网格员) who legally lie under the command of Public Security but, in fact, tend to work under the authority of the residents committee. These grid managers collect data on everyone living within a certain area, by knocking on doors and registering their phone numbers through a QR scan. In the places that had such systems in place during the outbreak, these grid managers were tasked with assisting the residents committees in the containment of the pandemic.

Local police precincts are the official extension of the state's repressive capacities in an area. They are the official local-level organizations of the Public Security Bureau (公安局), which lies under the authority of the Ministry of Public Security (公安部), both of which are often colloquially referred to as *gong'an* (公安).[48] By law, each local precinct

48. The *gong'an* has its own higher-level political and national security police (国保—*guobao*) who operate in a similar capacity to organizations like the FBI in the US. They keep their own records and have access to a wider array of government data, but there are continual mismatches in data-sharing between different branches and between localities and higher authorities. Almost all accounts of national biometric systems being rolled out in China include the caveat that they only exist right now in local instances. They are most developed in areas like Xinjiang and Tibet and these are where the databases appear to be the largest and best integrated. The single largest national Automatic Fingerprint Identification System (AFIS) in China still appears to be owned by a private company (海鑫科金) and individual cities and provinces apparently contract with separate AFIS companies rather than using an integrated system. Though the exact extent of centralization is unclear, it's almost certain that China still lags behind the widespread centralization of fingerprinting, criminal and general background records gathered by local police and accessible by organizations like the FBI in the United States. See Han Congying "Fingerprint recognition system curbs crime in China," *Orms Today*, Feb. 5, 2019. If the *guobao* need to obtain information from local arms of the *gong'an*, they are often met with data collected according to inconsistent standards and sequestered behind various veils of local corruption and decades of *de facto* autonomy. Separate from either the *gong'an* or its *guobao* arm is the Ministry of State Security (国家安全部, abbreviated to 国安—*guo'an*), which operates somewhat like comparable international state intelligence and counter-terrorism agencies such as the CIA in the US or MI5 in the UK, but also tends to have a more expansive domestic purview as well, often stepping in to handle particularly high-level political cases or issues of national security. More commonly, though, political cases are pursued on the ground the *guobao* (they are usually the agency that does the actual arresting, for instance) with investigative support from the *guo'an*. Even in cases of interest, however, it's often surprising how begrudging and inefficient local police arms of the *gong'an* can be with their resources and information—as when local police officers came

lies under the authority of a public security office that lies at or above the county level, which is itself further nested within higher levels of command. But in many places this extension of power is not particularly direct. Policing in China is still surprisingly decentralized and local police often have extreme amounts of autonomy. This autonomy goes well beyond minor differences in how to interpret the law or prioritize certain activities over others. Instead, the decentralization extends to the more fundamental structure of the national policing infrastructure. On one hand, this is a matter of insufficient cooperation and administrative integration. While certain criminal activities will today more regularly lead to higher-level police attention, and therefore some degree of tracking from city to city and coordination between police departments, basic police records and command chains remain heavily balkanized in many areas. For many years, it was possible, for example, for individuals who might be arrested for political organizing in one region to simply move to some other city in a distant province and not be bothered by the local police. Recent efforts at national integration of policing infrastructure have made this less and less possible, however, for more serious crimes—especially those of a political nature.[49]

On the other hand, this is also a question of more fundamental material decentralization, which has seen less progress. A good example can be found in the recent expansions of digital surveillance infrastructure throughout many Chinese cities — including cellphone tracking, facial recognition and now public-health QR codes—which is treated in the foreign press as a particularly egregious example of China's authoritarianism. In reality, these forms of surveillance in China all lag far, far behind that of the United States, for example, where the NSA has built one of the world's biggest spy centers in Utah and aggregated immense amounts of surveillance data domestically and, apparently, on people worldwide.[50] Similarly, since 1999 the FBI has overseen a centralized

---

and essentially just begged one of the feminists of interest to higher-level political police (during the crackdowns in the mid-2010s) to move out of their jurisdiction simply so that they themselves did not get in trouble. Peng X, "Drinking Tea with China's 'National Treasure': Five Questions," *Chuang Blog*, Aug. 28, 2017.

49. Chuang, "Picking Quarrels," *Chuang Journal*, Issue 2: Frontiers, 2019.

50. James Bamford, "The NSA is Building the Country's Biggest Spy Center (Watch What You Say)" *Wired*, March 15, 2012.

national computer database of fingerprint data and, since 1998, DNA data, gathered from local criminal records, military records, and federal employment records, as well as other likely sources today. They were then given enhanced data gathering and information sharing powers after the first Homeland Security act was passed in 2001.[51] In contrast, examining the actual fiberoptics infrastructure of the most advanced surveillance networks in places like Shanghai reveals that the cables themselves run straight to the precinct-level police station, which has no cables of comparable capacity running anywhere else from there, inhibiting the ability to aggregate such data and even implying that it may be getting regularly deleted, given the likely storage requirements.[52]

Policing infrastructure is not only administratively fragmented at the level of command, then, but also literally fragmented, insofar as it has no material ability to centralize the many small fiefdoms of locally gathered records into a single integrated system, except in instances where higher authorities step in to gather data on their own persons of interest. Nonetheless, these local precincts remain the essential point of contact with the population. Not only do they have responsibility for enforcing basic laws, but they also work closely with the residents or villagers committees, and they're the agencies tasked with primary demographic record-keeping: when moving to a new area, you're still legally required to register your ID or passport, if you're a foreigner, with the local precinct.[53] The precinct shares this information with the relevant local committee, but they do not seem to have consistent standards for

51. See: "Automated Fingerprint Identification System (AFIS) overview—a short history," *Thales*, Jan. 10, 2021.

52. This information comes from on the ground research into the telecommunications infrastructure of Shanghai, not yet available in any published form.

53. In reality there are many ways around this and the registration is only necessary for certain types of paperwork. Thus, many people simply never register or they register by other means—through an employer, or a driving school, for instance. The rules have been more strictly enforced for foreigners, but even in these cases it's increasingly easy to get around them. Ultimately, it is the landowner's and employer's legal responsibility to make sure that all those living on a property or working at a firm (especially foreigners) are registered. It also does not change your *hukou*, however, since the *hukou* doesn't record actual residence but instead one's "home" residence, which gives rights to welfare resources in that location. They are notoriously hard to transfer from rural to urban areas. See our summary of the recent *hukou* reforms here: "Free to move, forced to move," *Chuang Blog*, May 18, 2020.

sharing it with higher levels of government unless it is specifically requested. During the pandemic, contacts from the local precinct worked with the neighborhood resident committees to oversee those who had reentered the area and were undergoing the mandatory fourteen-day quarantine period in their apartment. This was applied to both foreigners and Chinese nationals. Often, individuals from high-risk areas, like Wuhan or certain foreign countries, were assigned a particular contact at the local precinct who they interacted with daily via WeChat, using the app's location-sharing feature to confirm that they had not left home.

One important variant of the state's policing capacity can be found in the less formal but much larger army of uniformed **security guards** that populate every Chinese city, usually just referred to by the name embroidered onto their navy-blue uniforms: *bao'an*.[54] One of the most immediately noticeable features of the Chinese city for foreigners who have never travelled to the country before is the sheer number of security guards. At first, these guards appear to be police officers since they tend to wear nearly identical uniforms. They stand at the entryways of buildings, protect shops, walk patrols through shopping centers or staff official-looking guard stands at subway stops, train stations and airports. This gives newcomers the sense that there are "police" everywhere in China. However, these are private employees of security companies (保安公司) and they have about as much legal power as mall cops or "loss prevention" employees do in any other country—and quite a bit less right to be armed or use lethal force. The only thing that makes them more common than similar security officers in places like Europe or the US is the fact that Chinese cities tend to be highly compartmentalized. They are organized into more of a gated-community cellular structure, within which apartment, shopping and factory complexes are walled or fenced off and have only a certain number of gates leading in and out, staffed by security guards.[55]

---

54. We will refer to them here as security guards. It should be kept in mind, however, that their precise legal status and sheer numbers make them somewhat distinct from similar workers in other countries. Particularly important is the fact that, in certain settings, they can instead be tasked with "auxiliary police" functions.

55. Urban space is also patrolled by *chengguan* (城管) or "urban management officers" who are under the authority of the Urban Management Bureau. During the

Normally, these guards have essentially no power. In almost every case, you can simply walk by them and not be bothered. The exception is if you are trying to enter into high security areas such as a factory complex, but even in these instances the filtering process is fairly lax and you're only likely to get stopped if you appear like you should not be there (i.e. you are obviously a foreigner, beggar or schoolchild). Even if a security guard harasses you, you are usually within your legal right to ignore them. Meanwhile, since they are organized into various companies, they are even more unintegrated than the local police, and their rights and training vary enormously depending on who is employing them. In terms of demographics, the average guard tends to be an older male migrant worker. Culturally, they're often portrayed doing nothing more than sitting around smoking and chatting. That said, every security company is legally subject to the authority of the Public Security Bureau, where they must register and assist with maintaining social peace in times of emergency, even though they lie outside the bureau's command structure.[56] During the pandemic, individual security guards on the ground were suddenly mobilized by their own companies to begin engaging in basic forms of population control. They were essentially deputized to serve as a second, far more expansive police force. Suddenly, the guard working the gate at any given housing complex would actually stop people, ask what they were doing and prevent entry to those who didn't live there or weren't on essential business. In other instances, they had thermometers and took the temperature of those who entered the stores that remained open, often while they also staffed the QR health code scanning stations. They were probably the most common point of contact that ordinary people had with the partitioning of the city. As time went on, they slowly began to revert back to their earlier status, with people more confident that they could just ignore the guards and go where they pleased. Nonetheless, the particular role

---

pandemic, they could be mobilized in the same way as security guards but had more legal authority.

56. Or in more carceral territories, like Xinjiang, where a special "auxiliary police" recruitment effort essentially deputized thousands of security guards. This is reviewed in more detail below. For information on the nexus of private and public security in China, see: Susan Trevaskes, "The Private/Public Security Nexus in China," *Social Justice*, No. 3–4, Aug. 2007, pp. 38–55.

they played during the pandemic proves that traditional separations between "the state" and "the private sector" do not adequately capture the nature and extent of state power and, in particular, fail to grasp the deployment of that power through informal means.

In many cases the most aggressive guards who limited entry were those employed by a given housing complex's **property management** authority (物业管理). These are mostly private companies for managing the upkeep of a housing complex, though certain residential buildings have retained slightly different administrative systems—for example, some buildings will have appointed "building committee leaders" (楼组长) for each building in the complex, or the *shequ* residents committee might have an actual office in the complex. Sometimes the property management company may also manage sales of empty units or advertising. Their core duties, however, are things like security, cleaning common areas, and maintenance. Legally, they are subject to all kinds of other authorities: their security guards are legally under the jurisdiction of the Public Security Bureau, and administrative personnel in the property management company for any given complex are in regular contact with the residents' committees for those neighborhoods. These jurisdictional facts are what ultimately allowed the property management authorities to be deputized in a fashion similar to the security companies. Representatives from an area's property management authority would work with the residents committee to try and keep track of who was actually in the complex since many residents had left early in the holiday and underwent lockdown elsewhere; make sure that people had things like cooking gas, arrange safe systems for food delivery or mobile market days; and manage home quarantines for those returning from outside the area.

Finally, there was the **local medical system**, which tended to only become a point of contact for those entering an area from outside, especially high-risk areas, those who had become sick or failed a temperature check (or whose housemates or family members had) and foreigners undergoing mandatory quarantine after entering the country. Temperature checks became common when returning to work, but these often did not involve direct interaction with medical staff.[57] It was

---

57. Instead, it was common for them to be overseen by the company itself (often

common for medical staff to work alongside representatives from the local government at major entry points into the city such as airports and train stations.[58] At these checkpoints, medical staff were also tasked with conducting free testing—initially just to those who requested it, but later this became mandatory—and facilitated the transport of anyone who failed a temperature check to local hospitals.[59] After being admitted to the hospital, it often became clear that the chain of authority had been unevenly and inconsistently delegated. Even if an individual had just taken a COVID test at the border or other entry point, the hospital would re-administer it. Frequently, one only found out if a test was positive and simply didn't receive any result if it came back negative, though foreigners and Wuhan residents often needed proof of a negative test in order to rent rooms at hotels or buy bus and train tickets. Other tests were often required at this point as well, though the exact requirements seemed to be up to the discretion of the local medical facility. If someone still failed to pass temperature checks despite having consistently negative COVID results, they were often bounced back and forth between multiple hospitals, makeshift quarantine zones and entry points for weeks at a time without being able to get through—even if they had a registered address in China. Foreigners who had a smoother experience getting across the border and quarantining at home were often still required to send daily temperature checks (via their phone) to a primary-contact nurse (alongside confirmations of their locations, sent to an assigned contact at the local precinct).

---

the HR department) which would then notify medical authorities of anyone with a fever.

58. The government staff at these checkpoints were often individuals drawn from various low levels of administration who were also often party members. They frequently volunteered for this responsibility out of an earnest sense of duty and belief in the work and tended to be fairly helpful and straightforward.

59. It's also worth noting that their official cut-off for a "fever" was 37.3 °C (99.14 °F), or sometimes even 37.0 °C (98.6 °F), compared to 38 °C (100.4 °F) in Hong Kong (which follows the standard set by the CDC in the US).

Volunteer Organizations

Even with the vast mobilization of all the formal organs of local government and the deputization of various informal agents for more widespread management of the population in the pandemic, the outbreak
likely could not have been contained if not for the willing mass mobilization of that population itself surging far beyond the existing capacity
of the state. At the most minimal level, this entailed a general social
trust, not necessarily a trust in the government, so much as a trust in
the need for everyone to work together if they wanted to overcome the
virus. This required active, earnest participation or at least a begrudging acceptance of the various forms of fumbling and poor management
evident in almost every aspect of the official response. In many cases,
for example, it was extremely easy to fake one's temperature while quarantining at home and reporting temperature via WeChat, to avoid scanning one's QR code, or to craft a legitimate excuse as to why you might
be outside of your apartment during the lockdown. In most cities
after the lockdown lifted, the QR-scan requirement so essential to the
contact tracing system was only inconsistently enforced—you might
be asked to scan to enter a large grocery store or office building, but
small, migrant-worker restaurants quickly stopped asking patrons to
scan their health code. These persistent inefficiencies at the level of enforcement meant that the entire system essentially relied on people taking the threat seriously and actively self-reporting their own locations,
health status and social contacts. Even if many still may not have actively
participated, the ultimate success of containment was not due to the
state's "authoritarian" measures, later surpassed by even more rigorous
lockdowns in Italy, France and elsewhere. Instead, the pandemic was
contained in China largely because most people were earnestly engaged
in the effort, even if passively.

But many went the extra step and became actively engaged as well.
This took numerous forms. The most common was a sort of self-depu-
tization, where certain individuals took it upon themselves to question
anyone they thought was out of place in a particular area. It's important to intervene early here and argue against applying prefab theories
of "totalitarianism" and the resulting paranoid, self-policing populace
to this sort of phenomenon. Instead, it's something much more similar

to everyday activities familiar to readers in any other country: equivalent to having a nosy neighbor, an intrusive landlord or an overbearing homeowners association. In fact, in these other countries the same phenomenon often takes more nefarious forms and often results in extreme violence, such as in the US, when property owners or white people strolling in the park call the police on black people who appear "out of place." In China, this attitude remained mild and mostly amounted to being lambasted in public for not wearing a mask or walking around during the height of the lockdown without a good reason. This was rarely followed by police violence. Throughout the country it also stoked a latent xenophobia toward outsiders or foreigners in general but expressed with far more vigor against Africans. In Guangzhou, African migrants were subject to extended quarantines regardless of whether or not they had left the country, while landlords conducted mass evictions of these migrants. All of this was paired with an outpouring of explicit racism on the Chinese internet. Ultimately, the government was forced to issue an apologetic diplomatic statement and to call on local officials to apply equal standards.[60] At its most extreme, this sort of neighborhood watch attitude escalated to voluntary cordons often condoned by local committees and set up by villagers in certain rural areas or by residents of particular housing complexes. They essentially walled these areas off from their surroundings and prohibited almost all entry by anyone outside the community. These blockades did become violent in some instances, but the violence was almost always against or between factions of police representing different local authorities. Sporadic clashes became somewhat common along these divisions as official reopening commenced, with some areas refusing to take down their barricades even after government representatives had told them to.[61] Overall, in many places mutual aid efforts were successful not simply because of their cooperative character but instead because their inherent

60. Li Hangwei, "Mistreatment of Africans in Guangzhou threatens China's coronavirus diplomacy," *The Conversation*, April 17, 2020.

61. Sidney Leng, "Coronavirus: police, public clash as border reopens between Hubei and Jiangxi provinces," *South China Morning Post*, Mar. 28, 2020. The most widely publicized of these was a clash at the Jiangxi and Hubei border, where police from two different jurisdictions (alongside members of the public) ended up fighting when authorities on the Jiangxi side set up a barricade to stop people from Hubei (the most virus-stricken province) from crossing the border despite that border being officially reopened.

communitarianism entailed exclusion of outsiders. It is in these cases that we see the most conservative edge of the mass mobilization campaign that succeeded in containing the virus.

Volunteers were integral at a broader level as well. Local government and property management authorities rarely had sufficient staff to conduct all the necessary check-ups on those quarantining at home, keep track of who was returning to their apartments and run the necessary checkpoints. Volunteer labor was the foundation on which these local administrative organs relied. In some instances, these volunteers were low-level party members who were earnest true believers in the party's social mission—here meaning nothing more than the type of belief exhibited by canvassers, social justice activists or phone-bank volunteers in any other country. But far more often they were just regular people who wanted to help. Assisting formal organizations in their work was one way to do this. But less official volunteering was even more common and composed the bulk of mutual aid efforts. Above, we argued that these activities could be split into two broad categories: (1) **self-organization for survival** and (2) **self-organization against the pandemic.** Below, we'll anatomize each category in more detail, exploring what sort of activities they entailed and to what degree they can be characterized as truly autonomous.[62]

62. We used a wide array of sources for this section, drawing on both English-language literature, Chinese-language literature and reports from our own interview respondents. A few resources were particularly helpful. The first was the "Workers Organizing in the Pandemic," which we translated and include as Chapter 2 of this book. The second was an article posted to the Chinese liberal web platform *Matters*, the first and second parts of which are now available in English translation via *Lausan*: 栗子、几何、蜜糖子弹、百无一用、K、晤、Ноябрь、水母 [Chestnut, Geometry, Honey Bullet, Useless, K, Ng, November and Jellyfish], 疫情时刻的自组织：民众如何重塑社会 [Self-Organization during the Pandemic: How the People Can Rebuild Society], *Matters*, March 5, 2020; Third, this report in English by the Stanford Social Innovation Review, which gives a little more background on the involvement of pre-existing NGOs in the "civil society" response to the pandemic: Eva Woo, "COVID-19 and Chinese Civil Society's Response" *Innovation Review*, April 14, 2020; Finally, this piece by the UN's Food and Agriculture Organization provides some important background data on the Chinese food system under the pandemic, which we reference at various points throughout this summary: Fei Shulang and Ni Jia, "Local food systems and COVID-19: A look into China's responses," Food and Agriculture Organization, Aug. 4, 2020.

1. Survival

1a. General Medical Services

These overlap with pandemic protection somewhat, but they mostly capture activities undertaken to help alleviate the overloading of the formal healthcare system. Technically the medication groups below would belong here, but they were distinct enough to merit their own mention (especially insofar as they operated alongside LGBTQ+ NGOs). The more general medical services groups in this category were organizations such as the NCP Life Support Network, founded by Hao Nan, "China's leading disaster relief social entrepreneur." This was clearly an outgrowth of existing civil society networks, since Hao had played a similar role organizing aid from civil society for the 2008 Sichuan earthquake. The network ran an online clinic to help with all kinds of common medical consultations and provide mental health support and end-of-life support for families who had lost people during the pandemic. Similar groups existed with more specific focuses, such as a mutual aid group for pregnant women, who could no longer go to the doctor for regular pre-natal checkups.

1b. Essential Medication Groups

This category includes a number of makeshift organizations, many of which were more aligned with pre-existing NGOs. Basically, the problem was that normal supplies of necessary life-saving medication were constrained by the lockdown and the overload in the medical system. In addition to this, restraints were often placed on even basic painkillers like ibuprofen because of their capacity to reduce fever and thereby allow individuals to disguise the fact that they were sick. As of January 2021, individuals in most cities are still required to use real name registration to obtain fever reducing medicines. A side effect of all this was that people living with conditions that required regular medication could not easily access that medication. These groups coordinated the distribution of such medication outside the bounds of the formal medical system. The best-documented case of this activity was the distribution of medicine to those living with HIV/AIDS, where even temporary interruptions can lead to severe deteriorations in health. In Wuhan, LGBTQ+ and AIDS support groups mobilized to coordinate the distribution of medicine. One way this worked was that those with access to a larger personal store of medication couriered their access to those whose supplies were low. It's unclear how, exactly, medication was accessed in other instances, but some practice of bulk buying and informal supply from local medical facilities was likely.

1c. Labor Organizing

Chapter 2 covers this subject in detail, but the summary is that labor organizing under the lockdown was sporadic and small. It then tended to pick up after the lockdown lifted. There was at least one example of a strike among healthcare workers in Xuzhou, Jiangsu. Smaller protests began among delivery drivers and some others in the logistics sector. These efforts culminated in the fall with a series of widely publicized slowdowns, mass resignations and a series of small strikes leading up to "Singles Day" on November 11, 2020, when online shopping hits its annual peak.[63] There were also some more minor labor disputes in manufacturing and service sectors generally, almost all focused on cut bonuses and missing back wages. The most common factor was individual-level refusal to return to work in dangerous conditions. This resulted in companies having to charter labor in the early stages of the reopening to ensure that their factories would be staffed. In general, however, the fact that the lockdown occurred during the Spring Festival holiday meant that most workers had already planned on taking time off. In fact, for most migrant workers employed in low-end services or manufacturing, the holiday is often an opportunity to switch jobs anyways and they often leave early. This is why strikes have tended to peak in the months prior, as workers demand all their back wages before moving on. After the holiday ends, workers frequently take some extra time in their hometown or look for work in a new city. Many migrants who had come home early for the holiday ended up trapped there for longer than planned, but the timing of the pandemic made the experience much less onerous than it would have been otherwise. In the interview

63. "Delivery Workers, Trapped in the System," *Chuang Blog*, Nov. 12, 2020.

printed above, the construction worker "W" notes that workers' access to land and savings were essential here. If current trends continue, rising consumer debt and gradual dispossession of land will ensure that such a response will be less feasible in the future.

1d. Informal Resource Sharing and New Apps

This is a very broad category including an amorphous assortment of volunteer activities, some of which were later commodified. Much of this can hardly even be categorized as "volunteering" or "self-organization," since it occurred mostly within extended family networks or in the form of a general neighborliness. For example, those who had stocked up on food tended to share it when other residents of the same building or village ran out. What's notable here is, in part, the old anarchist lesson that in moments of general social strain cooperation still appears to be much more common than ruthless black-market bartering. This also demonstrates the essential role taken by informal reproductive labor in general and during the crisis specifically—a fact now clearly visible to much of the world's population forced into a mandatory confrontation with questions of housework and food preparation under lockdown. It should be noted, however, that food supply chain problems in China were less severe than those that arose later elsewhere, where initial disruptions led to widespread shortages of particular goods, even while the massive decrease in demand overall (largely due to the closure of restaurants) has led to extreme overproduction, requiring the liquidation of not only food meant for final consumption but also the production of things like seed potatoes. In India, all these factors contributed to the widespread participation of farmers in the world's largest general strike to date, involving some 250 million people and including a march of tens of thousands of farmers to New Delhi.[64] In China, by contrast, the formal food system was kept operating at its agricultural base throughout the lockdown. Initial strangulation of logistics networks meant there were some issues of supply—particularly in Wuhan and other parts of Hubei. But very quickly all kinds of informal and formal methods

64. Julia Hollingsworth, Swati Gupta and Esha Mitra, "Tens of thousands of farmers swarm India's capital to protest deregulation rules," CNN, Dec. 6, 2020.

arose to solve these issues. Food shipments were officially given prior-
ity status on roadways and were some of the few vehicles allowed to pass
through checkpoints. Similarly, there was an enormous amount of intervention here on behalf of the e-commerce sector, where all kinds of
mechanisms quickly composed to create new ways of contactless or risk-
reduced shopping. These included the forms of "community group
buying" mentioned above and sometimes facilitated by the resident committee. In these cases, there was no real e-commerce innovation, you'd
just pool orders in a single group chat and one person would put in
the order, then all the food would be delivered to the community the
next day. This was a safer version of the early example where the mobile
market would come to the community, since it didn't require any interaction between sellers and most residents. But there was also a wide
proliferation of different apps serving similar functions, such as being
able to buy groceries online while getting gas and have the order placed
in your trunk. Many of these apps actually began as volunteer efforts by
tech workers and were then spun off as privatized entrepreneurial ven-
tures and sold to larger firms.[65]

2. Pandemic Containment

2a. Fundraising and PPE Distribution Groups

Probably the most prominent of any of the volunteer efforts, these
groups raised money for supply of PPE or coordinated donations of
PPE to medical professionals and undersupplied hospitals. They then
either distributed these themselves or worked with other groups, like
mask groups, private car service groups, to do so. In many ways they were
the most makeshift of organizations with the greatest local variation
in who founded them, who participated and what scale they reached.
The majority seem to have been based among student groups or alumni
networks. But many became quite large and grew into substantial
web platforms to coordinate donations. For example, the Hubei Medical Resource Supply-Demand Platform, founded by a small group of

---

65. Examples of this are mentioned in the *Matters* article and in the collaborations
listed in the Stanford Social Innovation Review piece on civil society measures.

volunteers but growing into a network that included more than a thousand people, with regular information on supply needs in 308 Hubei hospitals. Such organizations helped to address some of the resource misallocation that occurred due to the state's emphasis on central economic areas. One important sub-category here were the fundraising and PPE groups that focused on supplying women medical workers specifically, such as "Sisters Against the Virus Support Group," which not only donated additional necessities like sanitary pads but also argued publicly against the sexist portrayals of women medical workers who were referred to in the media as "mothers, girlfriends, and wives making immense sacrifices."

All the above groups were technically operating outside the bounds of the legal restrictions on fundraising laid out in the relatively new Charity Law. Some of them therefore aligned themselves with formal groups already in compliance with the law, like pre-existing NGOs sanctioned by the state. Others simply flew under the radar and were surveilled but not cracked down on. But this has also led to cooperation with (or even buying-up of many such activities by) large e-commerce and logistics platform. The group Wuhan2020 mobilized thousands of volunteer tech developers and thousands of on-the-ground volunteers to help solve supply shortages among hospitals. This effort was led by a Stanford Business School graduate, Xue Wu, and the group then went on to collaborate with IBM. Similar efforts extended globally through business networks, such as the Blazing Youth Community, "formed by young entrepreneurs, study-abroad students and professionals, and researchers in Wenzhou," a city known for its early entry into global markets and its substantial connections across the global supply chain. Blazing Youth drew on extensive Wenzhou capital networks (via the Global United Wenzhou Society) to extend aid to other countries hit by the pandemic.

2b. Mask Distribution Groups

These were related to the fundraising groups but in many places they took on a distinct form. Instead of attempting to distribute general PPE to medical facilities, these volunteers focused on masks specifically and tended to offer their resources to the population at large as well. These volunteers were particularly active in the earliest weeks, when mask supplies were extremely limited, had sold out quickly and were further constrained by the shutdown. It was very common in the first month of the lockdown for people to be completely without masks and, with production stalled, these groups helped facilitate a more equitable distribution of existing supplies. Like the fundraising groups, these seem to have initially been based among students. In certain places, this led to a notable expansion of the group beyond the coordination of resources. In one example, a Beijing-based mask distribution group formed to distribute PPE to street sweepers whose job left them particularly exposed to infection and then used these contacts to produce an investigative report on the city's street sweeping industry through a detailed survey of the workers.[66]

2c. Private Car Services

More colloquially referred to as "carpools" (车队), these volunteers helped drive medical workers to and from their workplaces and periodically delivered the medical supplies gathered by the groups discussed above. This was made necessary because the lockdown cancelled bus and subway service in many places and the availability of ride-share services substantially declined, meaning that anyone who was, for example, a rank-and-file nurse who couldn't afford their own car had essentially no way to easily get to work or home again after. This was a major structural weakness of the healthcare system in the context of lockdown. These volunteers covered the cost of gas, disinfectant and face masks for the

66. 疫情之下：北京环卫工人防护情况调查 [Under the Pandemic: An Investigation on Health and Safety among Beijing Sanitation Workers], 品葱 [*Pincong*], January 31, 2020; Some of their results are worth quoting here: "The majority of the interviewees, 56.52%, were between 50–65 years old; the second largest cohort was 40–50 years old, making up 28.26% of the interviewees; while the share of both 30–40 year old interviewees and interviewees older than 65 was 6.52% for each of these two cohorts. Not being able to return home for Chinese New Year is a very common situation for cleaners. Three fourths of the interviewees were not registered as Beijing locals—among these cleaners coming from Hebei, Henan, Shandong and Shanxi made up one half. As they maintain the deserted Beijing streets the 'state of exception' does not apply for them, unlike other city dwellers. Being overburdened with work is the normal state of things. More than one half of the workers interviewed reported that they worked more than eight hours. One of the workers reported that they start working at 4 am and finish at 7 pm."

drive out of pocket. Though the actual trip only required one driver, the infrastructure to connect those in need of rides to these drivers meant that the services were organized by entire teams of volunteers. According to one source, "over 4,000 volunteers participated in these transport teams."[67] And despite protections, a few people died doing this. In fact, it was likely the deadliest of all the volunteer activities.

2d. Pandemic Information Groups

These were organizations of higher-educated volunteers who tried to help spread accurate information on the pandemic. This need was conditioned by the fact that the government's official pronouncements were initially contradictory and, paired with its active suppression of information from early whistleblowers, its recommendations were often seen as not entirely reliable. This information problem was aggravated when detailed instructions for the handling of the lockdown in Hubei were not provided in a timely manner. As stated in Chapter 3, the initial lockdown ordinances merely announced the closure of mass transit and most shops but gave no detailed instructions on how the lockdown would be managed or what health protocols should be implemented. It wasn't even clear how people were supposed to get food. Two weeks into the lockdown, the Wuhan Municipal government finally released a series of more detailed instructions, via the newly-formed Epidemic Prevention and Control Center, on the basic ways that the lockdown would work and the expected public health practices. At the same time, behind the scenes, the state had finally given at least basic instructions for its local delegates in village committees or neighborhood-level residents committees, who were also the official organs tasked with distribution of masks, disinfectant and other supplies—but again, this wasn't until two or three weeks after the lockdown had begun. This was the context in which volunteers mobilized to produce, gather and distribute reliable information on the pandemic and the proper public health practices, ranging from basic instructions on how to wear masks or properly disinfect a space to more complex ideas about the nature of the virus and how containment of an epidemic was supposed to work. Such groups

---

67. Quoted in the *Matters* article, cited at the beginning of this section.

often saw themselves as fulfilling a broader social mission. For example, the A2N Volunteer Organization was founded to "promote scientific literacy and refute rumors" but grew quickly to include "collating data about the pandemic, mapping the spread of the virus, writing and editing popular science articles, debunking rumors, verifying hospitals and suppliers, and providing information about how to donate resources."[68]

2e. Petition Groups and Citizen Journalism

At times, the more general-purpose information groups spawned more specific initiatives geared toward citizen journalism or petitioning the government for policy changes. Similar initiatives also periodically grew out of other volunteer activities like mask distribution. These were driven by a broader mandate than the pandemic information groups, since they tended social media channels, gathered data on people's views of the state's handling of the pandemic and published articles summarizing their social research. This included overseeing and promoting public discussion via online platforms. One of their biggest channels was the WeChat feed "Delay Going Back to Work, Control the Pandemic," where they demanded that the State Council extend the official Spring Festival vacation. Ultimately, the resumption of work was delayed, though it is not clear how much of this was in response to such demands and how much was simply seen as necessary for containment of the outbreak. Similar groups were founded to petition for increased worker protection after the lockdown was lifted as well as to advocate for workers' rights and payment of wages. These groups also had to face the problem of being constantly censored, because citizen journalism was treated as "rumor." So, they also formed an infrastructure to compile and archive pandemic-related posts in regions of the internet outside the Great Firewall.

---

68. Also quoted in the *Matters* article.

2f. Volunteer Blockades

While many volunteer efforts helped to improve the circulation of necessary personnel and equipment in the context of general constraints on movement, there was also widespread volunteer participation in the segmentation of space itself. These included volunteers working for property management companies and neighborhood resident committees to seal off entire housing complexes, volunteers staffing road blockades to prevent traffic from entering or exiting certain cities, and various makeshift barricades that arose across rural China, sealing villages off from their surroundings. These became particularly visible symbols of the lockdown. In part, this was due to the widespread circulation of humorous images of some of the more absurd blockades, like those staffed by "old uncles" carrying traditional pole arms (关刀—*guandao*) in "defense" of their village. But it was also because these volunteers were an integral element of the everyday segmentation of urban space, represented at the most basic level by the fact that anyone wandering around on the streets might be accosted by locals and asked what business they had to be outside. These forms of self-organization were by far the most conservative, in that they tended to work directly alongside the official organs of the government, and insofar as they exposed the exclusionary dimension of such communitarianism.

In general, the lifecycle of volunteer organizations was such that the most truly independent forms of mutual aid tended to be the shortest-lived. Even if they were momentarily tolerated by the authorities, all the groups that engaged in any activity, such as citizen journalism, that was more oppositional toward the official management of the pandemic simply failed to find any foothold after the lockdown lifted. None of these groups seem to have (at this point) suffered any strong direct repression on the part of the state aside from the normal internet censorship and reprimands given to those "spreading rumors." That said, the government has detained several professional journalists and a few other already well-known activists, it hasn't to our knowledge cracked down on any organized volunteer effort. The closest it has come to doing so are cases where groups have explicitly been asked to stop distribution, but not punished for it.[69] Instead, these organizations have tended to merely evaporate after their initial goals were met and the need for their services decreased. At the same time, many of those engaged in even moderately oppositional activities operated with a reckless naivete and failed to follow any of the security practices that have long been common necessities for those in labor and/or feminist organizing circles. If the state had cracked down on any of these organizations (or decides to in the future), very little would have stood in its way.

These are all the exact opposite of the features necessary for any type of self-organization that builds political power. Such self-organization should exhibit inertia, antagonism and at least a basic awareness of security. **Inertia** means that such organizations would have a staying power beyond their momentary function and independent from official administration or private sector philanthropy and profiteering. In this regard, the mutual aid efforts were far more ephemeral than small-scale labor actions. **Antagonism** means that such organizations could potentially be—either at the level of awareness or activity or both—poised against the state and the present organization of society. This would not need to be explicit (in fact, it should not be, for security), but would have to exist in some form. The citizen journalist groups give some indication of how this might take shape, and it is an important fact that such groups essentially forced the public rehabilitation of Li Wenliang and other heroic doctors who had initially been reprimanded by the state, for which they became some of the only mutual aid organizations that saw participants detained. Nonetheless, most volunteer efforts had far less potential for opposition than even the most mundane labor actions or populist folk religions. **Security** is essentially awareness of the potential for antagonism, leading to the conscious preservation of self-organization through secrecy. This dimension is both particularly important and particularly difficult in China, where crackdowns against any potential opposition are swift and thorough. In this case, however, the unobjectionable nature of many volunteer efforts would have posed

---

69. This was the case with the "Masked Angels" group mentioned in the interview with our friends in Wuhan. The group was officially asked to stop distributing masks and therefore pivoted to the distribution of food.

an excellent opportunity to expand the capacity of secure forms of self-organization.

As for any relationship between mutual aid and political awareness, the evidence is sparse. For the most part, volunteering either remained largely apolitical or even tended to reinforce faith in the social and civilizational mission of the Chinese state—a perception that only grew after China was able to contrast its own success in containing the outbreak with the spectacular failure of the much wealthier US, UK and EU. This informal, autonomous mobilization of the population has never stood in stark theoretical opposition to the state in China. This mobilization is only understood to be a distinct threat when it is engaging in active opposition to the interests of the bureaucracy or is evidently consolidating its power and privilege in a self-serving manner. The key factor is therefore not the formal vs. informal, or governmental vs. autonomous character of any organization, but instead the direction that its action tends toward—namely whether or not its activities run parallel or perpendicular to that of the organized capitalist class, embodied in the party-state bureaucracy. At best, the most oppositional groups seemed to agree with liberal authors like Fang Fang and offered unthinking support for the introduction of Western style "civil society" institutions to act as checks and balances on state administration and economic interests. In particular, such groups have pointed to the spectacular information failure of the early pandemic to push for a more open media, the argument being that freer information flows would help state administration and assist central authorities to root out corruption. The fact that these were the most prominent, automatic political positions even among the more oppositional groups makes sense, given that many such groups were staffed by urban professionals. The exception here, again, was the small ripple of labor actions throughout the year, peaking in the fall. Meanwhile, many of the groups that cooperated most actively with the state, civil society, the e-commerce and logistics platforms, or various capitalist charity networks have had the longest staying power and tended to build the most robust tools and networks, many of which persist today.

Spatial Splintering

Now that the basic organs of local administration, the most prominent examples of self-organization and each sub-category's respective functions within the pandemic have all been illustrated, we can proceed to discuss the more general picture of how, exactly, the lockdown was implemented and experienced on the ground. Here, the most important factor was how space was segmented. In this regard, the urban geography of China was an enormous advantage, since Chinese cities are typically organized in a cellular fashion: residential complexes, shopping areas, industrial campuses, schools and universities are all already built with walls and fences separating them from the outside and only a few official gates, often staffed by security guards. At first, this might appear to be a more recent inheritance of the autarkic economic units of the developmental regime, where each individual urban factory had an affiliated residential complex that included localized, communal reproductive services, all distributed according to one's inclusion or exclusion from particular work-units (单位). In fact, this autarkic urban geography was itself influenced by much older practices in architecture and urban design, where cellular structures had long been a norm in built space across the region. More importantly, these norms were integrally linked to Chinese cosmology and political philosophy in that they tended to gesture toward the ideally subdivided, orderly and quantifiable population curated and overseen by the sagely state imbued with the mandate of heaven.

The prototypical example was Chang'an (today Xi'an) as rebuilt from scratch in 582 CE right before the inauguration of the Tang Dynasty (in 618 CE), which soon became the most populous city in the world and provided the paradigm emulated by other cities across the region. Chang'an was designed at its most fundamental level to be cellular, with its gridiron layout cut up into a nested hierarchy of functional zones, each walled off from the others. Helmed by the palace complex, these functional zones included government compounds, market areas and urban parks. But the bulk of the city was given over to residential wards, which were similarly walled off from other functional zones and from one another. Moreover, the wards were then internally parcellated into distinct plots dominated by walled structures, including temples, government offices and courtyard housing compounds.[70] At every point of entry and exit from these walled zones, there was often a gate and frequently also a guard. Meanwhile, at night the wards essentially closed, their gates overseen by a nightwatch who allowed no passage except for in the case of emergencies and high-level official business. Though subsequent centuries saw transformations to this basic urban structure and to the political philosophy that underpinned it the essential geographic form retained a powerful inertia. Not only would this cellular urban logic again predominate in the cities of the socialist developmental regime—enhanced by the autocratic nature of production and everyday life—but a similar logic of parcellation and subdivision then returned at a larger scale in the transition to capitalism. The cellular organization of the average Chinese city then became particularly visible in the response to the pandemic.

Urban development cannot be understood without reference to the economic logic driving it. On the one hand, this is defined by the pragmatic, material requirements of production and population management. We might think of this as the organic dimension of urbanization, in the sense that it is driven by essentially impersonal material incentives. On the other, the class relationship generates its own grander political rationality, which manifests in intentional urban administration and takes influence from its contingent cultural heritage. This administrative dimension is therefore split between its primary functions: serving the impersonal requirements of production, giving spatial expression to the class relation and in particular providing for the security of the wealthy; and its ancillary function: weaving the prevailing political rationality of the ruling class into the fabric of the city. Thus, we can argue that the cellular structure of contemporary Chinese cities is an outcome of distinctly capitalist development in a simultaneously organic and administered sense and that it is also *incidentally* shaped by the political logic of a ruling class that has increasingly portrayed itself in continuity with the past. The material conditions that underpinned the hyper-cellular logic of ancient Chang'an no longer prevail.

---

70. Heng Chye Kiang, "Visualizing Everyday Life in the City: A Categorization System for Residential Wards in Tang Chang'an," *Journal of the Society of Architectural Historians*, 73 (1), 2014. pp. 91–117.

Nonetheless, such places are still upheld as prototypical examples of the "Chinese city" in discourse today, since they are paradigmatic of the political rationality of the ruling class. Geography, urban planning and architecture departments still use these as models of a distinctly "Chinese" urban logic and train scholars, designers and administrators with these points of reference in mind. Meanwhile, recent administrative efforts to further subdivide the city into "grid" structures echo the pattern.

Of course, as the circulation of commodities and the movement of the population has increased with the transition to capitalism, Chinese urban geography has also become more permeable. This is certainly true at the large scale, with the population no longer strictly fixed to rural hometowns or the compounds of autarkic urban work unit. The rapid spatial opening of the city was also visible on the ground in the early period of transition to capitalism, when these flows were newest. At the same time, old cellular geographic divisions have taken on new functions serving capitalist accumulation and entirely new ones have taken shape: the capitalist enterprises founded in places like the Pearl River Delta tended to also form themselves into walled-off compounds, for instance, and the greenfield residential complexes built in that era operated according to the same logic — only now rendered as upscale gated communities. Altogether, the mega-urban complexes such industrial development shaped tended to take on the character of exploded cities marked by a deep balkanization. But now, instead of self-sufficiency, this balkanization was driven by capitalist imperatives and built to facilitate flows of labor and goods between different segments of the city. These divisions initially took shape through competition. Some villages were able to successfully attract investment and therefore to finance its affiliated infrastructure earlier; others were not and became relegated to agricultural production or even left to lie fallow. Within the rapidly developing urban core, meanwhile, old courtyard houses were demolished at record speed, but they tended to be replaced by larger housing, shopping or administrative complexes that were often literally still walled off or, at minimum, were built such that entire segments of the city could be easily sealed from others. This was particularly true of the encirclement of remaining poor districts dominated by informal housing (the "villages in the city" or 城中村), where entries were few and easily controlled.[71] Similarly, the most fundamental logic of spatial segmentation embodied in things like one's *hukou* status — which is, after all, a deeply geographical category, linking social rights to one's place of origin — remains integral to production (disciplining labor and driving down the wage bill) and the maintenance of social order (sequestering the "low-end" population in easily sealed-off industrial districts).[72]

Many features of this older, cellular logic have been retained or reproduced precisely because they make sense both within the political rationality of the ruling class, drawing from and referring to inherited presumptions about the nature of urban space, and within the material logic of capitalist production. In fact, if the early reform era seemed to hint at a more general opening, this was only because the autarkic, small-scale, fixed-in-place cellular structures of the developmental regime — which were at least, in their own way, still distinctly human spaces built on intimate social bonds — were in the process of being razed to make way for a new cellular subdivision of the city that retained, reinforced and even created further segmentation within the population, all while ensuring the dynamic movement of money, goods and labor. In other words, the urbanization of China saw the dismemberment of whatever remained of deeply inhabited spaces defined by intimate social relationships. These remnants were then uprooted and replaced by a cold terrain of alienated economic interactions, administered by an aseptic state scoured of any mandate to tend to human needs except in an ancillary fashion, as one step in an algorithm ultimately serving the inhuman imperatives of capital. This is in no way a process unique to China. It defines capitalist urbanization everywhere. But, as elsewhere, these baseline imperatives are accompanied by distinct contingencies of history, culture and geography, including the peculiarities of how the ruling class understands itself and rationalizes its

71. During the pandemic, this fact would become particularly relevant in cities like Guangzhou and Shenzhen, which have higher numbers of urban villagers. From late January onward the villages' few entrances were blockaded with random construction materials affixed with ropes and zip ties. As late as November of 2020, guards still took everyone's temperature at the entrance of each urban village and barred entry by outsiders even though the rest of the city had by then returned to normal.

72. Lu Bu (卢布), "Adding Insult to Injury: Beijing's Evictions and the Discourse of 'Low-End Population,'" (*Trans*: Ignatius Wu), *Chuang Blog*, Nov. 24, 2017.

political practice. The bureaucracy was itself restructured in this period in largely the same fashion as the razing and rebuilding of urban space, but with an even greater emphasis on orderly partition and subdivision. In recent decades, the rebuilding of the bureaucracy has accompanied both invocations of tradition and new, increasingly aggressive subdivisions of urban space.

According to this logic, the *shequ* was made the basic level of urban governance, which increased the granularity of administration by further subdividing the urban fabric down to the neighborhood level, where functionaries responsible for seeing through the implementation of key policies were assigned. In the countryside the village continued in this capacity, but now with its new "autonomous" administrative organs and restructured party branches. At the same time, these base-level administrators often lacked the resources to implement such policies in any systematic fashion and were therefore effectively expected to rely on informal networks. In many places, they remained essentially inoperative or had so little capacity to enforce policy that temporary *shequ* committees would have to be established in their place when the pandemic broke out. In one sense, then, this was a "vertical" extension of the state since it better integrated these areas with the upper echelons of the command structure and linked them back directly to the central bureaucracy. At the same time, this was also an extension of the state's traditionally balkanized, "horizontal" governance, since these new administrative subdivisions were expected to form their own rhizomatic plateaus of informal government in order to be able to implement policies in the first place. Thus, the *shequ* (and, to a lesser extent, the village) and the administrative divisions (subdistrict, district, county) immediately above it became the main site at which the outbreak was contained. Though this containment involved the vertical chain of command, any authority transmitted through that chain was slow, incomplete and often contradictory. The effort was primarily successful through the horizontal mobilization of relational government, most visible in the massive numbers of volunteers who staffed essential positions and their open coordination with these base-level organs of the state.

The ease with which space could be splintered and sealed off was a great advantage in containing the outbreak. At the same time, it also exhibited a persistent incapacity since the very splintering of space necessary for wide-ranging quarantine was only manageable through reliance on informal networks and masses of volunteers. This also meant that attempts to vertically integrate various local mobilizations continually ran up against the reality of *de facto* horizontal autonomy, which produced numerous non-commensurate public health measures that simply could not be packaged together into a single standard. In its ideal form, the model to be implemented across China was called "closed management" (*fengbishi guanli*—封闭式管理). In most of the areas where this came into effect, villages, communities and other divisible spatial units, such as housing complexes, would only keep one entrance and exit point open, and each household was allowed limited numbers of entrances and exits. In some places, night-time access was prohibited, instituting a local curfew despite there being no similar city-wide requirement. In extreme cases, access was prohibited throughout the day. The most stringent application of the closed management system was in Wuhan, where the early lockdown was particularly extreme. It effectively limited most people to their housing complexes unless they were essential workers.[73] But a fairly rigorous example of the system also arose in Beijing, where direct administrative links to the central government were already more common. Elsewhere, "closed management" was aspirational, at best. In many areas, its successful implementation was not achieved through rigorous enforcement but simply because people were earnestly concerned about the virus and didn't venture outside more than necessary. This sort of geographical and administrative fragmentation was by far the most salient feature of the containment effort.

Maybe the best example of this problem was the contact-tracing QR codes. Colloquially, the QR code is simply referred to as a "health code" (健康码) and that's what we'll call it here. Health codes were intended to track population movement and rank people as "safe" or "unsafe" based on the places that they'd travelled to. This system was itself modelled on similar QR scans that had been rolled out in Xinjiang in

73. It's worth remembering that in this earliest period it was not yet clear how contagious the disease was or what the major vectors were for human-to-human infection. There was still widespread concern about aerosol transmission outdoors and infection through surface contact, so it also makes sense that the areas that locked down earliest tended to also pose more limits on any sort of travel outside the household—and people in general were far more wary about leaving the house for any reason.

the name of "anti-terrorism" and that were being experimented with in
the "grid-style social management" system operational in a few key cities. On the surface, this seems to be precisely the kind of "totalitarian"
measure that the Chinese state should be capable of, especially if one
accepts the predominant media narrative about the CCP's overarching
control over society and over Chinese telecoms and internet infrastructure specifically.[74] This is not simply a myth cultivated in the foreign
press. Instead, the central state itself has talked about the health codes
as if they were part of a unified system of contact tracing like that deployed in neighboring countries, where they were highly effective, not
only in similar single-party states like Vietnam, but also in South Korea,
Taiwan and Japan, hinting that success here had nothing to do with
undemocratic political institutions.[75] In reality, this claim was also mostly aspirational. China was substantially larger than any country where
such systems were effectively implemented, it had a much more widely
distributed outbreak, and it could not restrict domestic travel as easily
as places like Taiwan, which could simply cancel international flights.
Thus, a public health system overseen by a state with substantially less
command capacity was stretched far thinner. The result was that the
health code was not a single, unified system, but instead a multi-level
maelstrom of semi-overlapping systems, the bulk of which either didn't
work or were incredibly easy to falsify.

This is best illustrated by the fact that almost no one had a single
health code that they scanned everywhere. Even though shops, residential complexes and all sorts of transit centers (bus and railroad stations,
airports, etc.) all technically required those entering to scan their code,
they also used different systems and codes frequently would not work
between them, requiring most people to download multiple apps (there
were three, each of which then required different mini-apps) in order to
scan in and, if this didn't work, usually just being waved through

74. Here the QR Code might be placed alongside myriad other examples such as
the social credit system, facial recognition ticketing jaywalkers or Huawei's military connections as a favorite tech touchstone in the new yellow peril journalism, bulwarked by
similar academic accounts common in International Studies departments bankrolled by
the US State Department.

75. For an overview of these systems, see: Dyani Lewis, "Why many countries failed
at COVID contact-tracing—but some got it right," *Nature*, Dec. 14, 2020.

anyways. Technically, these codes all functioned in the same way, using data from your phone's SIM card (and thereby your cell carrier) to determine if your cell phone had been in an "unsafe" place with ongoing infectious activity. Green codes meant you'd never been in contact with anyone infected, yellow meant you'd been in an infectious space and red that you'd received a positive test, which should have led to formal quarantine until you'd tested negative multiple times. Similarly, the scan of your health code outside your residential complex while you were supposed to be in isolation, if you'd just travelled to the area from a hotspot, for instance, indicated to local authorities that you might be breaking your quarantine. Ideally, this was meant to be a granular measurement that would let you know if you'd come into contact with anyone who later tested positive. Certain health code systems picked up other clusters and effectively traced them, but it was far more common for poor information sharing across systems to result in "missed" contacts. Ultimately, local authorities tended to just focus surveillance on anyone from a foreign country or from Hubei and Wuhan especially, who had recently entered the area. Based on all our interviews, the only reported cases of individuals having a "red" code indicating high risk were those whose cell carriers had placed them in Wuhan. Though presumably those who had contracted the virus, tested positive *and volunteered to self-report that fact across multiple health code platforms* would have also had a "red" status until they were no longer contagious.

The health codes also demonstrate the fragmentation of state authority and the substantial untracked seepage between supposedly sealed-off segments of urban space. Since the codes relied on detailed access to one's SIM card and the locational data, the first fracture occurred at the level of telecom infrastructure. Different carriers seemed to work better with one or another of the three major apps (WeChat, Alipay and one used in government buildings) and, in most cases, you were required to scan a code specific to your carrier and for the city you were registered in. One irony of this was the fact that even non-Chinese respondents who had re-entered China from a foreign country with high caseloads in the early months of the pandemic were never given a "red" or even "yellow" status, simply because they had never used their Chinese SIM card outside of China, and when they put it back in after crossing the border, the telecom had no record of them ever having left. Similarly, the array of health code mini-programs was bifurcated between WeChat and Alipay.[76] This meant that, when scanning a code, you'd not only have to frequently install a separate mini-program but also make sure you were operating within the right platform environment. But it was at the level of the mini-program that the real fragmentation of the system became evident: every different local jurisdiction essentially had its own health code. At airports and train stations, those travelling between different areas would be met with bulletin boards that had numerous printed-out QR codes pinned to them prior to boarding, each for a different destination. These let travelers apply for a valid local health code before departure, rather than relying on WeChat or Alipay to suggest the correct code based on the location of the device after landing, though this latter system also worked and was presumably used by anyone driving long distances in a personal vehicle. Meanwhile, an entirely separate system operated in government buildings and required carrier-specific codes to be scanned which then prompted a site-specific query of your device's ID and ostensibly cross-checked it with more detailed contact tracing records kept by that carrier.

On the ground, the system was further separated by uneven implementation and reinforced at every level by much more mundane methods, which were likely far more important in the ultimate containment of the outbreak. During the early period of lockdown, health code scans (or just showing a picture of the code, which was easier to fake) were mandatory to enter most public spaces, including restaurants and subways, and they were accompanied by temperature checks. But this varied significantly by the degree of formality of the space and by location. Malls and hotels, for instance, tended to more stringently enforce the checks, while neighborhood restaurants run by migrants rarely checked. Similarly, certain cities seem to have been more stringent than others. In Beijing, requirements remained extremely strict, codes were checked with greater consistency, mask-wearing was strictly enforced, and space

76. Common on Chinese smartphones, these small applications can only be installed within the environment of larger all-purpose apps like WeChat and Alipay. The vast majority of e-commerce transactions, in everything from food delivery to Taobao purchases to ordering a taxi, occur through such mini-programs running on one of these master platforms.

was extensively policed by security guards and numerous individuals who had taken on the duty of questioning passersby about their business. In Shanghai, this was true early on but lightened up quickly and never seemed to apply to more informal spaces like small restaurants. In Guangzhou and Chengdu, restrictions were lax to begin with and tended to focus on those who had entered from elsewhere, though many people never talked to volunteers from their local residents committee or property management authority, at most maybe sending in some paperwork confirming they were living in their unit or working in a particular location, and never had to report their temperature to anyone other than the HR department at their workplace or upon entry to airports or government buildings. In these cities, some guards and neighborhood watch types would accost people early on, but the habit seems to have faded more quickly. Most security guards reverted to their normal laziness, standing right next to the sign posted at the shopping mall saying that health code scans were required as everyone simply walked past without scanning.[77]

In part, this fragmented system was overcome by the extreme focus placed on those who entered the area from elsewhere, in particular Wuhan, Hubei more generally, or any foreign country. These are the individuals who would be given a contact from the local police precinct and whose period of isolation would be monitored most stringently. Depending on their initial temperature check and housing status, this either meant home isolation where they would have to send in their temperature to a local nurse via WeChat once or twice a day, or monitored isolation at a quarantine hotel where their temperature would be taken by staff. These are also the people who bore the brunt of the more aggressive quarantine controls at the border, often forced to choose between sequestration at designated quarantine hotels and makeshift hospitals or deportation. At worst, individuals who failed temperature

---

77. In later outbreaks, these requirements would return, with the system having been smoothed out somewhat in the interim. By the winter of 2020–2021, the fragmentation of the system itself had been alleviated somewhat but travelling to and from a city like Beijing still required that you meticulously input the names of all the counties you had passed through manually, though you'd often only be prompted to do this days after your return. Your answers would then presumably be checked against the locational data on your cell phone and you would be given a "green" status if you answered correctly. It is unclear why the information was not just logged automatically.

checks, even those within the normal range of human body temperature, since the threshold was low, were shuttled between various quarantine and testing sites for weeks, even if they were consistently testing
negative. At best, it meant a monitored quarantine period at one's home.
During further travel, it was common for those from foreign countries
to have to carry physical copies of paperwork showing that they had
completed quarantine and tested negative, since the paperwork would
almost never come up automatically on your phone. Meanwhile, even after the outbreak had largely been contained and travel restrictions lifted,
many locales had inconsistent policies when it came to housing foreigners and people from Wuhan. It was common for certain districts in a
city to periodically ban such people from all hotels or assign them all to
a single "approved" hotel in the district. But if one were to simply go to a
different district in the same city, no such restriction existed.

These decisions were, for the most part, made by local government
officials acting alone and attempting to fulfill the vague directives hand-
ed down from above with very few resources and almost no guidelines
about how to do so. The role played by these local officials gave the post
facto impression that the state had successfully mobilized its chain of
command to orchestrate the containment and this myth was readily
repeated by official media outlets after the fact, especially when it became
evident that far wealthier countries were being hobbled by the same virus that China had successfully defeated. Thus, a typical account of the
containment became something like:

> there has been a proliferation of subdistrict Neighborhood
> Committees and rural Village Committees. Cities extending
> this form of social management have split their neighbor-
> hoods into grids. Each grid manages the workspaces and the
> comings-and-goings of tens, and in some cases, hundreds
> of households, through daily surveillance. People have to show
> their IDs and obtain temporary permits just to enter or exit
> their neighborhoods.[78]

78. This quotation comes from the *Matters* article cited above.

As we've already seen, this was an ideal never quite met for the vast majority of Chinese cities, even if it was approximated for a brief time in areas under closer central scrutiny (essentially just Wuhan and Beijing) and independently reproduced on the ground by volunteers and eager local authorities in particular areas of other cities. But this didn't stop the government from claiming it to have been the general case afterward. For example, in September, the Central Committee of the CCP issued awards to 150 "progressive grassroots party organization" leaders from around the country for their efforts in epidemic prevention and control, and nearly all of these individuals were either doctors or residents committee leaders.[79] This is an extremely common pattern in Chinese statecraft, in which myriad makeshift local responses to a crisis are systematized in later narratives and reframed as if they were the product of central planning. Every weakness is, after the fact, claimed as a strength.

The Anatomy of the Coming State

The pandemic was contained in China not by the all-seeing power of the party-state but instead by the massive, voluntary mobilization of ordinary people. It is incorrect, however, to characterize this mobilization as an enormous outpouring of "mutual aid" in the Leftist sense. Though it certainly proves the old anarchist adage that people thrown into catastrophe will tend to cooperate rather than ruthlessly compete with one another, this cooperation was also cooperation with the state. Only rarely did such groups find themselves positioned against the government and, even then, only in the mildest fashion. Despite—or, in fact, because of—widespread distrust of the competency of government administrators, the volunteer efforts of people in general served to buoy the state itself, as they have historically. At the same time, the catastrophe and the state's incapacity in the face of it has provided further justification for the bureaucracy to accelerate its attempt to develop and extend its local presence. The government now retroactively claims its

79. 新華網 [*Xinhua*], (受權發布) 中共中央關于表彰全國優秀共産黨員和全國先進基層黨組織的決定 ["The Central Committee's Decision to Commend the Nation's Outstanding Party Members and Advanced Local-Level Party Organizations"], Sept. 8, 2020.

containment practices to have been a massive success relative to the truly monstrous failures visible in many much wealthier countries with far
more health resources per capita. This is merely the public face of what
appears to be a deeper recognition that state capacity proved dangerously limited.

On the one hand, a true success would have seen the virus detected
significantly earlier, with containment efforts following much more
quickly afterwards. The process of containment should have begun with
the exact sort of public announcements from doctors and nurses which
were so quickly cracked down on and silenced by local officials. On
the other, the central state is certainly aware that its "base-level organs"
proved flimsy when pressure was finally applied. In many areas, makeshift "temporary" neighborhood-level residents committees had to be
composed at the last minute where official committees had atrophied,
not yet formed, or even seen their seats never filled. Ultimately, if the
population had not willingly and often vigorously participated in the
containment effort, especially by staffing necessary administrative
positions, China would today find itself in straits far worse than those
of the United States. This sort of catastrophic failure is still possible,
depending on the results from the vaccines currently being rolled out,
and remains a threat in any future pandemic. While the state will never
acknowledge this incapacity publicly, it does appear as if the present
catastrophe is already beginning to serve as a significant inflection point
in the ongoing state-building process and may prove as important to
the consolidation of state power as the great recession and its aftermath
a decade prior. In contrast to the 2010s, however, it seems that this is
the juncture at which this new state, increasingly centralized and now
reconstituted around capitalist imperatives, will now begin to truly determine the nature of its local governance.

There is no reason to believe that the new state being constituted
on the initiative of the Chinese capitalist class organized in the body of
the CCP will necessarily resemble the democracies of the West or even
those of the East Asian nations developed under the military tutelage
of the US. The only hard requirement for this state is: that it protect
the class interests of the bloc of capitalists that it represents; and that
it helps maintain the baseline conditions for accumulation. But there is
enormous room for experimentation in exactly how these capitalist

imperatives are pursued. This experimentation is itself a necessity, producing innovations to better facilitate the social reproduction of the capitalist system at ever larger scales and intensities. Crises that threaten this social reproduction often induce the rapid mutation or exaptation of vestigial administrative mechanisms to confront the crisis and its symptoms. This is not a mindless evolutionary process, but an intentional one composed of myriad social innovations commissioned by those in power, formulated by experts in relevant fields, or sometimes invented out of necessity by common people trying to survive the crisis on their own. The majority are failures, but those adaptations that do help overcome that crisis often become enshrined in future governance and take on integral roles in the political philosophy of those who wield power.[80] At the same time, they are also mythologized such that even the most incidental of their institutional dimensions are exaggerated out of all proportion by both critics and proponents. This is clearly visible in the phenomenon of "neoliberalism" and its associated constellations of theories and policies, wherein even the most minor social transformations are easily analogized to amorphous non-concepts such as "neoliberal subjectivity," which is about as rigorous and functional a concept for academics today as "original sin" was for medieval scholastics. It would be a major error, then, to see in the Chinese state-building process any evidence for a "new type" of capitalism.

We might argue instead that the CCP functions as something of a vanguard for the global capitalist class. Its experiments are important precisely because they lie at the forefront of the expansion of capital today, in both its industrial and financial dimensions, and are adapted for confrontation with the foremost limits to accumulation at the largest scales. Thus, high-level experiments to found larger conglomerates better integrated with one another through willing coordination between

80. Nonetheless, no single "regime of accumulation" can really be said to prevail globally at any given time, and most attempts to periodize capitalism according to these regimes are doomed to fail. The only functional periodizations are the most minimal ones and those that include seemingly contradictory geographic variation in their basic equation: the era in which capitalism had a non-capitalist periphery vs. the era in which the few shrinking non-capitalist territories have become utterly encircled; eras of increasing growth in global trade vs. eras of decreasing growth in global trade; or simply eras defined by the alternation of periods of rapid movement and periods of relative geographic stability in the location of the global center of gravity of production.

Chinese capitalists have already shown some success in their ability to mobilize capital profitably at large scales and with greater stability than equivalent financial mechanisms in the West, though the conglomerates are of course also interdependent with these foreign institutions. On the one hand, this certainly validates the classical Marxist prediction that long-run capitalist development entails increasing socialization to accommodate the ever-greater scope of production. This socialization nonetheless remains fundamentally private and fundamentally geared toward accumulation, meaning that its various institutional and infrastructural mechanisms cannot simply be seized and used for more rational purposes without systematic restructuring. On the other hand, every means of overcoming one crisis can become the cause of the next or, at minimum, a hindrance to ongoing accumulation. Since these institutions are relatively new, it is not yet clear whether the structural contradictions they have generated—namely a sequence of debt bubbles centered on local governments and an immense increase in global industrial overcapacity—can be reconciled in the coming decades. This is one reason why new extensions of the bureaucracy are increasingly necessary, and why the building-up of its local capacity for governance remains essential to state construction.

The present pandemic represents the first of the major catastrophes to test the new organs of local government. After this, they will see another process of systematic reform and adaptation, only now with far more resources and closer attention paid to the clear apportionment of control rights and chains of command. But this does not mean that the goal is to integrate everything within a single, vertical structure in the fashion of the fictional Leviathan that the Chinese bureaucracy has always been portrayed as. Nor does it entail the formation of vertical systems homologous to federal governments in most wealthy countries, though in certain respects these have proved useful models from which to cherry-pick particularly functional institutional mechanisms.[81]

81. The most glaring example is the recent turn toward Western-style institutional models of depoliticized multiculturalism in Tibet, Xinjiang, Mongolia and other regions with large concentrations of non-Han ethnolinguistic groups, as advocated by the proponents of the "Second Generation Ethnic Policy," which is explicitly modelled on that of the United States. This has included both a dismantling of older rights of "autonomy" allowing for things like bilingual education (most recently in Mongolia, where the rollback

The state currently being constructed seems to resemble neither these western states, nor the floating state of the imperial era, nor the aspirational universal state of the developmental regime with its roots sunk mangrove-like into the populace. Instead, a state without any real precedent is forming, structured by the need to serve capitalist imperatives under increasingly catastrophic global conditions and informed by new currents of distinctly Chinese political philosophy which developed out of both the failure of the developmental regime and the reinvigorated engagement with foreign theories of statecraft and governance that accompanied the transition to capitalism. To conclude, then, we will first speculate on the practical anatomy of what this coming state might look like and then finish with a more general overview of these new currents of political philosophy in order to demonstrate how such theories are relevant not only to understanding the state-building project currently underway in China but also to theorizing the nature of the state as such.

There is now a widespread recognition that more resources must be committed to local administrative organs and that even this will fail to guarantee effective capacity to govern such a large population. Regardless, there seems to be a consensus that the new forms of *shequ* and village administration piloted in the last three decades should be retained rather than reinvented. There is an effort to integrate them more rigorously into vertical chains of command, but also to reinforce their informal capacity so long as this informality can be effectively wielded and monitored. But again, the formality-informality dyad has never been a particularly good characterization within Chinese statecraft. Not only are the two better understood as existing on a spectrum rather than in diametric opposition — the bureaucracy gives way to customary forms of authority at its base and is interpenetrated by informal social obligations

---

of bilingual education has faced immense opposition) and the rise of an ethnically-targeted mass incarceration system designed to both sequester populations deemed "dangerous" and to force their cultural assimilation. The latter, of course, is also modelled on examples from the United States, both in its rendering as an "anti-terror" measure in Xinjiang and in its assimilation policies, which resemble both the "Americanization" policies imposed on immigrants in America in the first few decades of the 20th century and, of course, the notoriously brutal boarding schools used to strip indigenous peoples of their languages and cultural practices in the US and Canada.

at every level—but they are also not the only poles in the spectrum. It is better to characterize the bureaucracy as simultaneously operating through formality and the alternation between informality and what might be thought of as a para-formality. If informal relations retain a stronger allegiance to customary authority than to official authority, or if relational social obligations exert more power than formal bureaucratic commitments, then they are deemed informal in a negative sense, as instances of corruption or potential sites of rebellion. This portrayal of informal authority is more common in times and places where the bureaucracy is particularly weak, since it is forced to rely on these mechanisms even while it fears them because they lie outside of its control. This sort of informality therefore exists in mutual interdependence with the formal bureaucracy, but it is an oppositional interdependence. By contrast, in times of stability or in places where the bureaucracy exerts the most direct influence, a second kind of informality is actively cultivated by the formal institutions of the state. For example, customary power becomes a means by which the bureaucracy conducts taxation and informal social obligations become the threads stitching together the upper echelons of the state. We can think of this as a sort of para-formality, also in mutual interdependence with the formal bureaucracy, but no longer in opposition to it. It is a sort of fully domesticated informality capable of reverting to its feral form, but only if it is abandoned by the formal sphere that tends it.

With this in mind, we argue that the extension of the regrouped state down to the local level is an attempt to domesticate the productive informality that arose during the transition to capitalism and to mobilize it as a para-formal apparatus for formal governance. A similar procedure was initiated in the upper echelons of the bureaucracy immediately after the ascent of Xi Jinping, who led a crackdown on "corruption" that extended higher and further than any earlier effort. This was necessary because the very forms of local informality that had once enabled the transition to capitalism, ensured industrial profitability and thereby developed once-poor regions of the country were now becoming hindrances to further accumulation. But this was not an attempt to systematically uproot the sort of informal ties that composed this corruption. Instead, the campaign cracked down most harshly on those who were seen as being in potential opposition to the bureaucracy and its long-term interests. These were cases where customary ties were perceived as being stronger than official ones and a rebellious form of opposition seemed to lie just over the horizon. In other cases, similarly informal mechanisms were systematized by the state and effectively converted into para-formal means of government. For example, previously "corrupt" practices in which resources would be preferentially allocated to select enterprises with ties to particular bureaucrats were transformed into a semi-formal standard for lending. In this new system, preferential credit is formally allocated through the major state banks that compose the bulk of the financial system. But loans now go to an even narrower subset of major conglomerates with close ties to the party apparatus.

The pandemic has proved essentially the same point at the level of local administration, and we would expect to see a similar approach applied to "base-level organizations" of government. At the same time, the pandemic was already preceded by far more nefarious extensions of the state into the local sphere in places like Tibet and Xinjiang, which were already acting as the foremost testing grounds for the government's mobilizational and technical capacity. In a certain sense, some of the practices observed in response to the pandemic were even prefigured in Xinjiang, where the lack of sufficient police to staff the new carceral infrastructure saw instead an almost identical mobilization of glorified security guards,[82] only operating under a different name and taking on a para-formal character:

> the data janitors of the Safe City system in Shawan and
> throughout the region were 90,000 police contractors or
> assistants (*xiejing*, 协警) hired at the beginning of 2017.
> According to job listings, most of these recruits would not
> receive formal training in police academies as Public Security

---

82. Elsewhere in the article quoted immediately below, the author argues that the assistant police would be categorized as security guards or civil police elsewhere. But that's not quite true. Assistant police designated as *xiejing* already operate throughout China as untrained or minimally trained laborers hired to assist the police in simple tasks. They can regularly be seen on the streets in many cities. The difference is their sheer number in Xinjiang and the specific tasks they have been assigned. In any case, they lie under the immediate command structure of the police and this is the key thing that distinguishes them from security guards.

Bureau employees do. Most would not be authorized to carry
lethal weapons. [...]

> [these] assistants conduct spot checks centered on actively
> profiling passersby, stopping young Turkic people and
> demanding that they provide their state-issued IDs and open
> their phones for automated inspection via spyware apps
> and external scanning devices. Policing contractors monitor
> face-scanning machines and metal detectors at fixed check-
> points. All of these activities assure that information forcibly
> collected from Uighur and Kazakh residents continues to
> feed the dataset of the system, making "extremism assess-
> ments" conducted by neighborhood watch units more and
> more precise.[83]

These practices, however, don't represent exact models to be applied to
the general population in China any more than stop-and-frisk policies,
deportation cages and massive prison cities do in the US. Instead, they
resemble the American case—including its overseas military interventions, which utilize much of the same "anti-terror" infrastructure—in
the way they create militarized, carceral territories where more extreme
methods of surveillance, policing and interventionist local administration can be piloted on designated minority populations, after which
certain elements of these new technical and administrative systems, like
"smart cities," can then be watered down and rolled out at a broader scale.
This is hinted by the fact that, even in their most carceral applications,
these systems have consistently been justified not only in anti-terror
language but also in terms of their ability to increase the "efficiency of
governance."[84]

83. Darren Byler, "'Because There Were Cameras, I Didn't Ask Any Questions': Chinese Government Documents Provide New Details on a Small Xinjiang Town's Extensive System of Surveillance," *ChinaFile*, Dec. 30, 2020.

84. In addition to the above-quoted article, further details on Xinjiang can be
found in Byler's other work and in his forthcoming book, which represents some of the
best on-the-ground scholarship studying events in the region, and in Adam Hunerven's
piece printed in the second issue of our own journal: Adam Hunerven, "Spirit Breaking:
Capitalism and Terror in Northwest China," *Chuang Journal*, Issue 2: Frontiers, 2019.

Altogether, then, we might expect future reforms of local organs of government across China to entail the better integration of existing organs with higher authorities, a more systematic and non-overlapping distribution of control rights between different agencies and a general weeding-out of particularly inefficient and corrupt local administrators. At the same time, it also means the open cultivation of informal capacities and their conversion into para-formal mechanisms to amplify the reach of the state. This will include plenty of seemingly "totalitarian" features and many seemingly "democratic" ones, but neither term is particularly informative. For instance, we might expect that new surveillance technologies will, in fact, become more centralized, but not in the direct way that this centralization operates in the US, where such data is siphoned directly by federal agencies who store and sift through it. Instead, this centralization will likely proceed in a "trickle-up" fashion, where new large infrastructural channels are opened to enable the transmission of surveillance data upward to higher levels of the state, but filtered by lower levels on the way, with all kinds of associated loss and horizontal seepage, as when local officials provide information to local employers who happen to be relatives. Similarly, these efforts will require the massive extension of both the formal police apparatus and its less formal security guard counterparts, which will in all likelihood be para-formalized. This might look like a repurposing of the pre-existing "urban management officers" who have long harassed migrant street hawkers, or it could mean the extension of more rigorous organizing and oversight infrastructure into the companies that currently employ security guards. But the extension of policing could also conceivably be undertaken in a more aggressive fashion, resembling the para-formal infrastructure of the "assistant" or "auxiliary" police already piloted across Xinjiang.

We should also expect new, seemingly democratic evolutions of local "autonomy" that are nonetheless designed to bulwark the official bureaucracy. More emphasis might be placed on the election of residents committees—which are legally already subject to elections, but most are simply appointed—or new mechanisms developed to mobilize volunteer labor and coordinate donated resources, similar to those created by tech workers in the course of the pandemic and since absorbed into e-commerce infrastructure. Numerous local experiments already

underway seem to point in this direction, allowing people to report instances of corruption through an app or to contribute to the patchwork
of collaboratively produced credit scores used by certain locales and
within certain companies.[85] But, again, such examples exist alongside
similar mechanisms of digitized community surveillance that encour-
age individuals in places like Xinjiang to actively inform on neighbors
and family members. While some of these mechanisms may at first
appear to be democratic, their "democracy" is that of the social media
platforms they are most obviously inspired by. In other words it is a tyran-
nical form of constant participation that offers little genuine autonomy
and instead increases surveillance, snitching and self-censorship. Beyond the digital sphere, it's perfectly possible that various cooperative
forms of local democracy will arise and elections will be conducted,
so long as they don't take on an oppositional character. Such organs
will likely be cultivated in order to more efficiently coordinate volunteer labor in times of crisis and "local self-government" will coexist in
harmony with even the most egregious surveillance systems imported
from Xinjiang.

These vertical integrations and local reforms will then be paired
with the additional cultivation of horizontal linkages between formal
and para-formal institutions of authority that operate at the same level.
For example, the central role played by property management companies and various other organized groups of landlords or homeowners
during the lockdown has already led for calls to extend party infrastructure
more thoroughly into these organizations:

State media quoted one scholar as saying that the party must
"thread" [neighborhood residents committees] together with landlords'
associations and property-management firms. In recent years, the party
has been laying the groundwork for this by forming cells within these
groups. The central city of Hefei wants at least half of those sitting on
landlords' committees to be party members, according to Legal Daily.

---

85. These are often misreported as the rollout of a single, national "social credit
score" that ranks all citizens. Not only does no such thing exist, but in the locations that
local variations of the concept have been experimented with they've tended to have
less impact on people's everyday lives than the much more systematic and thoroughly
enforced influence of one's combined credit score and criminal record in any Western
country.

State media often use the term "red property-management" to refer to firms that use their party cells to interact with property owners and try to keep them happy.[86]

This threading-together will doubtless be conducted both through formal mechanisms, such as direct placement of party cells within these groups, and through the informal cultivation of mutual social obligations between these distinct formal institutions, such as through nepotistic placement of family members in parallel horizontal positions. In fact, these informal familial linkages have already been integral to the expansion of policing in Xinjiang, since the recruitment of police "assistants," who are themselves predominantly hired from the Muslim minority populations that they are then employed to target, relies on familial networks in hiring and verifies applications not simply through a criminal background check but also by determining whether or not their family connections prove "trustworthy." Thus, in addition to integration between *shequ* residents committees and property owners, we might expect to see a similar cultivation of further horizontal linkages between the local police precincts and the various companies employing security guards within their territory as a potential first step in the process of para-formalization.

The Philosophy of the Coming State

The new currents of political philosophy that began to take shape in the reform period were deeply shaped by the various administrative transformations piloted in the 1980s and 1990s. They then contributed to these reforms insofar as they helped to lay out the general problematics of governance in the era and created new readings by new interlocutors through which those rising to power might both study Western political philosophy and return to classical texts on statecraft. But the intellectual sphere also tended to exaggerate the potentials of the reforms then underway. An example of this can be found in the proliferation of the concept of "autonomy" to describe local administration. On the one hand, autonomy as a synonym for local self-government in the

---

86. "On every street: China's Communist Party worries about its grassroots weakness," *The Economist*, June 11, 2020.

context of the rollback of state resources was a simple conceptual extension of the term as it had been used in the developmental regime to
define ethnic minority policy, where "autonomy" did not really mean self-
government so much as the application of a separate set of legal expectations, preferential access to certain resources and the ability to retain
some culturally-specific practices, particularly in the language of in-
struction in schools. The term came to take on its new meaning in 1980s
and 1990s as it was used to describe the reduced role of government in
the countryside. On the other hand, these administrative changes were
themselves occurring amid renewed debate on the nature of government. Though this debate was conducted with its formal veneer still
rooted in the then-prevailing orthodoxy of official "Marxism," its fundamental concepts began to be drawn more explicitly from both classical
texts on Chinese statecraft and various Western theories of governance
and direct democracy.

In both its theoretical and practical aspects, the debate on "the changing function of government" (政府职能转变), as it was known, was a
hybridization that openly used terms imported from foreign political
philosophers but subtly transformed their meanings:

> The plethora of new governmental terms and concepts that
> have emerged in Chinese discourse over the last two decades
> [i.e., the 1980s and 1990s] at first glance appear to have
> direct and obvious links to foreign counterparts, and no doubt
> many of these have been "imported" through closer working
> links with international governing institutions and the domes-
> tic resurgence of social sciences. A closer reading, however,
> reveals that Chinese notions such as *zizhi* and *zhili* [治理],
> which are generally rendered as "autonomy" and "governance"
> respectively, must be understood within the complex socio-
> historical terrain of modern China.[87]

Similar attentiveness must be paid to the transformation of the official
"Marxist" orthodoxy inherited from the developmental regime, guided

---

87. Gary Sigley, "Chinese Governmentalities: Government, Governance and the
Socialist Market Economy," *Economy and Society*, Vol. 35, No. 4, Nov. 2006. p. 489.

now by its mission to build a "socialist market economy." This was accompanied by other subtle changes in the vocabulary used to describe the function of the state, with terms like planning (计划), administration (行政) and government (政府) giving way to the more modern-sounding management (管理) and governance (治理) over the course of the 1990s. In the same way, autonomy and even terms such as "egoism" (自我主义) began to be used to describe ideal actors under the socialist market system, including individuals, institutions and industrial enterprises. Such terms became the norm among those leading the reforms and within various strains of Chinese liberalism that began to emerge in the period, including that of the supposedly "Maoist" thinkers of the Chinese New Left.

The liberal critique that developed in these years would form the seed for the type of politics advocated, at the popular level, by authors like Fang Fang today. Such thinkers essentially argued for a higher degree of emulation of foreign governance through "civil society" or through a particularly westernized notion of local democracy, though almost always with continuing emphasis placed on the centrality of the bureaucracy. While the classical liberal position has grown less common in the years after the great recession, in the 1980s and 1990s the proliferation of experiments in local self-government that accompanied the regrouping and temporary rollback of the central state led Chinese liberals to place enormous emphasis on the development of local "autonomous" organs that allowed for mass participation in governance. This was particularly true in rural areas, where these thinkers saw immense potential in the state's implementation of village democracy. Today, these dreams seem laughable. But their inheritance is clear even in contemporary liberal accounts of the volunteer efforts that arose in response to the pandemic. In one of the most popular of these pieces, posted to the liberal blog *Matters*,[88] the authors offer an intricate critique of the older style of institutional liberalism that advocated the cultivation of Western-style civil society in China as a sort of cure-all to be carried out alongside further marketization. But the authors' alternative is to turn instead

---

88. This is the piece cited several times above, thus far only partially translated into English via *Lausan*. The relevant section referenced here is Part III, still untranslated at the time of writing.

to a subset of New Left and left liberal scholars, such as Wen Tiejun and Zhao Xueguang, who have long advocated for the central state to culti-vate genuine organs of rural self-government via cooperative forms of di-rect democracy. Alongside these Chinese theorists, the authors gesture toward well-known Western thinkers like Murray Bookchin, Erik Olin Wright and Michael Albert, as well various technocratic-liberal boost-ers of the "sharing economy" and the potential of cryptocurrencies to create "radical markets." Articles such as this represent the general im-poverishment of Chinese liberalism in recent decades and its displace-ment by new strains of conservatism that have tended to emphasize the centrality of state-building above all else.

But this new conservatism did not appear out of thin air. Instead, its emergence indicates that deeper changes were already underway with-in intellectual circles. One important component of this conservatism has been a new political philosophy of statecraft less reliant on terms imported from the West, enabled by the revival of interest in the Chi-nese literary and philosophical tradition. The rise of Chinese liberalism and the debate on the "changing functions of government" took place in the midst of two other important intellectual trends: the "culture craze" (文化热) of the 1980s, which saw foreign philosophy rapidly translated into Chinese and thinkers from Taiwan, Hong Kong and even Republican-era China re-introduced to the mainland; and the "national studies craze" (国学热) of the 1990s, culminating in the found-ing of "national studies institutes" at universities and the reincorpora-tion of the classics into lower level school curricula.[89] In the intellectual sphere, this process was defined by numerous attempts to resurrect and grapple with classic questions in Chinese philosophy and to put them in-to conversation with current scientific knowledge, modern governmen-tal techniques and China's own more recent inheritance of "socialist" philosophy. In later years, this would be portrayed as a "revival of Con-fucianism," epitomized by the proliferation of classical quotes and aes-thetic flourishes that populated the public image of the Hu-Wen admin-istration and its notion of the "Harmonious Society." In one respect,

89. Song Xianlin, "Reconstructing the Confucian Ideal in 1980s China: The 'Cul-ture Craze' and New Confucianism," *New Confucianism: A Critical Examination*, (Eds: John Makeham), pp. 81–104; Chen Jiaming, "The National Studies Craze," *China Perspec-tives*, No. 1, 2011, pp. 22–30.

this is a fair characterization, since "Confucianism" does not refer to the specific body of works produced by Confucius and his immediate inheritors but instead to the continual process of synthesis within the Chinese philosophical/literary tradition. This has tended to be conducted under the banner of "Confucianism" even as it has been marked by the incorporation of non-Confucian elements into both the general philosophical inheritance and the specific body of Confucian practice.[90] At the same time, the more recent visibility of this trend on the political stage disguises the fact that the resurgence began much earlier in the academic sphere and, like other returns to "Confucianism" in the past, is better understood as a broader revival of interest in the Chinese-language philosophical tradition in general.

One of the most representative figures throughout the whole period was Gan Yang (甘阳), whose individual intellectual journey traces larger changes within Chinese political philosophy more broadly. Gan first grew to public prominence in the 1980s as the editor of one of the first book series (*Culture: China in the World*) since the early years of the PRC that sought to systematically translate Western philosophy for a Chinese readership.[91] He was a student of Western philosophy at Beijing University and became involved in the liberal student politics of the time. According to Gan, his essays on Isaiah Berlin were some of the earliest attempts to re-introduce classical liberal political philosophy to China. These political sympathies would ultimately see him leave the country after the Tiananmen Incident, going on to conduct research at the University of Chicago and then the University of Hong Kong before finally returning to China to take up a position at Sun Yat-sen University in 2009.[92] While in the US, he was introduced to the thought of modern conservatives like Leo Strauss via the classicist Alan Bloom, under whom he studied. Throughout these decades, he grew more and more critical of his youthful liberalism and was drawn instead toward the more conservative social democracy of the early Chinese New Left. In

---

90. Hui, *The Question Concerning Technology in China: An Essay in Cosmotechnics*, 2016.

91. Zhang Xudong, "On Some Motifs in the 'Cultural Fever' on the late 1980s: Social Change, Ideology and Theory," *Social Text*, No. 39, Summer 1994. pp. 129–156.

92. William Sima and Tang Xiaobing, "Translator's Introduction to Gan Yang, 'Liberalism,'" *Reading the China Dream*, 1999.

this role, he contributed to the popular polemical debates between Chinese liberals and the New Left in the later 1990s.[93] Though this often saw Gan classed among New Left thinkers like Wang Hui (汪晖) or Xu Jilin (许纪霖), his influence on more avowedly conservative traditionalists was equally important. Meanwhile, Gan continued in this role as a major interlocutor for Western philosophy, but now with an emphasis on conservative thinkers, joining Jiang Shigong as a major interpreter of Carl Schmitt.

Gan's influence is particularly relevant here, however, because of the way that his 2005 essay on "Unifying the Three Traditions" (通三统) provided the almost universal point of reference for anyone seeking an integration of traditional political philosophy and official state policy. In this piece, Gan argues that "three traditions" coexist in contemporary China. The first is a socialist tradition defined by "its emphasis on equality and justice." The second is a liberal tradition cultivated in the reform era and defined by concepts such as "freedom and rights." The third is "the tradition of Chinese civilization, forged over thousands of years," which can also be thought of as "Confucian culture" and is expressed "in terms of interpersonal relationships and ties of locality."[94] Meanwhile, the very idea of "unifying the three traditions" is itself a historical reference to Dong Zhongshu (董仲舒), a political philosopher from the Han dynasty who argued that the synthesis of a single civilizational practice from the "three traditions" of the Xia, Shang and Zhou dynasties was a necessary precedent for the emergence of the imperial polity in the Qin and Han.[95] In echoing this formulation, Gan is arguing that

93. For a summary of these debates, see: Li Shitao 李世涛 (ed.), 知识分子立场：自由主义之争与中国思想界的分化 [*Intellectual Positions: Debates on Liberalism and the Splintering of the Chinese Intellectual World*], Changchun: Shidai wenyi chubanshe, 2000.

94. Gan Yang, "'Unifying the Three Traditions' in the New Era: The Merging of Three Chinese Traditions," Lecture at Tsinghua University, Trans: David Ownby, *Reading the China Dream*, May 12, 2005.

95. For more detail, see the translator's introduction in ibid. The Xia, Shang and Zhou dynasties were all pre-imperial polities that existed in the East Asian mainland. The Zhou (1050–771 BCE) was ruled according to a *fengjian* (封建) system, which was a sort of confederated religious monarchy based on a system of enfeoffment (受封). Later, influenced by Marxism, *fengjian* would become the Chinese word for "feudalism," despite historical differences. Something like a *fengjian* system likely prevailed in the preceding Shang (1600–1046 BCE) and Xia (~2000–1600 BCE) dynasties, but this is more difficult to determine since information about both is partially mythical. Very little clear

China today is poised for a similar qualitative leap. The precise traditions he sees as being unified are certainly vague, but this is part of their appeal. The fact that they are open to interpretation and modification is what would make them a functional template for both religious neo-traditionalists and more secular defenders of party orthodoxy such as Jiang Shigong.[96]

The neo-traditionalists on the mainland had the benefit of being able to draw on the unbroken lineages of philosophy that existed in Taiwan, Hong Kong and elsewhere in the Chinese diaspora. The most important of these thinkers were the New Confucians (新儒家),[97] a school of thought that is neo-conservative in its general contours but can be sub-divided by geography—namely newer mainland thinkers vs. older philosophers in greater China—and into liberal-democratic and more traditionalist interpretations. The most important New Confucian thinkers are likely Mou Zongsan (牟宗三), who represents those who fled the mainland after the revolution, and Jiang Qing (蒋庆) who became one of the preeminent thinkers in the mainland revival of Confucianism in the reform period. But both currents trace their roots to the Republican era, which saw an earlier attempt to revive and modernize Confucianism led by scholars like Xiong Shili (熊十力). While Mou

---

archeological evidence yet exists for the existence of the Xia. Nonetheless, the importance here is that these were the three loose pre-imperial polities that formed the basis for the region's civilization, which the Qin (221–206 BCE) would unify into a single imperial state, giving way to the Han (202 BCE–220 CE).

96. For Jiang, the three traditions are similar, but not identical. He sees Xi Jinping Thought as the active integrator of its socialist era and reform era predecessors with classical Chinese statecraft. This fusion takes place entirely through the party, which is no longer merely the supposed vanguard of the Chinese proletariat but instead the vanguard of Chinese civilization as such. Throughout, he claims to maintain fidelity to Marxist orthodoxy.

97. Not to be confused with the Neo-Confucians of the Song and Ming dynasties. In English the two terms sound similar, but in Chinese they are completely different: Neo-Confucianism is 宋明理学, meaning something like "Song-Ming Rationalism," while New Confucianism is 新儒家, a literal translation of the Chinese. This distinction is important because, while Song-Ming Rationalism was concerned with excavating what it conceived of as an authentically Han philosophical lineage defined by Confucianism, it did so in an openly syncretic fashion that incorporated elements of Daoism, Buddhism and other intellectual currents. In contrast (and as hinted in its name), New Confucianism is more concerned with tracing out and reviving core aspects of Confucianism as such, even while it engages with both Western and non-Confucian Chinese thinkers.

and other diaspora New Confucians preserved and perpetuated key debates within Chinese philosophy and also laid the groundwork for an extensive engagement with Western philosophers, their work took on a particularly rarefied character and tended to emphasize moral cultivation above political transformation. This was natural, given the fact that such thinkers were working under either a slowly reforming dictatorship, in Taiwan, or a colonial regime, in Hong Kong, in the context of the Cold War. But it also meant that their thought tended to engage with explicit questions of statecraft far less frequently than that of thinkers on the mainland.

In contrast to Mou, Jiang Qing denies the title of New Confucianism, which he categorizes as too influenced by liberal democratic presumptions and too concerned with existential questions of individual moral development. This is part of a broader distinction in his philosophy between what he characterizes as Mou's "Mind Confucianism" and his own "Constitutional Confucianism" (or "Political Confucianism") which emphasizes the institutional dimensions of Confucian philosophy and explicitly advocates that these be taken up by the state. Jiang's body of work is complex, and his own biography is itself a fascinating narrative that illustrates a gradual transition from dissenting humanist socialism, to a dalliance with secular liberalism and, finally, concludes in an embrace of a particular brand of neo-traditional conservatism. At every point he is critical of the existing government, leading to eventual voluntary self-exile in rural Guizhou. Jiang's work takes politics as its explicit object and argues that the current state-building effort must be informed by the distinctly Chinese philosophical tradition, rather than just modelled on Western precedents. This is the basis of his critique of liberals and even other traditionalists, who have penned numerous draft constitutions since the late Qing dynasty: "Their basic ideas and systems are, without exception, purely Western [...] not one of them includes any place for China's own historical and cultural specificity in their basic ideas or in their constitutional format [...]."[98]

Against this, Jiang offers a constitutionalism rooted in Confucian

98. Jiang Qing (蒋庆), *A Confucian Constitutional Order: How China's Ancient Past Can Shape Its Political Future*, (Trans: Edmund Ryden), Princeton University Press, 2013. p. 45.

tradition which understands questions of sovereignty and legitimacy in a distinctly indigenized sense rather than in the meaning such terms have inherited from the West: "Sovereignty refers to an authority that is sacred, absolute, exclusive, and supreme. Such authority can belong only to heaven, not the people."[99] This fact guides his concrete political prescriptions arguing that China must be administered by a renewed class of scholar-gentry, organized into a coherent Academy composed of various institutions and operating at multiple levels of governance, with the entire system helmed by "sage-kings" and cohered around a symbolic monarch. The system incorporates Western elements such as a tricameral legislature and institutional features of a constitutional monarchy modelled on the British and Japanese cases. But emphasis is placed throughout on the administration of society by enlightened scholars. Though Jiang offers a variant with explicitly religious overtones, this turn to authoritarian intellectualism has been common among former liberals of all schools, especially those involved in student politics in the reform era, and has thereby become an almost universal element of the Chinese new right. A secular variant of the same basic idea can be seen today in state propaganda emphasizing informed rule by experts and in popular culture, such as in the conservative Prometheanism (工业党) underpinning the work of major authors like Liu Cixin.[100]

This authoritarian intellectualism is also evident in Jiang Shigong's[101] synthesis of Xi Jinping Thought. In all cases, the basic logic is that relying on popular legitimacy alone leads to catastrophe. Thus, the political infrastructure must be governed by intellectuals who, in the secular version, have access to particular expertise and foresight not prevalent in the general population or, in the Confucian version, are able to act in a "sagely" fashion as mediators between the sovereignty of

99. Ibid., p. 48

100. Yuyan, "*The Wandering Earth*: A Reflection of the Chinese Right," *Chuang Blog*, Feb. 13, 2019.

101. In order to not confuse the reader by jumping from one Jiang to another, Jiang Shigong will be referred to by his full name throughout this paragraph. In Chinese there is no ambiguity between the two scholars, whose surnames are different written characters and are pronounced in two different tones. Similarly, Jiang Qing the New Confucian is not to be confused with Jiang Qing (江青), famous actress, designer of revolutionary operas, member of the Gang of Four during the Cultural Revolution and wife of Mao Zedong.

heaven and the human sphere of the state. Jiang Shigong, meanwhile, offers a synthesis of the two, seeing the party as the *de facto* integration of the old secular socialist mission with the spirit of Confucianism, expressed through the living political practice of Xi Jinping:

> What we must pay particular attention to is the fact that when Xi Jinping emphasizes a return to Communist principles, he is not talking about the "communist society" that was of a piece with scientific socialism but is instead using the idea that "those who do not forget their original intention 初心 will prevail," drawn from traditional Chinese culture. In so doing, he removes communism from the specific social setting of the Western empirical scientific tradition, and astutely transforms it into the Learning of the Heart in Chinese traditional philosophy, which in turn elevates communism to a kind of ideal faith or a spiritual belief. [...]

> Precisely within the context of traditional Chinese culture, the understanding of this highest ideal is no longer that of Marx, who thought within the Western theoretical tradition; it is no longer in humanity's Garden of Eden, "unalienated" by the division of labor within society. Instead it is intimately linked to the ideal of "great unity under Heaven" 天下大同 from the Chinese cultural tradition. The last section of the report to the Nineteenth Party Congress begins with the phrase "when the Way prevails, the world is shared by all" 大道之行，天下为公, an ultimate ideal that encourages the entire Party and the people of the entire nation.[102]

Jiang Shigong's synthesis is one wherein communism itself is mystified even while the secular character of "socialism with Chinese characteristics" is upheld through the historical centrality of the party itself, which acts as the dialectical vehicle integrating theory and practice.

102. Jiang Shigong, "Philosophy and History: Interpreting the 'Xi Jinping Era' through Xi's Report to the Nineteenth National Congress of the CCP," *Open Times* (开放时代), *Translators*: David Ownby and Timothy Cheek, *Reading the China Dream*, Jan. 2018.

Not all thinkers engaged in the general revival of interest in the Chinese philosophical tradition explicitly branded their work as Confucian. In fact, the interest of Chinese liberals in questions of autonomy and self-organization was mirrored at a deeper level in the reappraisal of fundamental concepts more often associated with Daoism, which has always been the strain of Chinese philosophy most explicitly concerned with the processual and self-generative theories of nature. Though some point to the publication in the early 1990s of Dong Guangbi's (董光壁) text *Neo-Daoism* (当代新道家) as a turning point, there was no real "Neo-Daoist" current with anything like the consistency of the New Confucians.[103] Part of the reason this consistency was lacking was precisely because the loose proliferation of non-denominational texts which emerged in these years was less concerned with making explicit political prescriptions and tended instead to produce more general, existential meditations and engage with modern science, though this sometimes verged on reproducing the worst, Western-style New Age mysticism. Often, the effort was led by philosophers who were experts on major figures in Western schools of thought, putting this work into conversation with the Chinese tradition through their expertise, as in the work of Deng Xiaomang (邓晓芒), who was among the foremost Chinese interpreters of Kant.[104]

A number of central philosophical concepts were revived in these years, but maybe the most relevant here, already partially evident in Jiang Shigong's usage above, was the reappraisal of the core concepts of *wuwei* (无为) and the *dao* (道) itself.[105] Meaning something like "non-action" and "path," respectively, these terms take on a different valence depending on the school or thinker deploying them. Their relevance for statecraft is central, however, as in the role of *wuwei* in

103. This text and the informal group of philosophers who can, in this period, be characterized as Neo-Daoist are not to be confused with the Xuanxue (玄学) school of the Six Dynasties period (which is also called Neo-Daoism), though many authors in this current do draw influence from Xuanxue.

104. For a more general text of Deng's, see: Deng Xiaomang (邓晓芒), 人论三题 [Three Topics of Discourse on Humanity], 2008, Chongqing: Chongqing University Press.

105. See, for instance: Cai Degui (蔡德贵) 道家道法自然的和评论 [Daoist Naturalism and the Theory of Peace], *Journal of Anhui University (Philosophy and Social Sciences)*, 26(5), Sept. 2002.

Daoist political philosophy: governing without intervening (无为之治). While the founding texts of Daoism approach the concept from two different angles, these represent inward and outward dimensions of the same thing: "Laozi... places more emphasis on societal change and governing the world, while Zhuangzi emphasizes more the internal transformation and spiritual freedom of the individual person."[106] Similarly, the Daoist approach to statecraft is complementary with the Confucian and, according to the philosopher Yuk Hui, the two should be seen as integrally linked despite their apparent contradictions, which are, in fact, the form of their linkage.[107] Both are, after all, concerned with the central question of the *dao*. For Confucianism the *dao* "is recognized as the coherence between the cosmological and moral orders" and, for Daoism, it is fundamentally linked to the self-generative capacity of nature. While "according to conventional readings, they seem to be in tension" since Daoism is "critical of any imposed order" while "Confucianism seeks to affirm different kinds of order," the pair can also be seen as approaching the same topic by different routes, "as if one asks after the 'what,' and the other the 'how.'" Thus, taken together, "both embody ... a 'moral cosmotechnics': a relational thinking of the cosmos and human being, where the relation between the two is mediated by technical beings."[108] This relationality is essential to understanding the way that such concepts have been translated into a certain approach to statecraft.

One of the most relevant points here is how contemporary appraisals of *wuwei* place emphasis on the fact that its self-organizing capacity, like the generative dimension of the *dao* itself, is not something that happens automatically—as in the romantic misunderstanding of the concept as "going with the flow"—but instead requires systematic

106. Wang Hongyu, "*Wuwei*, self-organization, and classroom dynamics," *Education Philosophy and Theory*, 2019.

107. Yuk Hui's interpretation of the fundamental concepts used throughout the Chinese philosophical tradition is among the best overviews of the topic available in either English or Chinese. Though his concern with the question of technology guides his work in a particular direction, many of the same observations can be applied to Chinese political philosophy's conception of the state which is, after all, composed of similar social technologies and rituals.

108. Yuk Hui, *The Question Concerning Technology in China: An Essay in Cosmotechnics*, Urbanomic, 2016. pp. 64–65.

structuring to ensure.[109] In other words, the enabling of a "non-interventionist" form of governance via the self-organization of *wuwei* requires a series of preceding, systematic interventions in order to rectify social institutions, ensuring that they lie in accord with the *dao* and are capable of cultivating wisdom among sage-like leaders.[110] Thus, both the Daoist and Confucian traditions have always been concerned with a deeply processual approach to statecraft (at least as one dimension of a larger "moral cosmotechnics") and concepts like *wuwei* have been mobilized in even the most bureaucratic Chinese political philosophies. The notion was central to the way that Legalists such as Han Fei (韩非) and his precursor, Shen Buhai (申不害), conceived of the nature of autocratic rule. Thus, *wuwei* and its related constellation of concepts have consistently contained seemingly contradictory imperatives, entailing aggressive intervention in the name of non-intervention. This is evident in the state's own continually contradictory attitude toward local self-government and the higher-level informal networks that have long buoyed the bureaucracy. In times of stability, these features are cultivated and even enshrined, constituting not so much informal governance as a para-formal state that coexists with its formal counterpart.[111] In times of chaos, though, these para-formal institutions are reduced again to

109. There is certainly an unconditional or cosmic dimension to *wuwei* which inheres in the self-generating force of the universe. But the emergence of consciousness implies a different form of *wuwei*, which is conditional and requires effort in order to rectify the practice of the conscious being (individually or collectively, both are part of the same moral fabric in Chinese cosmology) with the *dao*, which can be lost or forgotten by consciousness.

110. A few examples can be quoted from the *Tao Te Ching* (道德经): "*Governing a great state is like cooking small fish*" (治大国若烹小鲜); "*A state may be ruled by (measures of) correction; weapons of war may be used with crafty dexterity; (but) the kingdom is made one's own (only) by freedom from action and purpose*" (以正治国，以奇用兵，以无事取天下).

111. For example, in the early 1980s a nationwide anti-crime campaign was launched, called "Strike Hard" (严打). In order to improve the efficacy of the campaign, the right of death penalty review (死刑复核权), at the time exclusive to the supreme court, was delegated to local People's Courts so that suspects of serious accusations could be sentenced to death pursuant to the judgment of the local court. This was initially portrayed as a temporary policy, but the devolution of authority was soon formalized (in 1983) in law. Similar powers were later given to provincial courts to deal with drug crimes in later decades. Tracing the same pattern we describe throughout, this localization of authority was then rolled back (in 2006) after the transition to capitalism was complete and the state-building effort was beginning.

informality, systematically treated as threats and supplanted, but always in the name of their future cultivation. Despite being structured to serve specifically capitalist imperatives, then, there is every reason to believe that the current state-building project will incorporate a similar processual logic, defined by these moving contradictions.

Though all this philosophical detail might seem irrelevant to understanding the nature of political dynamics in China today, the reality is that many seemingly straightforward concepts became willfully mangled via a sort of contextual short-circuiting as they were taken up in Chinese administration. The issue is not that terms like autonomy / self-organization, community, governance, etc. are themselves mistranslated, but rather that they carry implications in English which link them to presumptions within Western philosophy or even actual institutional practices that are not implied in their Chinese usage. These false contexts then help to obscure the actual contextual implications and other subtleties carried by these terms. More importantly, they give the false impression that China's state-building project is nothing more than a gradual subsumption into the logic of "governmentality" as it emerged through early capitalist state formation in Europe, and this itself is often traced back to Roman jurisprudence in order to link the logic of the capitalist state with its civilizational precursors. At the most basic level, it should at least be acknowledged that anyone attempting to compose a long-run theory of civilization and the self-reflexive state logics that it produces must be as familiar with the political philosophy of ancient China as they are with the legal theory of ancient Rome.[112] But even this attempt tends to lose sight of the fundamental changes induced

112. And we would add that any general theory of civilizational governmentality is obligated to explore commonalities that extend across all civilizational sequences, including those that existed in Africa and the Americas. The failure to do so represents not simply the "Eurocentrism" of Western political philosophy, though this is certainly the case, but also the tendency of philosophers to over-generalize from historical particularities—a practice that they quite ironically justify in the same breath that they reject a supposedly "totalizing" Marxism. The communist method of inquiry embodied in the work of Marx, however, entails abstraction from the general case. This is an active abstraction, continually attentive to changes in the particular and capable of also intervening to coherently explain the dynamics of these particular instances, as in Marx's historical writings, by referring to their underlying logic but without schematically reducing them to it. Marx's method also allows for the identification of "real abstractions" unique to social-scientific inquiry.

in the nature of the state when the mode of production shifts, transforming both the class structure of society and the governing logic of everyday life, defined by participation in and dependence on production. This then changes who, exactly, composes and controls the state and what, exactly, they do with it.

In other words, the perception that states are governed by a strict and universal governmental logic that can be traced by a silver thread back through history is only true in the broadest sense and is at every point obligated to demonstrate the material substrate of such a genealogy. Civilization is one such substrate, defined by certain population dynamics and a general dependence on domesticated crops and livestock, but this is so generic as to be not particularly informative if we are inquiring into the specific ways in which states are organized today.[113] For European states and their colonial offshoots, a closer genealogy is self-evident, and even the Roman connection is reasonable given that early modern governments actively sought to model themselves on the region's last great imperium — or even in some cases derived basic administrative infrastructure from centuries-distant political fragments of the empire's collapse.[114] That said, the existence of certain logics of statecraft linked to such a civilizational genealogy cannot override the new imperatives driving the function of states under capitalism. At best, precapitalist moral or cosmological attitudes embedded in the state prior to the transition to capitalism are adapted to new uses during this transition. This, however, means that they do not retain whatever necessity they may have had in pre-existing government — nor does capitalism itself emerge from incidental cultural features, such as the Puritan work ethic. The only true necessities for the state under capitalism are the

113. This general theory was formulated first in what would come to be known as the Marxist tradition by Engels, who was essentially just quoting the work of past anthropologists, who were themselves essentially just repeating in descriptive contrast the political theory and practice of indigenous people. It has since been taken up in the academic sphere by anthropologists like James C. Scott, who explored the historical formation of "paddy states" dependent on domestic rice production in Southeast Asia. Meanwhile, the anti-civilizational critique has long formed the basis of indigenous anarchist and communist politics in the Americas and elsewhere.

114. Edward D. Re, "The Roman Contribution to the Common Law," *Fordham Law Review*, 29(3), 1961. pp.447–494. On the European continent, modern legal systems often bore a direct, ancestral relationship to Roman law. But even the case of English common law operated within the same general frameworks of statecraft.

two, broad functions laid out above—maintenance of baseline conditions for accumulation and management of conflicts within the ruling class—both involve general social reproduction.

This does mean that the management of life and death among governed subjects (i.e., "biopolitical" and "necropolitical" aspects of "governmentality") is an integral aspect of capitalist statecraft, but only in a general and indirect sense, serving to maintain the input of labor into the system and to guarantee enough overarching social stability to enable the circuit of capital to continually complete itself. There is no reason to believe, however, that specifically European cultural, moral or institutional methods of managing population—or the affiliated discourse on this management—would be necessary to serve this function. Similarly, any universalization of Western notions of sovereignty, right, governance or other aspects of the state's moral genealogy has been incidental, driven more by the material reality of imperialism and colonization than by any logical necessity. Thus, there is no reason to believe that capitalist states with different genealogies would inherently mirror these European precedents, their colonial offshoots or the states that developed under their direct military tutelage short of colonization. The case of Imperial Japan already began to gesture at this fact, but its defeat and subsequent reorganization under the military hegemony of the United States has tended to obscure this divergence.[115] The ascent of

115. Similar local divergences have always been visible in the areas more distant from the economic core but, due to this distance, have tended to be explained in terms of low levels of development and an incomplete transition to capitalism, the presumption being that, if economic development were to advance, the state and affiliated social institutions would grow to resemble those seen in the developed nations. The problem here is that local genealogies of statecraft only really gain relevance insofar as they become successfully fused to capitalist imperatives, through which they then spark debates about the precise divisions between "Western" influence and this local cultural/philosophical inheritance. In Japan, this reached its peak in the formation of the Kyoto school. Similar debates have marked development in numerous other countries, however, even if their economic power has never been great enough to exert much influence on the larger trajectory of global capitalism: Thailand and Ethiopia are two prominent cases with their own long histories of statecraft, though many post-independence and post-dictatorship nations in Africa and the Americas that have seen a similar discourse could be included here as well: Bolivia, Venezuela, Tanzania and Ghana, to list only a few. These are not purely discursive matters, either, since they've exerted real power on the re-writing of constitutions and the establishment of various land tenure systems. The difference with China is more a difference of degree in relative influence on the global economy.

a powerful bloc of Chinese capitalists has again created the material prerequisites for a powerful state to emerge, which, although serving the same capitalist imperatives, also incorporates incidental institutional logics from its own indigenous genealogy of statecraft.

There is no space here to pursue a philosophical inquiry into this genealogy in any detail, though such a project is worthwhile. Meanwhile, none of the various philosophers cited above (even Jiang Shigong, despite his claims) should be portrayed as filling some sort of leading role relative to those in the bureaucracy who are most actively shaping the reform of government administration. There is no single school of political philosophy on which the current state-building effort is modelled. Instead, the relevant point is the fact that the construction of the state has been taking place in an intellectual climate marked by the revival of many schools of Chinese thought, all inhabiting a general conceptual universe distinct from the Greco-German lineage but now also in more direct conversation with it. This is the context in which the terms and institutions that have defined reforms in local governance must be understood. Placing such terms in context then allows us to speculate in a more accurate fashion about the character of the state currently being constructed. This is not because the fanciful goals of political philosophers have any chance of becoming fundamental imperatives of the state, but instead because elements of this thought may become incidentally useful in the pursuit of accumulation. What we have offered here is by no means any conclusion. We simply suggest that this inquiry be initiated with the correct foot forward. If this is not done, then a theory of the Chinese state will, at worst, tend to unthinkingly transplant the most mundane accounts of "totalitarianism" into foreign soil or, at best, try to capture the dynamics arising between the Chinese state and the global economy with loose approximations formulated to describe extremely different political formations from the history of Europe or the anglophone nations. Thus will you hear the claim that China deploys "Keynesian" measures, or is a "corporatist" state in the sense first used by Mussolini. We humbly suggest, instead, that China is making its own, original contributions to the brutality of global capitalism as it advances into the twenty-first century.